INTRODUCTION TO AGROMETEOROLOGY

Introduction to Agrometeorology
Second Edition

HS Mavi
Professor of Agrometeorology
Punjab Agricultural University
Ludhiana

Oxford & IBH Publishing Co. Pvt. Ltd.
New Delhi
(*A Unit of* CBS Publishers & Distributors Pvt Ltd)

CBS Publishers & Distributors Pvt Ltd

New Delhi • Bengaluru • Chennai • Kochi • Kolkata • Lucknow • Mumbai
Hyderabad • Jharkhand • Nagpur • Patna • Pune • Uttarakhand

Introduction to Agrometeorology Second Edition

ISBN-13: 978-81-204-0910-1
ISBN-10: 81-204-0910-8

© 1986, 1994, 1996, 2001, HS Mavi

Reprint: 2017, 2018, 2019, 2022

OXFORD & IBH
New Delhi
(A Unit of CBS Publishers & Distributors Pvt Ltd)

Published by **Satish Kumar Jain** and produced by **Varun Jain** for

CBS Publishers & Distributors Pvt Ltd
4819/XI Prahlad Street, 24 Ansari Road, Daryaganj, New Delhi 110 002, India.
Ph: 011-23289259, 23266861, 23266867   Website: www.cbspd.com
Fax: 011-23243014   e-mail: delhi@cbspd.com;
cbspubs@airtelmail.in.

Corporate Office: 204 FIE, Industrial Area, Patparganj, Delhi 110 092
Ph: 011-4934 4934   Fax: 011-4934 4935
e-mail: publishing@cbspd.com; publicity@cbspd.com

Branches

- **Bengaluru:** Seema House 2975, 17th Cross, KR Road, Banasankari 2nd Stage, Bengaluru 560 070, Karnataka, India
  Ph: +91-80-26771678/79   Fax: +91-80-26771680   e-mail: bangalore@cbspd.com
- **Chennai:** 7, Subbaraya Street, Shenoy Nagar, Chennai 600 030, Tamil Nadu, India
  Ph: +91-44-26680620, 26681266   Fax: +91-44-42032115   e-mail: chennai@cbspd.com
- **Kochi:** 42/1325, 1326, Power House Road, Opp KSEB, Power House, Ernakulum Kochi 682 018, Kerala, India
  Ph: +91-484-4059061-65,67   Fax: +91-484-4059065   e-mail: kochi@cbspd.com
- **Kolkata:** 147, Hind Ceramics Compound, 1st Floor, Nilgunj Road, Belghoria, Kolkata-700056, West Bengal, India
  Ph: +033-25633055, 033-25633056   e-mail: kolkata@cbspd.com
- **Lucknow:** Basement, Khushnuma Complex, 7 Meerabai Marg (Behind Jawahar Bhawan), Lucknow-226001, UP, India
  Ph: +0522-4000032   e-mail: tiwari.lucknow@cbspd.com
- **Mumbai:** PWD Shed, Gala no 25/26, Ramchandra Bhatt Marg, Next to JJ Hospital Gate no. 2, Opp. Union Bank of India,
  Noorbaug, Mumbai-400009, Maharashtra, India
  Ph: 022-66661880/89   e-mail: mumbai@cbspd.com

Representatives

• Hyderabad	0-9885175004	• Jharkhand	0-9811541605	• Nagpur	0-9421245513
• Patna	0-9334159340	• Pune	0-9623451994	• Uttarakhand	0-9716462459

Printed at Chaman Enterprises, Daryaganj, New Delhi, India

Preface to the Second Edition

Since the first edition of the book was published, the science of Agrometeorology has progressed fast, both in its contents and applications. New instruments, new techniques and new areas of studies have emerged. The computer-based simulation has expanded scientific methodology in knowing the previously unknown of the crop eco-systems and in providing quantitative insights into the interactions between crops, environment and management. A chapter on Modelling Crop Growth and Production, has, therefore, been added with the objective of making the students familiar with the types of models and major areas of their applications. Climate change and its implications on the eco-systems has emerged as a serious scientific concern and is a key topic of research and study in future agricultural planning and food supply. The chapter on Climate Change and Crop Production has been added to acquaint the students with the probable causes of climate change and the serious implications of green house effect and global warming on eco-systems and crop production.

 I am grateful to my colleagues in the Department of Agrometeorology for their help in this work.

March, 1994
Deptt. of Agrometeorology   **H.S. Mavi**
P.A.U.

Preface to the First Edition

Weather is the most important input in agriculture. In spite of this fact, not many quantitative crop-weather relationship studies have been conducted till recently. Agronomists and other agricultural scientists have been aware of the effects of weather on various aspects of agriculture, but did little to understand and highlight these effects. In fact, agricultural scientists focussed their entire attention on the tapping of soil and improving agronomic practices, not caring to understand climate, even as a resource in agriculture. A majority of them have been of the view, that the studies on crop-weather relationships are of little practical value when compared with the knowledge of soil potentials. Scientists in meteorology, on the other hand, concentrated their attention on the measurement of the atmosphere, and on giving mathematical expressions to the various phenomena occurring in the atmosphere. They did not highlight the importance and usefulness of their findings to agriculture. Thus, agriculture and meteorology remained self-contained disciplines till very recently.

In the rigid compartmentalisation of agriculture and weather science, the full potential of climate as an agricultural resource has not been used or even realised. As a result, several crops are grown traditionally in areas without any consideration for the suitability of the climate. Thus, on the one hand, poor yields of crops are being obtained, and on the other, much of the production potential of this vast resource, is left unutilised. Doubtless, it is impossible to tame the weather on a large scale, or even be in complete harmony with it. However, it is more than possible to make adjustment with the weather to extract the maximum benefit from this resource.

There now exists full realization that except for climate, all other resources in crop production can be exploited only to a limited extent. A fuller exploitation of the weather resource, therefore, is the major hope for greater agricultural production to meet the demands of the staggering increase in population. It has been demonstrated that, apart from weather forecasting which solves a number of our daily problems—meteorology has some other very useful applications to various agricultural activities. For example, the selection of crop production sites, irrigation control, soil and water conservation, amelioration of field climate, and the adoption of the most appropriate agronomic and cultural practices in crop production.

The increasing utility of agrometeorology, together with an integrated approach of scientists of different disciplines during the past few decades, has greatly contributed to the development of this field into a broad-based inter-disciplinary subject. Micrometeorologists and biologists have greatly contributed to the development of this subject. The former, by providing quantitative expressions to the available thermal energy and water balance, and the latter by bringing to light plant response to the climatic environment.

Agrometeorology has now developed into a fullfledged discipline and a researcher in the subject requires a thorough knowledge both of meteorology and agriculture.

With the certainty that the science of agrometeorology has an important role to play in modern day agriculture through education, research and extension services, Departments of Agricultural Meteorology are fast coming up in agricultural universities in India. This book will serve the purpose of both, a text for undergraduate students, and a first book for the graduate level students who wish to major in agrometeorology.

Solar radiation is the primary source of energy for the biosphere. Its various aspects are discussed in Chapters 2 and 3. A brief reference of the role of other meteorological factors in photosynthesis has also been made in Chapter 3. The significance of temperature and moisture in plant growth has been presented in Chapters 5 and 6 respectively. In Chapter 9, quantitative approximations are supplied, for the desired climatic elements for optimum crop and animal production.

The rest of the book deals with the agrometeorological techniques which can be used for improving crop production. Since water is the most important input in crop production, and is a precious resource to be used very carefully, some methods of estimation of its loss to the atmosphere, and its availability in the root zone of crop plants, have been given in Chapters 7 and 8. In Chapter 10 various techniques have been briefly mentioned, which are currently being used or attempted to modify the weather at the macro level, as well as at the field scale.

An important utility of the subject is in minimising losses through timely weather forecasts. Guidelines to prepare weather forecasts for farmers have been given in Chapter 11. Additionally, a few models of other agrometeorological forecasts are given.

One of the methods used to improve farm production is by making adjustments with the prevailing climate, to make the best possible use of it. This can be done by understanding prevailing agroclimates. Agroclimates, properly understood and scientifically integrated into agroclimatic regions, can serve as valuable tools for harnessing climate potentials of the areas, for crop production. In the last chapter, some techniques and methods, used for delineating agroclimatic regions, have been summarised.

Assistance, rendered by a number of friends, in the preparation of diagrams and reading the manuscripts, is acknowledged with thanks.

H.S. Mavi

Department of Agrometeorology
P.A.U.

Contents

CHAPTER 1

AGROMETEOROLOGY

Agrometeorology, abbreviated from Agricultural Meteorology and also referred to as Agroclimatology, has been defined in several ways. The name itself implies that it is the study of those aspects of meteorology which have direct relevance to agriculture. Agrometeorology puts the science of meteorology to the service of agriculture, in its various forms and facets, to help the sensible use of land, accelerate production of food and to avoid the irreversible abuse of land resources (Smith, 1970).

The meeting of Agrometeorologists in Moscow in 1951 (Molga, 1962) defined agrometeorology as a science investigating the meteorologic, climatologic and hydrologic conditions which are significant for agriculture owing to their interaction with the objects and processes of agriculture production.

The task of an agrometeorologist is to apply every relevant meteorological skill to help the farmer to make the most efficient use of his physical environment for improving agricultural production both in quality and quantity (Bourke, 1968).

1.1. Scope of Agrometeorology

For optimum crop growth specific climatic conditions are required. Agrometeorology thus becomes relevant to crop production because it is concerned with the interactions between meteorological and hydrological factors on the one hand and agriculture, in the widest sense including horticulture, animal husbandry and forestry, on the other. Its objective is to discover and define such effects and thus to apply knowledge of the atmosphere to practical agricultural use. The field of interest of agrometeorology extends from the soil surface layer to the depth up to which tree roots penetrate. In the atmosphere he is interested in the air layer near the ground in which

crops and higher organisms grow and animals live, to the highest
levels in the atmosphere through which the transport of seeds, spores,
pollen and insects may take place.

1.2   Inter-disciplinary Aspects

Agrometeorology is an inter-disciplinary science in which the
main scientific disciplines involved are atmospheric sciences and soil
sciences which are concerned with the physical and chemical environment, and the plant sciences and animal sciences (including
their pathology, entomology and parasitology, etc.) which deal with
the contents of the biosphere. Though inter-disciplinary in nature,
agrometeorology is now a well-defined science. It has a set approach in theory and methodology. Its subject matter links together
the physical environment and biological responses under natural
conditions. Using a four-stage approach, an agrometeorologist first
formulates an accurate description of the physical environment and
biological responses. Secondly, he interprets biological responses in
terms of the physical environment. Thirdly, he makes crop and
weather forecasts. His final goal is the control of physical environment of crop fields and animal houses.

1.3   Practical Utility

The science of agrometeorology has great practical utility in protection against, or avoidance of adverse climatic risks. The dangers
to crops and livestock which have a meteorological content include
the incidence and extent of pests and diseases; the pollution of air
and soil, crop growth, animal production; all farm operations, the
incidence and effects of drought; soil erosion from wind or water;
incidence, frequency and extent of frost; the dangers of forest or
bush fires; and losses during storage and transport.

Out of the total annual crop losses, a great proportion is due to
direct weather effects such as flash floods, untimely rains, hails and
storms. Losses in harvest, storage and also those due to parasites,
insects and plant diseases are highly influenced by the weather.
When specifically tailored weather support is readily available to
the needs of agriculture, it greatly contributes towards making short
term adjustments in daily agricultural operations which minimise
losses resulting from adverse weather conditions and improve the
yield and quality of agricultural products (Mavi, 1974). The weather
support also provides guidelines for long range or seasonal plan-

ning and selection of crops most suited to anticipated climatic conditions.

Weather elements which influence agricultural operations and crop production can be forecast for different time spans; however, with an increase in time span, the accuracy of the forecast decreases (Newman, 1974). Hail, tornados and flash floods can be forecast up to 12 hours in advance; heavy rainfall, blizzards and thunderstorms up to 24 hours in advance; and wind velocity and rainfall forecasts can be made up to 36 hours in advance. Weather elements like rainfall and temperature intensity can be predicted for five days. Departures from the normal temperature and precipitation can be predicted for the coming season. Based on the forecasts of these elements, decisions can be taken in advance in agricultural operations and planning so as to make the best use of favourable weather conditions and make adjustments for adverse weather.

Other applications are through improvement in techniques based on sound interpretation of meteorological knowledge. These include irrigation; shelter from the wind or cold; shade from excessive sun; anti-frost measures including choice of site; anti-erosion measures; soil cover and mulching; plant cover using glass or plastic materials; artificial climates of growthrooms or heated structures; animal housing and management; climate control in storage and transport; and efficient use of herbicides, insecticides and fertilisers. Agrometeorological methods can be used in efficient land use planning; determining suitable crops for a region; risk analysis of climatic hazards and profit calculations in farming; production or harvest forecasts; and in adoption of farming methods and choice of farm machinery.

1.4. Future Thrust

The use of weather science has contributed considerably towards increased efficiency of agricultural operations. The increased efficiency has been due to laboratory and greenhouse studies in which biological responses have been measured under controlled conditions and later transferred to the field.

Because of its economic importance, there is a definite need to expand the sphere of agrometeorological knowledge. Greenhouse experiments, controlled climatic studies and bioclimatological models need more thrust (Russel, 1976). The other areas which need to be pursued vigorously by agrometeorologists are:

1) Identification and ecological importance of droughts;
2) Water balance analysis as an index of crop production potential.
3) Soil micro-climate; and
4) Agroclimatic classifications.

In livestock production, the thrust has to be to:

1) Stengthen the agrometeorological network to meet the special needs of livestock raising; and

2) Conduct research on the adaptation of animals to varying climatic conditions and in the design of animal shelters.

More agrometeorological research stations need to be established in typical agroclimatic regions to record data on weather and crops for preparing agrometeorological models and agroclimatic indices.

REFERENCES

Bourke, P.M. Austin, 1968. The Aims of Agrometeorology. Agroclimatological Methods—Proc. Reading Symposium, UNESCO: 11-15.

Mavi, H.S. 1974. Agricultural Meteorology, PAU, Ludhiana: 1-5.

Molga, M. 1962. Agricultural Meteorology. Part II—Outline of Agrometeorological Problems. Warsaw: 5-8.

Newman, J.E. 1974. Applying Meteorology to Agriculture. Agric. Meteorol. 13: 1-3.

Russell, E.W. 1976. Agricultural meteorology and tropical agriculture. Agric. Meteorol. 16: 1-3.

Smith, L.P. 1970. Aims and Extent of Agricultural Meteorology, Agric. Meteorol. 7: 193-196.

Chapter 2

SOLAR RADIATION

All matter, at a temperature above the absolute zero, imparts energy to the surrounding space. This transferring of energy and its mode of transfer are known as radiation. Every organism at the surface of the earth is thus immersed in an environment of radiation consisting of short wave radiation from heavenly bodies and long wave radiation from nearby surfaces, including the earth. The total radiation flux within a given site is highly variable, changing with the time of day, season and weather. The variations of the total radiation flux from one site to another on the surface of the earth are enormous and the distribution of plants and animals responds to this variation.

2.1 Sun

The ultimate source of practically all of the energy for physical and biological processes occurring on the earth is radiation received from the sun.

This is the nearest star to planet Earth and is the original source of most of the earth's energy. The diameter of the sun is 1.39×10^6 km. It rotates on its axis about once every four weeks. However, the rotation is not that of a solid body. At the equator it takes 27 days and at the poles 30 days for each rotation. The sun is on an average 1.5×10^8 km away from the earth. The surface temperature of the sun is 5762°K. In the central interior it is estimated to range between 8×10^6 and $40 \times 10^{6°}$K. The interior mass of the sun has a density 80 to 100 times that of water (Duffie, 1974).

Fusion reactions take place in the sun. These reactions supply the energy radiated by it. The one which is most important is the process in which hydrogen is transformed to helium. The energy through this fusion reaction is produced in the interior of the sphere of the sun at a temperature of several million degrees centigrade.

The energy is first transferred to the surface of the sun and then radiated into space. The radiation from the core of the sun is thought to be in X-rays and γ-rays. The wave length of radiation increases as the temperature falls at increasing distances from the core. The central region of the sun which extends from 0 to 0.23 R (R is radius of the sun) contains 40 per cent of the mass and 15 per cent of the volume of the sun, and generates 90 per cent of the energy of the sun.

At a distance of 0.7 R from the centre, the density of the sun mass drops to 0.07 g cm^{-3} and the temperature drops to 1,30,000°K. From 0.7 R in the interior to the outer surface, the zone is called the *Convective Zone*. Here the temperature is about 5000°K and the density approximately 10^{-8} g cm^{-3}. The upper layer of the convective zone is called the *Photosphere* and has sharply defined edges. In spite of the fact that it has low density (10^{-4} that of air at the sea level), the photosphere is opaque because it is composed of strongly ionised gases. The photosphere is the source of radiation flux to space because it has the capability to emit and absorb a continuous spectrum of radiation.

Outside the photosphere is the solar atmosphere which is several hundred km deep and is almost transparent. This solar atmosphere is referred to as the *Reversing Layer*. Outside the reversing layer is the *Chromosphere* which is about 1,00,000 km deep. It is seen from the earth only during the total eclipse when it appears as a region of rosy colour. It is in this zone that the short lived, brilliant solar flares occur in the clouds of hydrogen and gaseous calcium. These flares are a source of intense bursts of ultraviolet and radio-wave radiation. The solar flares also eject streams of electrically charged particles called corpuscles which on reaching the earth's surface disturb its magnetic field. The outer ring of the sun is the *Corona* which is seen during a total eclipse. It has a temperature of the order of 10^{6}°K and has a very low density. The corona is believed to consist of very sparse ions and electrons moving at such high speeds as to generate a temperature of over 10,00,000°C. There is no sharp boundary to this outermost region (Lamb, 1972).

These zones suggest that the sun does not act as a perfect black body radiator at a fixed temperature. The radiation flux is the composite result of the several layers. For general purposes however, the sun can be referred to as a black body at a temperature of 5762°K.

The sun supplies more than 99 per cent of the energy to the biosphere. Small quantities of energy are available from other sources, some of which are given in Table 2.1.

Table 2.1   Thermal energy sources at earth surface relative to average solar energy of 263 kilo langley (kly) per year

(Sellers, 1967)

One-fourth solar constant	1
Heat flux from interior of the earth	18×10^{-5}
Radiation from full moon	3×10^{-5}
Sun's radiation reflected from the moon	1×10^{-5}
Energy from lightning discharges	6×10^{-7}
Total radiation from stars	4×10^{-8}

From Table 2.1 it is clear that the sun completely overshadows all the other sources of energy on the earth's surface.

2.2   Solar Constant

The sun is the source of more than 99 per cent of the thermal energy required for the physical processes taking place in the earth-atmosphere system. Every minute, the sun radiates approximately 56×10^{26} calories of energy. In terms of the energy per unit area incident on a spherical shell with a radius of 1.5×10^{13} cm (the mean distance of the earth from the sun) and concentric with the sun, this energy is equal to

$$S = \frac{56 \times 10^{26} \text{ cal min}^{-1}}{4\pi (1.5 \times 10^{13} \text{ cm})^2} = 2.0 \text{ langley min}^{-1}$$

where S is the solar constant. The solar constant is the flux of solar radiation at the outer boundary of the earth's atmosphere received on a surface held perpendicular to the sun's direction at the mean distance between the sun and the earth.

The solar constant is not a true constant, but fluctuates by as much as $\pm$ 3.5 per cent about its mean value, depending upon the distance of the earth from the sun. Solar constant has been measured directly with aircraft and satellites. The total radiation flux measured at a height of 82 km is 1.95 langley (ly) min^{-1}. Thirty-five per cent of this value is contributed by ultraviolet and visible parts and the remaining 65 per cent by the infrared.

The total solar radiation intercepted by the earth in a unit time is equal to $\pi r^2 S$ (where r is the radius of the earth and S is the solar constant). It amounts to 6.37×10^{21} cal day^{-1}.

If the energy is spread uniformly over the full surface of the earth, the amount received per unit area and per unit time is:

$$Qs = \frac{\pi r^2}{4\pi r^2}\frac{S}{} = \frac{S}{4} = 0.5 \text{ ly min}^{-1} = 263 \text{ kly year}^{-1}$$

Actually, the distribution is not uniform and the annual value at the equator is 2.4 times that near the poles. The solar energy incident upon a surface depends upon the geographic location, orientation of the surface, time of the day, time of the year and atmospheric conditions (Boes, 1981).

2.3 Nature of Solar Radiation

The behaviour of electromagnetic radiation may be summed up in the following simplified statements (Morris et al., 1973). Every matter with temperatures above the absolute zero emits radiation.

Substances which emit the maximum amount of radiation in all wavelengths are known as black bodies. Such bodies will absorb completely all radiation incident upon them. A black body is thus a perfect radiator and absorber.

Substances absorb radiation of wavelengths which they can emit.

The wavelengths at which the energy is emitted by the substances depend upon their temperature; higher the temperature, shorter is the wavelength.

Gases emit and absorb radiation only in certain wavelengths. The amount of radiation absorbed by a gas is proportional to the: (a) number of molecules of the gas, and (b) intensity of radiation of that wavelength.

2.4 Radiation Laws

Wavelength: The wavelength of electromagnetic radiation is given by the equation:

$$\lambda = \frac{C}{V}$$

where λ is the wavelength,

V is the frequency which means number of vibrations or cycles per second, and C is the constant equal to the velocity of light, 3×10^{10} cm sec^{-1}.

Wavelength (λ) is the shortest distance between consecutive crests in the wave trance.

PLANCK'S LAW

Electromagnetic radiation consists of flow of quanta or particles and the energy content (E) of each quantum is proportional to the frequency given by the equation

$$E = h\nu$$

where h is Planck's constant having a value of 6.625×10^{-27} erg sec^{-1} and ν is the frequency. The equation indicates that the greater the frequency, greater is the energy of the quantum.

KIRCHOFF'S LAW

Any grey object (other than a perfect black body) which receives radiation disposes off a part of it in reflection and transmission. The absorptivity, reflectivity and transmissivity are each less than or equal to unity.

This law states that the absorptivity a of an object for radiation of a specific wavelength is equal to its emissivity e for the same wavelength and the equation of the law is

$$a(\lambda) = e(\lambda)$$

STEFAN BOLTZMAN'S LAW

This law states that the intensity of radiation emitted by a radiating body is proportional to the fourth power of the absolute temperature of that body

$$\text{Flux} = \sigma T^4$$

where σ is the Stefan Boltzman constant

$$(5.67 \times 10^{-5} \text{ ergs cm}^{-2} \text{ sec}^{-1} \text{ K}^{-4})$$

WEIN'S LAW

The wavelength of maximum intensity of emission from a black body is inversely proportional to the absolute temperature T of the body. Thus,

Wavelength (λ) of max. intensity $(\mu) = 2897\ T^{-1}$

For the sun the wavelength of the maximum emission is near $0.5\ \mu$ and is in the visible portion of the electromagnetic spectrum.

About 99 per cent of the sun's radiation is contained between 0.15 and 4.0 μ and is referred to as short-wave radiation (Munn, 1966). A systematic division of solar radition according to frequency and wavelength is given in Table 2.2.

Table 2.2   Range of electromagnetic spectrum (Lapp and Andrew, 1954)

Type of radiation	Frequency range cycles/sec	Wavelength range (cm)
Gamma rays	$3 \times 10^{21} - 3 \times 10^{18}$	$10^{-11} - 10^{-8}$
X-rays	$3 \times 10^{22} - 3 \times 10^{16}$	$10^{-12} - 10^{-6}$
Ultraviolet	$3 \times 10^{18} - 7.5 \times 10^{14}$	$10^{-8} - 4 \times 10^{-5}$
Visible	$7.5 \times 10^{14} - 4 \times 10^{14}$	$4 \times 10^{-5} - 7.6 \times 10^{-5}$
Infrared	$4 \times 10^{14} - 10^{11}$	$7.6 \times 10^{-5} - 0.3$
Radio waves	$10^{11} - 10^{4}$	$0.3 - 3 \times 10^{6}$
Electric waves	$10^{4} - 0$	$3 \times 10^{6} - \infty$

An approximation of energy content in various segments of short-wave radiation is given in Table 2.3.

Table 2.3   Electromagnetic spectrum energy content

Spectrum	Wavelength (μ)	% energy
Gamma rays and X-rays	$0.005 - 0.20$	9
Ultraviolet rays	$0.2 - 0.4$	
Violet	$0.4 - 0.43$	
Blue	$0.43 - 0.49$	
Green	$0.49 - 0.53$	41
Yellow	$0.53 - 0.58$	
Orange	$0.58 - 0.63$	
Red	$0.65 - 0.70$	
Infrared rays	$0.70 -$	50

A more detailed picture of the energy content and nature of solar radiation spectrum is given in Table 2.4.

Table 2.4   Partition of solar radiation (Baumgartner, 1973)

Spectrum	Wavelength (μ)	Energy portion (%)	Photometric portion (%)	Sensitivity to human eye (%)
Ultraviolet A	0.28	0.5	—	—
Ultraviolet B	0.32	1.0	—	—
Ultraviolet C	0.40	6.5	—	—
Violet	0.44	5.4	0.4	1.0
Ultrablue	0.48	6.4	3.4	8.3
Ice-blue	0.49	1.5	2.0	20.8
Sea-green	0.54	7.5	32.3	66.8
Leaf-green	0.57	4.4	27.8	98.2
Yellow	0.59	2.9	15.2	81.4
Orange	0.61	2.8	10.2	56.8
Red	0.76	17.1	8.7	8.0
Infrared A	1.4	32.3	—	—
Infrared B	3.0	10.7	—	—
Infrared C	6.8	1.2	—	—

2.5   Disposition of Solar Radiation

The solar radiation intercepted by the earth is absorbed and used in

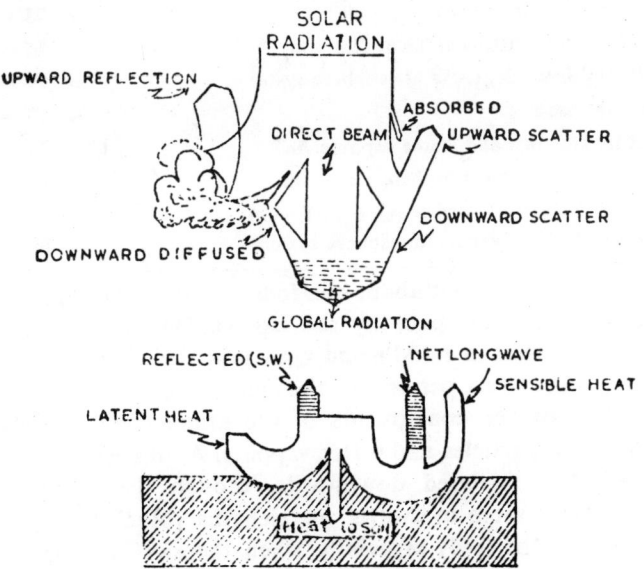

Fig. 2.1   Disposal of solar radiation.
(Rose, 1966)

energy-driven processes or is returned to space by scattering and reflection (Fig. 2.1).

In mathematical terms, this disposition of solar radiation is given by the equation

$$Qs = Cr + Ar + Ca + Aa + (Q + q)(1 - a) + (Q + q)a$$

where Cr is reflection and scattering back to space by clouds,

Ar is reflection and scattering back by air, dust and H_2O vapours,

$(Q + q)$ a is reflection by the earth, where

Q and q are respectively direct beam and diffused solar radiation incident on earth and a is albedo. Ca is absorption by clouds.

Aa is absorption by air, dust and water vapours.

$(Q + q)(1 - a)$ is absorption by the earth's surface.

The global disposition of short-wave radiation in terms of kly and also as per cent per year, is outlined in Table 2.5.

Table 2.5   Disposition of solar radiation

Solar energy incident on the top of the atmosphere Qs	— 263
Reflected by clouds Cr	= 63 = 24%
Reflected by air, dust and water vapours Ar	= 15 = 6%
Total reflected by atmosphere $Cr + Ar$	= 78 = 30%
Reflected from the earth's surface $(Q + q)a$	= 16 = 6%
Total reflected from the earth atmosphere system	= 94 = 36%
Absorbed by clouds Ca	= 7 = 3%
Absorbed by air, dust and water vapours Aa	= 38 = 14%
Total absorbed by the atmosphere $Ca + Aa$	= 45 = 17%
Absorbed by the earth's surface $(Q + q)(1 - a)$	= 124 = 47%
Total absorbed by the earth–atmosphere system	= 169 = 64%

Table 2.5 indicates that about one-fourth of the solar radiation is reflected back to the space by the clouds. On an average, the reflection is greatest in middle and high latitudes and least in the substropics. About six per cent of the incident radiation is scattered back to space by the constituents of the atmosphere, mainly air molecules, dust particles and water vapours. About 30 per cent of the radiation is scattered downwards, though the scattering is selective. This is more in shorter wavelengths (blue) than that in longer wavelengths (red) especially when the sky is clear. If the circumference of the scattering particles is less than about 1/10 of

the wavelength of the incident radiation, the scattering coefficient is inversely proportional to the fourth power of the wavelength of the incident radiation. This is known as Rayleigh scattering and is the primary cause of the blue colour of the sky (Wallace and Peter, 1977). For larger sizes of particles with circumferences of more than 30 times of wavelength of the incident radiation, scattering is independent of the wavelength i.e. white light is scattered (Gates, 1965) The phenomena is known as Mei scattering.

The red colour of the sky at sunrise and sunset is because of increased path length in the atmosphere. As the path length increases the percentage of solar energy in the visible part decreases. Within the visible part itself, the ratio of the blue to the red part decreases with increased path length. This is because of the fact that the part of the spectrum with higher frequency is reflected to a greater extent than the part with lower frequency away from the horizon.

About 17 per cent of the solar radiation is absorbed by the atmosphere. The constituents of the atmosphere that absorb the solar radiation significantly are oxygen, ozone, carbon dioxide and water vapours. Oxygen atoms in the upper part of the atmosphere absorb the extreme ultraviolet wavelengths (0.12 to $0.16\,\mu$). Ozone absorbs the ultraviolet part of the spectrum in the wavelengths 0.20 to $0.32\,\mu$. Ozone also absorbs some quantities of radiation in the visible portion of 0.44 to $0.70\,\mu$. Water vapours absorb in the near infrared bands at 0.93, 1.13, $1.42\,\mu$. Carbon dioxide absorbs the infrared bands at $2.7\,\mu$. Thus solar radiation reaches the earth's surface in a depleted form. Practically, all the radiation in the ultraviolet part at wavelengths smaller than $0.33\,\mu$ is absorbed by the oxygen and ozone in the upper atmosphere. This absorption is of great significance to life on the earth's surface, because only very little of this radiation can be tolerated by living organisms.

Thus, after reflection, scattering and absorption in the atmosphere, about half of the solar radiation reaches the earth's surface. Even out of this, about six per cent is reflected back to outer space and is known as albedo. This albedo varies with the colour and composition of the earth's surface. The albedo values of some selected surface are given in Table 2.6.

The albedo varies with season and the angle of the sun rays. The values are highest in winter and at sunrise and sunset.

The albedo also varies with the wavelength of the incident

radiation. Very small values have been recorded in the ultraviolet part of the spectrum and higher values in the visible part.

Table 2.6 Albedo of short-wave radiation
(Munn, 1966)

Surface	Albedo (%)	Surface	Albedo (%)
Fresh snow	75–95	Coniferous forests	15–20
Human skin blond	43–45	Deciduous forests	10–20
Dry sand dune	35–45	Meadows	10–20
Clay or grey soil	20–35	Dark soil	5–15
Wet sand dune	20–30	Water surface at 30° latitude	6–9
Crop plants	15–25		
Dark human skin	16–22		

2.6. Outgoing Long-wave Radiation

The surface of the earth after being heated by the absorption of solar radiation becomes a source of radiation itself. Because the average temperature of the earth's surface is about 285°K, 99 per cent of the radiation is emitted in the infrared range from 4 to 120 μ with a peak near 10 μ, as indicated by Wein's displacement law. This is a long wave radiation and is also known as terrestrial radiation.

The average annual global disposition of infrared radiation is represented by the equations A, B and C.

(A) $I_{(e)} = I_a + I_s$

(B) $I_{(a)} = I_{\downarrow} + I_{a(s)}$

(C) $I = I_{(e)} - I$

Where $I_{(e)}$ is infrared radiation emitted by earth surface.

I_a is infrared radiation from earth's surface absorbed by the atmosphere.

I_s is infrared radiation from the earth lost to space.

$I_{(a)}$ is infrared radiation from the atmosphere.

$I_{\downarrow}$ is counter radiation.

$I_{(a)s}$ is infrared radiation from the atmosphere lost in space.

I is the effective outgoing radiation from the earth.

The average annual global disposition of infrared radiation in terms of kly per year from the earth atmosphere system is summarised in Table 2.7.

From the Table 2.7 it is clear that about 90 per cent of the outgoing radiation from the earth's surface is absorbed by the atmosphere. Water vapours absorb in wavelengths of 5.3 to 7.7 μ and beyond 20 μ; ozone 9.4 to 9.8 μ; carbon dioxide 13.1 to 16.9 μ and clouds in all wavelengths. The long-wave radiation escapes to

Table 2.7   Disposition of terrestrial radiation

A	Infrared radiation emitted by the earth's surface	$I_{(e)} = 258$ kly
	Lost to space	$I_s = 20$
	Absorbed by the atmosphere	$I_a = 238$
B	Infrared radiation emitted by the atmosphere	$I_{(a)} = 355$
	Lost in space	$I_{a(s)} = 149$
	Absorbed by the earth surface as counter-radiation	$I_\downarrow = 206$
C	Effective outgoing radiation from the earth's surface	$I = 52$
	Effective outgoing radiation from the atmosphere	$I_{(a)} = 117$
	Effective outgoing radiation from the earth atmosphere system	$I_{(g)} = 169$

space in between 8.5 and 11.0 μ and is known as the *atmospheric window*. A large part of the radiation absorbed by the atmosphere is sent back to the earth's surface as counter-radiation. This counter-radiation prevents the earth's surface from excessive cooling at night.

2.7   Radiation Balance

When averaged over the globe, the earth's surface absorbs about 124 kly of solar radiation every year and effectively radiates 52 kly of long wave energy to the atmosphere. The difference, 72 kly is the net radiation balance of the earth's surface.

Likewise the net radiation balance of the atmosphere comes to −72 kly per year. Thus the atmosphere losses as much radiative energy in a year as the earth's surface gains and the radiation balance of the system becomes zero. To keep this system in equilibrium, energy is transferred from the earth's surface to the atmosphere to keep the surface from warming up and the atmosphere from cooling down. This vertical heat exchange occurs mainly through the evaporation of water from the surface of the earth (heat loss) and through condensation in the atmosphere (heat gain) and by the conduction of sensible heat from the surface and transfer to the atmosphere through convection.

REFERENCES

Baumgartner, A. 1973. Estimation of the radiation and thermal micro-environment from meteorological and plant parameters. Plant Response to Climatic Factors. Proceedings of the Uppsala Symposium, UNESCO: 313–323.

Boes Edlon. 1981. Fundamentals of solar radiation. Solar Energy Hand Book. Eds. Jan F. Krieder and Frank Krieth. McGraw-Hill: 2-1 to 2-76.

Duffie, John. A. 1974. Solar Energy Thermal Process. A. Beckman: 1-7.

Gates, D.M. 1965. Radiant Energy, its Receipt and Disposal. Agricultural Meteorology. Meteorological Monograph Published by American Meteorological Society. 6: 1-26.

Lamb, H.B. 1972. Climate: Present, Past and Future. Methuen & Co., Ltd: 11-12.

Lapp, R.E. and H.L. Andrew 1954. Nuclear Radiation Physics. Prentice-Hall, Englewood Cliffs, N.D.

Morris, Neiburger, James. G. Edinger and William. D. Bonner. 1973. Understanding our Atmospheric Environment. W.H. Freeman & Co: 40-65.

Munn, R.E. 1966. Descriptive Micrometeorology. Academic Press: 8-16.

Rose, C.W. 1966. Agricultural Physics. Pergamon, London.

Sellers, William D. 1967. Physical Climatology. The University of Chicago Press, Chicago: 11-29.

Wallace, John M. and Peter, V. Holiles. 1977. Atmospheric Science. An Introductory Survey. Academic Press: 280-309.

CHAPTER 3

SOLAR RADIATION AND CROP PLANTS

Solar radiation is the source of energy which sustains organic life on the earth surface. Crop production is in fact an exploitation of solar radiation.

The three broad spectra of solar energy are significant to plant life. The shorter than visible wavelength radiation segment in the solar spectrum is chemically very active. When plants are exposed to excessive amounts of this radiation, the effects are detrimental. The atmosphere however, acts as a regulator in this type of solar radiation and none of the cosmic, gamma and X-rays reach the earth (Evans, 1973). The ultraviolet radiation of this segment reaching the earth surface is very low and is normally tolerated by plants.

Solar radiation in the higher than visible wavelength segment, referred to as infrared radiation, has thermal effects on plants. In the presence of water vapours, this radiation does not harm plants, rather it supplies the necessary thermal energy to the plant environment.

The third spectrum lying between the ultraviolet and infrared is the visible part of solar radiation, also referred to as light. Virtually all the plant parts are directly or indirectly influenced by this part of the spectrum. Light of the correct intensity, quality and duration is essential to normal plant development. Poor light availability is frequently responsible for plant abnormalities and disorders. Light is indispensable to photosynthesis. It governs the distribution of photosynthates among different organs of plants. It also affects the production of tillers; the stability, strength and length of the culms; the yield and total weight of plant structures; and the size of leaves and the root development. Again, there are critical stages of plant growth when solar radiation is especially important. For example, radiation intensity during the third month of maize plant growth, the 25-day period before flowering in the case of rice, and the flowering period in the case of barley has a vital effect on the yield of these crops. The length of the day or the duration of the light period determines the flowering and has a profound effect on the content of soluble carbohydrates present. A majority of plants flower only when exposed to certain specific photo periods. It is on the basis of this response that the plants have been classified as short day plants, long day plants and day neutral plants. When any other environmental factor is not a limiting one, the longer duration of the light period increases photosynthesis (Salisbury, 1981).

3.1 Reflection, Transmission and Absorption

Reflection and transmission from the leaves have similar spectral distributions as is shown in Fig. 3.2. The maxima for both is in the green light as well as in the infrared region. The impression of the green colour of the plants depends upon the high reflectivity, relatively high intensity of solar radiation and greater sensitivity of the human eye for green light. The strong infrared reflection from plants is an important natural device for protection of plant life against damage due to overheating.

On an average about 75 per cent of the incident radiation is absorbed by the plant canopy. About 15 per cent is reflected and 10 per cent is transmitted.

Due to their chemical components or physical structures, plants absorb selectively in discrete wavelengths. Ultraviolet radiation is first absorbed by the anthocyanins, flavones and tannins and to some extent by carotenoids. Light is scattered by the celluloses and absorbed by the orange-red carotenes, yellow xanthophylls, dark-green chlorophyll a and light green chlorophyll b. Chlorophyll absorption is maximum in the blue (0.45 μ) and in the red (0.65 μ) regions. Just near the border of visible light, absorption by the plants decreases but again increases in the infrared. Infrared radiation greater than 3 μ is completely absorbed by the plants. The plant bodies are thus black bodies for infrared radiation.

The quality of radiation affects flowering, germination and elongation. It has been demonstrated that red light with a wavelength of 0.66 micron is by far the most effective inhibitor of flowering in the case of long day plants. The red light helps the mature apples

Table 3.1 Green leaf response to spectral radiation components
(Baumgartner, 1973)

Wavelength (μ)	Reflection (%)	Transmission (%)	Absorption (%)
0.34	9	0	91
0.44	11	2	87
0.51	14	10	76
0.58	14	10	76
0.64	13	9	78
1.0	45	50	5
2.4	7	28	65

to turn red. The germination of the seeds is inhibited when they are exposed to green, blue and other short wavelength colours and then again in the infrared part of the spectrum. Germination is, however, induced when the seeds are exposed to the red portion of the spectrum. This follows that the red and the infrared parts of the spectrum have reversible effects on seed germination. Stem elongation is promoted by exposure to far-red wavelengths whereas the red part of the spectrum suppresses the elongation (Butler and

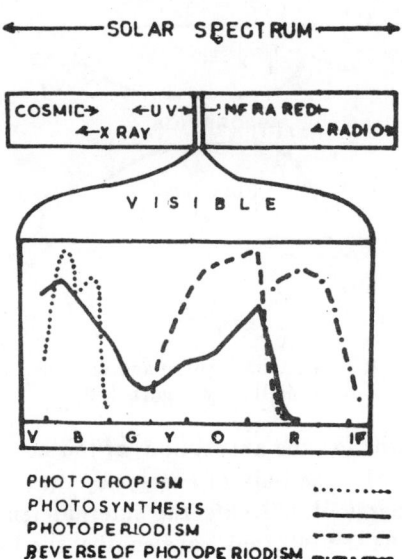

Fig. 3.1 Solar spectra and plant processes.

Roberts, 1966). The visible part of the spectrum also influences the orientation of shoots and the phenomenon is known as phototropism. When shoots turn towards the light, the phenomenon is known as positive phototropism. With increasing intensity of light positive phototropism turns into negative phototropism. The strongest influence on phototropism is by the blue part of the spectrum (.45 μ) and the weakest by the red rays (Fig. 3.1). The phototropism action of the visible spectrum increases from the red to the blue part, subsequently it declines again in the ultraviolet part.

The ultraviolet part of the spectrum has only a slight effect on the plant. This may be partly because very little of this part of the spectrum reaches the earth's surface. However, it is well known that these rays have biological effects. These rays may kill microorganisms, disinfect the soil and eradicate diseases. Experiments have proved that ultraviolet rays influence the germination and quality of seeds. These rays lead to many irregularities in the growth and development of plant (Caldwell, 1981).

Several studies have been conducted to find out plant responses to solar radiation. It has been established that a plant leaf strongly absorbs blue and red wavelengths, less strongly the green, and very weakly the near infrared and strongly the far

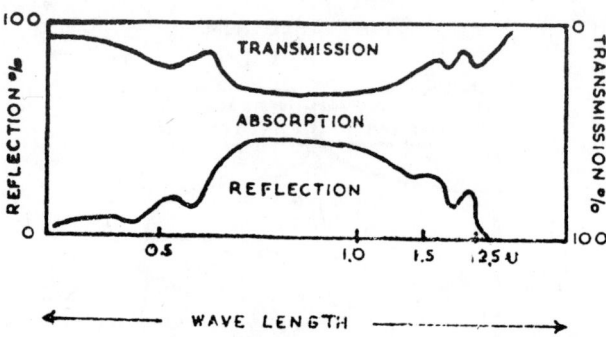

Fig. 3.2   Reflection, absorption and transmission of
solar radiation through a leaf.

infrared wavelengths. As the absorption of the near infrared wavelengths (which contain the bulk of energy) by the leaf is limited, by discarding this energy it prevents the internal temperature from becoming lethal. At the infrared wavelengths, the plant leaf is an efficient absorber. But in these wavelengths, the energy at the surface is small, with the result that the plant is a good absorber in the far infrared, it is equally a good radiator at these wavelengths (Fig. 3.2).

The Dutch Committee on Plant Irradiation (Wassink, 1953) has divided the solar spectrum into the following eight divisions or bands on the basis of the physiological response of plants to the incident radiation.

1st Band: Wavelength greater than 1.000 μ.

No specific effects of this radiation are known. It is acceptable that this radiation, as far as it is absorbed by the plants, is transformed into heat without interference in biochemical processes.

2nd Band: Wavelength 1.000 to 0.700 μ.

This is the region of specific elongation effects on plants.

3rd Band: Wavelength 0.700 to 0.610 μ.

This is almost the spectral region of the strongest absorption of chlorophyll and of the strongest photosynthetic activity in the red-region. In many cases, it also shows the strongest photoperiodic activity.

4th Band: Wavelength 0.610 to 0.510 μ.

This is the region of low photosynthetic effectiveness in the green and of weak formative activity.

5th Band: Wavelength 0.510 to 0.400 μ.

This is virtually the region of strong chlorophyll absorption and absorption by yellow pigments. It is also a region of strong photosynthetic activity in the blue-violet and of strong formative effects.

6th Band: Wavelength 0.400 to 0.315 μ.

It produces flourescence in plants and strong response by photographic emulsions.

7th Band: Wavelength 0.315 to 0.280 μ.

It produces antirachitic effects in the production of vitamin D from ergosterol. This radiation has significant germicidal action. Under natural conditions, practically no solar radiation of wavelengths shorter than 0.29 μ reaches the earth's surface.

8th Band: Wavelength shorter than 0.280 μ.

No such radiation reaches the earth's surface. This radiation has strong germicidal action. It is injurious to eyesight and below 0.26 μ has killing effects on some plants.

3.2   Radiation Distribution in a Crop Canopy

Three aspects of solar radiation are biologically significant. The first is the intensity of radiation i.e. amount of radiant energy falling on a unit surface area in a unit time. The second is the spectral distribution of radiation which governs the photochemical process of photosynthesis. The third aspect is the radiation distribution in time and is important for photoperiodic phenomenon.

The determination of intensity and spectral distribution of radiation within crop canopies is an important problem in agrometeorology because of its control on the photosynthetic process and on the microclimate of the plant community. The rate of photosynthesis is dependent upon the availability of photosynthetically active radiation intercepted by the leaves. The rate of transpiration taking place from the plant canopy is also controlled to a great extent by the radiation energy. Thus knowledge of radiation transmission through the elements of a plant community is necessary to know the use made by the crop of the incident radiation (Fig. 3.3).

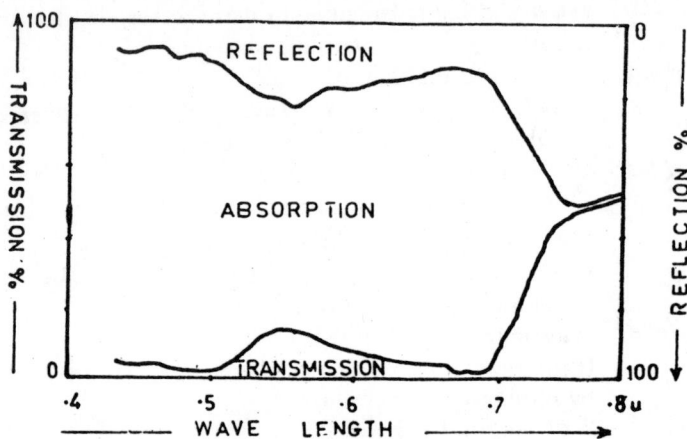

Fig. 3.3   Reflection, absorption and transmission of light through a leaf.

3.3   Factors Affecting Radiation Distribution Within the Plant Community

Although a single leaf is light-saturated at radiation intensity far short of full sunlight, because of the arrangement of leaf blades and stems in the fields, considerable part of the inner portions of the plant community remains short of light. To grasp the relationship between solar radiation and crop production, knowledge of radiation distribution within the crop canopy is required. The distribution of radiation is determined by several factors such as the transmissibility of the leaf, leaf arrangement and inclination, plant density, plant height and the angle of the sun.

The light transmissibility of the mature leaves of many species has been measured. Leaves of deciduous trees, herbs and grasses (including cereals) have a transmissibility ranging from 5 to 10 per cent. The broad leaves of evergreen plants have a value of 2 to 8 per cent.

Transmissibility varies slightly with the age of the leaf. The transmissibility of a young leaf is relatively high. With the maturing of the leaf, it declines but rises again as the leaf turns yellow.

The transmissibility of a leaf is directly related to its chlorophyll content. The logarithm of transmissibility decreases linearly with an increase in the chlorophyll content.

If the leaves that transmit 10 per cent of the radiation were horizontally displayed in continuous layers, only 1 per cent of light, mostly in the green region, could penetrate the second layer. However, leaves are rarely displayed horizontally. The relative light interception of horizontal and erect foliage is calculated in the ratio 1 to 0.44. Therefore, the actual light gradient within the canopy is much less steep as the transmissibility will suggest. It has been found that when the total leaf area equalled the area at the ground, the mean transmissibility was 74 per cent for the more upright leaves and 50 per cent for the more horizontal leaves.

In weak light, any departure of the leaves from the horizontal position reduces the net photosynthesis. In full sunlight, the optimum leaf inclination for efficient light use is 81° (Fig 3.4A, Chang, 1968). At full sunlight, a leaf placed at the optimum inclination is 4.5 times as efficient in using light as a horizontal leaf (Fig. 3.4B). For more efficient use of light, the upper leaves in a plant canopy should have a near vertical orientation, whereas the lower foliage should be almost horizontal. For the best results and in an ideal arrangement of the plant canopy, the lower 13 per cent of the leaves should be oriented at an angle of 0 to 30°, middle 37 per cent of the leaves should be at 30 to 60° and the upper 50 per cent leaves should be at 60 to 90° with the horizontal.

In the case of young plants, not only is the percentage of light interception small, but it is also variable with the time of day. It is minimum at noon and maximum during the morning and evening hours. When the plant height increases, the interception of light by the canopy also increases with only a small variation at different times of the day.

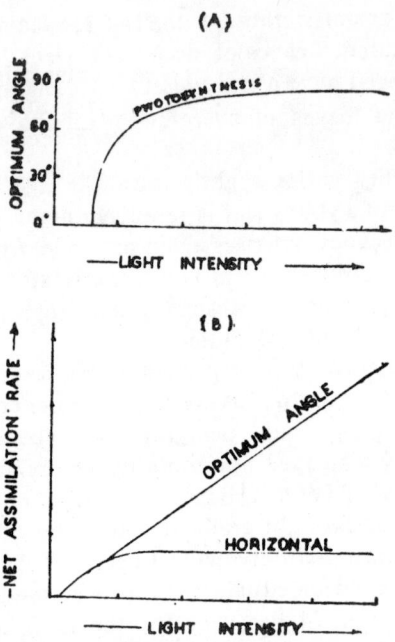

Fig. 3.4 (A, B) Light intensity and leaf angle for optimum net assimilation. (Chang, 1968)

3.4 Measurement of Radiation Distribution in a Plant Canopy

Several investigations have been made to determine the radiation and light profiles in a plant canopy and several equations have been put forward to determine the light at a particular height in a canopy.

The light distribution is expressed by Beer's law as:

$$I = I_a e^{-kf}$$

Where I is the intensity of light at a particular height within the canopy, I_a is the intensity at the top, k is the extinction coefficient of the leaf, f is the leaf-area index, and e is the base of natural log (2.7183). The extinction coefficient can be defined as the ratio between the light loss through the leaf to the light at the top of the leaf. The extinction coefficient varies with the orientation of the leaf. Its value is in the range of 0.3 to 0.5 in stands with upright leaves and 0.7 to 1.0 in stands with more or less horizontal leaves.

Monteith's equation expresses the radiation or light intensity within the crop canopy as

$$I = [S + (I - S)r]^f I_o$$

where I is the intensity of light at a particular height in the canopy, S is the fraction of light passing through a unit leaf area without interception, r is the leaf transmission coefficient and f is the leaf-area index. Figure 3.5 shows radiation balance in plant canopy.

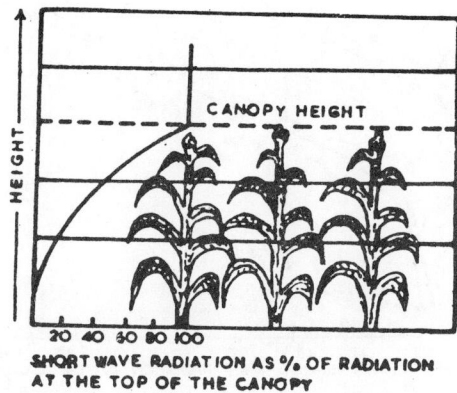

Fig. 3.5   Radiation balance in plant canopy

Both these equations are undoubtedly accurate. However, the main difficulty lies in the measurement of the leaf-area index for successive strata in the plant community.

3.5 Net Short Wave Radiation

The net short-wave radiation is the incoming short-wave radiation after reflection from the canopy and represents the amount of energy available for absorption and transmission. The short-wave radiation intensity decreases exponentially with increasing leaf area.

Profiles of net short-wave radiation in the Partap variety of maize crop on a clear day were measured at Ludhiana (Fig. 3.6). The measurements revealed rapid depletion in high density crops as compared with medium and low density crops. The per cent of net short-wave radiation which penetrated to the upper half of the crop varied from 10 per cent in high density to 30 per cent in low density stand. At the bottom of the crop canopy, the net short-wave

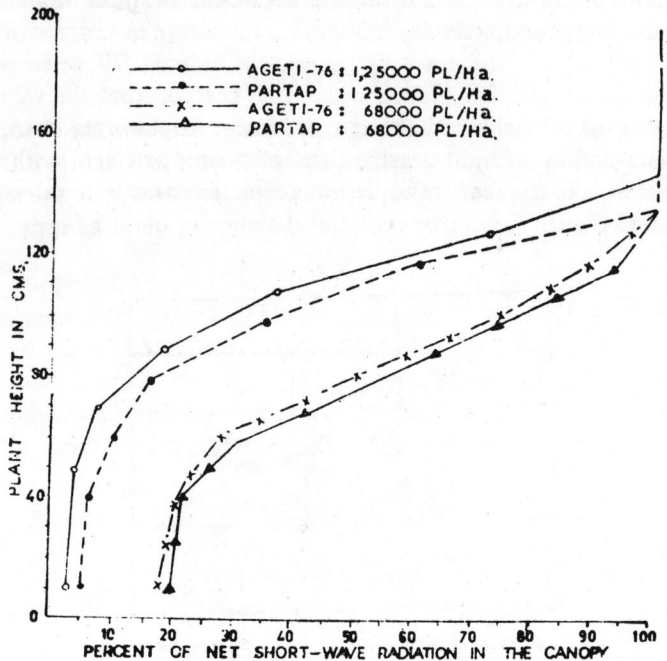

Fig. 3.6   Per cent depletion of net short-wave radiation in different stands of maize crop.

penetration was 5 per cent for the high density, 12 per cent for the medium density and 20 per cent for the low density stand of crop.

3.6   Net Radiation

The balance of energy after gain and loss of both short-wave and long-wave radiation fluxes is known as net radiation. Net radiation represents the amount of energy which is used for various kinds of activities within a crop. It is dispensed as sensible heat, latent heat and also in physiological processes such as photosynthesis and respiration. It has been demonstrated in a number of studies that the extinction of net radiation follows a similar law as for short-wave radiation. So the distribution of net radiation in a plant canopy can be explained with the equation of Beer's law.

The results of the study on maize crop (Babu Ranga, 1981) revealed that the pattern of depletion of net radiation was similar to that of net short-wave radiation with the only difference being the rate of depletion was lower. For example, the net radiation at the bottom of the crop canopy with high density stand was 17% as against 5% for short-wave radiation. Similarly in crops with low stand, the net radiation was 40 per cent as against 20 per cent of short-wave radiation. This is because of the fact that the values of the extinction coefficient for net radiation were lower as compared to short-wave radiation. Further, the crop canopy itself is a source of long-wave radiation which affects the net radiation values at a particular layer in the canopy.

3.7 Spectral Composition of Radiation in a Plant Canopy

After transmission through the plant community, the solar spectrum has a changed composition (Table 3.2). Radiation transmitted down through the leaves is mainly infrared with a small amount of the green part of the spectrum. The actual change in the composition depends upon the amount transmitted through the leaves plus that which passes through the gaps as sunflecks. In a tall alfalfa crop, it has been found that 30 per cent of the total radiation and 20 per cent of light reach the ground.

For a tall corn crop, the transmission of infrared radiation to the ground is 30 to 40 per cent. In the visible part of the spectrum, the transmission is only 5 to 10 per cent.

Table 3.2   Spectral variation of radiation after transmission through leaves (Baumgartner, 1973)

		$0.55\,\mu$	$0.70\,\mu$	$0.95\,\mu$
1	Leaf	0.14	0.20	0.42
2	leaves	0.020	0.04	0.18
3	leaves	0.0028	0.008	0.075
4	leaves	0.004	0.0016	0.032

The composition of solar radiation changes with the angle of the sun. The maximum visible spectrum penetration is at noon. Penetration of infrared is comparatively high soon after sunrise and just before sunset. The early morning and evening values are higher because of the greater amount of diffused light.

As solar radiation penetrates the canopy, its quality undergoes transformation in different layers. After every reflection and transmission, red and infrared radiation increases relative to the other wavelengths (Table 3.2). In the interior of the canopy there is relatively a greater decrease of light in the chlorophyll absorption bands at 0.45 µ and 0.65 µ ; a relatively small decrease in green at 0.55 µ and infrared at 0.80 µ.

REFERENCES

Babu Ranga. 1981. A Study of Agrometeorology of Winter Maize in the Punjab (Unpublished M Sc. Thesis) PAU, Ludhiana.

Baumgartner, A. 1973. Estimation of the radiation and thermal micro-environment from meteorological and plant parameters. Plant Response to Climatic Factors. Proceedings of the Uppsala Symposium, UNESCO: 313-324.

Butler, W.L. and Roberts, J. Downs. 1966. Light and Plant Development. Plant Agriculture. Readings from Scientific American. W.H. Freeman & Co: 78-85.

Caldwell, M.M. 1981. Plant Response to Solar Ultra-Violet Radiation. Physiological Plant Ecology. I. Response to Physical Environment (Eds. Lang. Noble, Osmond and Ziegler) Springer-Verlag: 169-198.

Chang, Jen. Hu. 1968. Climate and Agriculture. An Ecological Survey. Aldine Publishing Co.: 36-45.

Evans, L.T. 1973. The effect of light on plant growth, development and yield. Plant Response to Climatic Factors. Proceedings of the Uppsala Symposium, UNESCO: 21-31.

Salisbury, F.B. 1981. Responses to photoperiod. Physiological Plant Ecology. I. Response to Physical Environment (Eds. Lange, Noble, Osmond and Ziegler). Springer-Verlag: 135-168.

Wassink, E.C., 1953. Specification of radiant flux and radiant flux density in irradiation of plants with artificial light. J. Hort. Sci. 28: 177-184.

CHAPTER 4

METEOROLOGICAL FACTORS IN PHOTOSYNTHESIS

The dry matter of plants is produced through photosynthesis, a process through which carbohydrates are synthesised from carbon dioxide in the presence of solar energy. There are several environmental factors which regulate the rate of photosynthesis. Among these, solar radiation, environmental temperature, concentration of carbon dioxide in the atmosphere, moisture status and turbulence are the most important. In this chapter the relationship between these meteorological factors and photosynthesis is discussed briefly.

From the point of view of an agrometeorologist photosynthesis comprises three processes:

1) *The diffusion process* in which carbon dioxide is transported from the atmosphere towards the reaction centre in the chloroplast of the leaf.

The rate of this process depends mainly on the concentration of carbon dioxide in the atmosphere. The process is influenced mainly by wind and slightly by temperature. Light affects the diffusion rate indirectly—by influencing the temperature.

2) *The photochemical process* in which light energy is transformed into chemical energy. This energy is, in turn, used for the reduction of carbon dioxide to carbohydrates. This process is exclusively governed by photosynthetically active radiation (McCree, 1981,.

3) *The biochemical process* in which energy produced by light conversion is used for the reduction of carbon dioxide.

This process is strongly affected by temperature.

4.1 Solar Radiation and Photosynthesis

Photosynthesis is an inefficient process in the utilisation of solar radiation. This is because only the visible part of the solar spectrum is active in this process, additionally because the quantum required for photosynthesis is much higher than its theoretical needs.

For reducing one mole of carbon dioxide to the level of carbohydrates, about 1,12,000 calories of energy are required. The light is made available for this process in quanta with an energy content of about 41,000 calories per mole. Thus, the theoretical requirement for photosynthesis is three quanta. However, experiments have shown that actually eight to twelve quanta are absorbed. The excessive energy is released subsequently as heat.

It is estimated that ten quanta in the middle wavelength range of radiation, usefully absorbed by the chlorophyll, supply about 520 kcal. The reduction of one mole of carbon dioxide to the level of plant material, captures and stores only 105 kcal. The efficiency of the basic photosynthesis is therefore, $\frac{105}{520} \times 100 = 20$ per cent (approximately).

Assuming the incident radiation lost by reflection and transmission is 15 per cent, and that the energy in the visible range of the spectrum is 41 per cent—the maximum efficiency is $20 (1 - 0.15) \times 0.41$ i.e. about 7 per cent of total incident radiation.

4.1.1 SATURATION LIGHT INTENSITY

For many plants, light saturation occurs at about one-third the amount of the full sunlight, after a linear increase over a short range of low light intensity. Plants have been divided into sun and shade species on the basis of their marked differences in the saturation light intensity as shown in Fig. 4.1 (Moss, 1965).

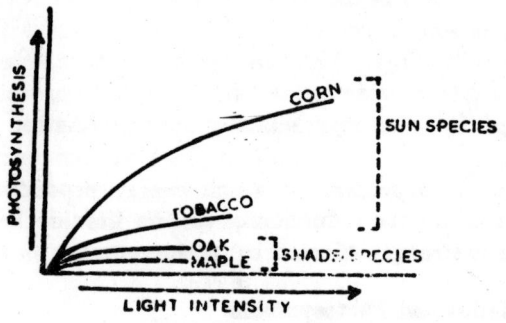

Most field crops belong to the sun species and reach light saturation at about 2,500 foot candles.

Shade species reach light saturation level at a maximum of 1,000 foot candles. They can be light-saturated in as dim a light as 500 foot candles.

The latest investigations have, however, shown that the values given above for the sun species are comparatively low. Even then, the highest value, of 6,000 foot candles given later (Table 4.1) is only about one-half of the full sunlight of the sun at its zenith — which may reach a value of 14,000 foot candles. Thus the unshaded leaves are light-saturated for about six hours at mid-day.

In the case of certain plants, the photosynthesis rate declines as the light intensity increases beyond saturation level. Saturation light intensity for some of the crop plants as reported in the literature (Chang, 1968) is presented in Table 4.1.

Table 4.1 Saturation light intensity of some crops

Crop	Saturation light intensity (ft. c)
Sugar cane	6000
Rice	5000–6000
Wheat	5300
Alfalfa	4700
Sugar beet	4400
Corn	2500–3000
Potato	3000
Apples	4050–4400

4.1.2. EFFICIENCY OF SOLAR RADIATION UTILISATION

The efficiency of solar radiation utilisation can be computed by comparing the calorific value of organic matter produced per unit of cultivated area, with the incident radiation on the same area during the same period. Some results of the studies on the effic ency of radiation utilisation are given in Table 4.2.

Table 4.2 Dry matter production, and efficiency of radiation
utilisation for several crops (Chang, 1968)

Crop	Yield (tons/hectare)	Efficiency (per cent)
Potato	9.6	0.5
Winter wheat	10.45	0.52
Sugar beet	16.00	0.92
Carrot	6.86	0.39
Turnips	3.60	0.51
Corn	15.52	1.05
Sugar cane	129.48	1.43

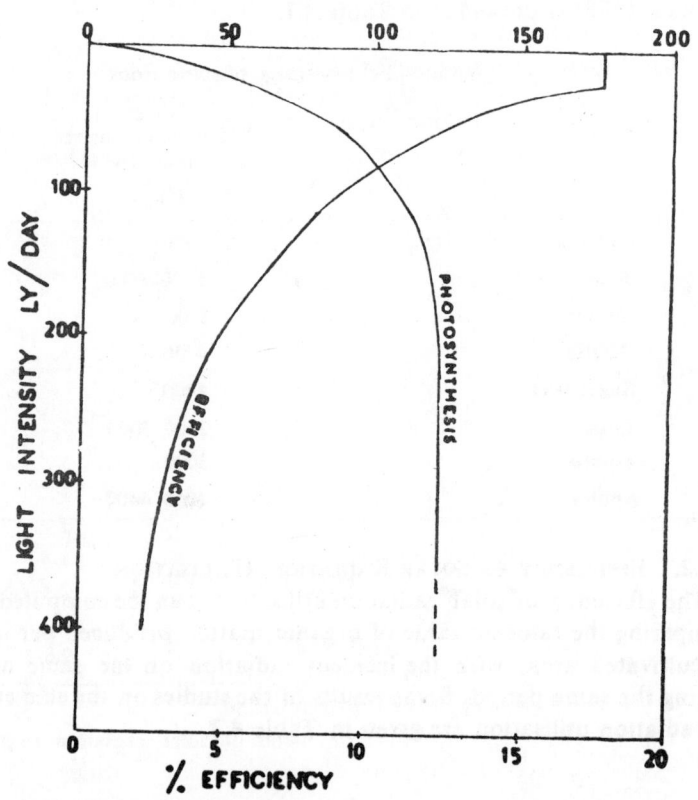

Fig. 4.2 Rate of photosynthesis and efficiency of radiation utilisation.

A leaf exposed to full sunlight cannot be expected to be completely efficient in the utilisation of light energy for photosynthesis. For example in sugar beet at very low light intensity, the efficiency is as high as 17 per cent, which declines to about 2 per cent when the light intensity is increased to 400 ly/per day. The decrease in the efficiency of radiation utilisation with increasing light intensity is caused by finite resistance to diffusion of carbon dioxide through the leaf, to the chloroplasts.

In the case of tomatoes, an efficiency of 10 per cent is obtained if the light intensity is reduced to one-tenth. Similar values are obtained in the case of sugar beet, alfalfa and sugar cane.

The photosynthetic efficiency, along with water use efficiency obtained under various farming systems in the world, is given in Table 4.3.

Table 4.3 Achievements and potentials for photosynthetic and water use efficiencies (Lemon, 1969)

System	Photosynthesis efficiency* (%)	Water use efficiency** kg/ton of H_2O
Subsistence farming		
Average	0.04–0.1	0.04–0.12
Best	0.08–0.2	0.10–0.24
Ranch farming		
Average	0.1–0.2	0.12–0.24
Best	0.2–0.4	0.24–0.48
Intensive farming		
Average	0.25–0.35	0.30–0.42
Best	0.6–1.0	0.72–1.2
Experimental		
Season	0.8–1.5	0.96–1.8
Week	1.5	1.8
Day	2–4	2.4–4.8
Theoretical upper limit	8–10	9.6–12

* On the basis of total incident solar radiation.
**On the basis of 60 per cent conversion of solar radiation to latent heat.

4.2 Temperature and Photosynthesis

Photosynthesis is influenced by temperature through the dark reactions, because the photochemical process is independent of temperature. The rate of photosynthesis and respiration increases with the increase in temperature, until a maximum value of photosynthesis is reached. This value is maintained over a broad range of temperature. Then at considerably high temperatures, when the enzyme becomes inactivated and various reactions are disturbed, photosynthesis decreases. This can be shown by the activities of two enzymes, RUDP carboxylase and PEP carboxylase which show a distinct and species specific dependence upon temperature. PEP carboxylase appear to be less efficient at low temperature than RUDP carboxylase.

4.2.1 LIMITING TEMPERATURES FOR NET PHOTOSYNTHESIS

Net photosynthesis is measured over a range in which increasing temperature has a stimulative effect. Beyond or below this range temperature acts as an inhibitor. These limits are referred to as the cardinal points — the cold limit or the temperature minimum (T min), the temperature optimum (T opt) and the heat limit or the temperature maximum (T max). The temperature limits for net photosynthesis for some plant groups are given in Table 4.4.

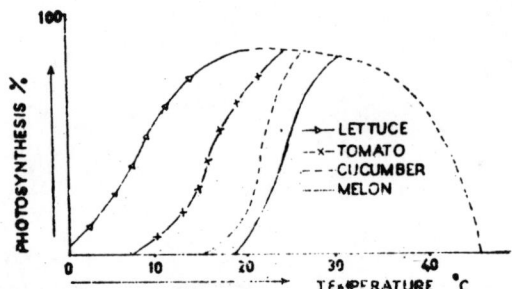

Fig. 4.3 Temperature limit for photosynthesis.
(Bierhuizen, 1973)

The low temperature limit for net photosynthesis in the case of tropical plants is 5–7°C, while the limit for temperate and cold regions is even below 0°C. In the case of higher plants carbon di oxide uptake is blocked as soon as the assimilatory organs like leaves begin to freeze, which occurs in the spring at − 2°C and in winter in the case of evergreens at − 5 to − 8°C. But lichens differ

Table 4.4   Temperature dependence of net photosynthesis during the growing season, under conditions of natural carbon dioxide availability and light saturation. (Larcher, 1980)

Plant Group	Low temperature limit for CO_2 uptake	Temperature optimum for net photosyn.	High Temperature limit for CO_2 uptake
1. Herbaceous plants			
C_4 plants of hot habitats	5 to 7°C	35 to 45°C	50 to 60°C
Agricultural C_3 plants	— 2 to over 0	20 to 30	40 to 50
Heliophytes	— 2 to 0	20 to 30	40 to 50
Sciophytes	— 2 to 0	10 to 20	40
Spring-flowering and alpine plants	— 7 to — 2	10 to 20	30 to 40
2. Woody plants			
Evergreen foliage trees of the tropics and sub-tropics	0 to 5	25 to 30	45 to 50
Sclerophyllous trees and shrubs from dry regions	— 5 to — 1	15 to 35	42 to 55
Deciduous foliage trees of the temperate zone	— 3 to — 1	15 to 25	40 to 45
Evergreen conifers	— 5 to — 3	10 to 25	35 to 42
Dwarf shrubs of heath and tundra	— 8	15 to 25	40 to 45
3. Lichens			
of cold regions	— 25 to — 10	5 to 15	20 to 30

from vascular plants i.e. they can take up and incorporate carbon dioxide at — 10°C and even at — 25°C i.e. even when the thallie are frozen.

At extremely high temperatures, the rate of photosynthesis decreases rapidly. However, the rate of respiration is increased which releases large amounts of carbon dioxide. For C_4 plants of hot habitats, the uptake of carbon dioxide stops at 50 to 60°C, whereas for C_3 plants this limit is between 40 and 50°C.

4.2.2 OPTIMUM RANGE OF TEMPERATURE

The range of temperature in which photosynthesis is more than 90 per cent of the maximum obtainable can be regarded as optimum. This range is narrower for net photosynthesis than for gross photosynthesis, because while gross photosynthesis is still operating at top speed in the optimum range of temperatures the rate of respiration increases, diminishing the net photosynthetic yield.

In the C_4 plants this range for net photosynthesis may be above 30°C and in some cases it may reach 50°C (Table 4.4). Thus, this optimum range is a specific or genetic character for C_4 plants.

But in case of C_3 plants, this optimum temperature is not a genetic character but is an adaptation to the thermal conditions in the natural habitat of the plant at the time when growth is proceeding actively. For example:

1) Sciophytes (plants growing under shade) function optimally between 10 and 20°C. Same is the case with spring blooming and high alpine plants which generally grow in these areas with low average temperature.

2) Herbs, in sunny habitats and trees of warm climates, achieve their highest photosynthetic activity between 20 to 30°C.

3) Lichens are confined to the cooler parts of the world growing in high mountains and polar regions. But folios and crustaceous lichens from warmer parts of the world also have optima at lower temperatures.

The net photosynthesis in the case of these lichens is greater when these are well supplied with water, or when dew, fog or humidity is high.

4.3 Photosynthesis in Relation to Carbon Dioxide Concentration

With an additional supply of carbon dioxide, both the saturation light intensity and the efficiency of light utilisation can be raised. For example, the saturation light intensity of a strawberry leaf increases from one-tenth sunlight at low carbon dioxide concentration, to about one-half sunlight at high carbon dioxide concentration

The results of studies (Nasser et al. 1982) with corn, sugar beet, soybean and radish, conducted in phytotrons with controlled carbon dioxide and light intensities, indicated that with an increase in concentration of carbon dioxide from 350 to 675 µl/l and photosynthetic photon flux density (PPFD) from 600 to 1205 $\mu m^{-2} s^{-1}$, total dry-matter production increased in all species of plants, at all growth stages with both, increased carbon dioxide concentration and PPFD levels. Maximum dry matter was produced at the highest combined levels of carbon dioxide and PPFD. The dry weight increase varied between the different species, and between plant parts within a species. High levels of carbon dioxide and PPFD caused a greater increase in net assimilation rate in plants during early growth stages than in later stages, because the first few young, rapidly growing leaves were very efficient photosynthetic organs. A high carbon dioxide or PPFD level resulted in decreasing leaf area ratios, with increasing plant age for all the species, due to a rapid increase in stem and root growth.

Corn having the C_4 pathway of photosynthesis, showed less response to increased carbon dioxide and PPFD than the three C_3 species, i.e. sugar beet, radish and soybean. Increasing the atmospheric carbon dioxide concentration from 350 to 675 μl/ litre at low and high PPFD levels produced dry matter increases of 72.7 and 76.4 per cent, respectively, in soybean, and 18.9 and 18.6 per cent respectively, in corn, at 50 days after planting. None of the species tested are light-saturated at levels available in the standard flourescent and incandescent lighting as was shown by the increased growth when higher PPFD levels were obtained with a combination of multi-vapour and sodium lamps.

Table 4.5 Rate of normal and enriched levels of CO_2
Mg of $Co_2/dm^2/hr$ (Bassham, 1977)

Plant	Normal level	Enriched level
Sugar cane	60–75	100
Rice	40–75	135
Sunflower	50–65	130
Soybean, sugar beet	30–40	56
Cotton	40–50	100

Theoretically, it has been computed (Table 4.5, Fig. 4.4) that the efficiency of light utilisation can be doubled if the limitations imposed by carbon dioxide deficiency are removed.

The concentration of carbon dioxide in the atmosphere is 0.03 per cent by volume. It is not more than one-fourth the saturation level of carbon dioxide concentration for optimum photosynthesis.

The atmospheric carbon dioxide is photosynthetically fixed by

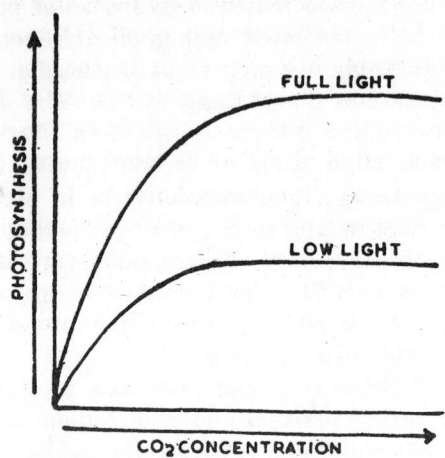

Fig. 4.4 Relationship between light intensity, CO_2 concentration and photosynthesis.

green plants. Simultaneously plants, their roots, micro-organisms and the organic matter present over the earth surface and soil, release carbon dioxide into the atmosphere through respiration and decomposition. Because of varying rates of photosynthesis during different seasons the carbon dioxide concentration in the atmosphere varies with seasons. It also shows marked variation with elevation in the atmosphere.

The seasonal variations in carbon dioxide concentration are well marked in the cold temperate climates where plant growth is at a standstill during winter, and no crops are grown in this season because of intense cold (Rosenberg, 1974). At the end of the winter season with almost no photosynthetic activity, the concentration of carbon dioxide is comparatively much higher near the earth surface, compared with that at the top of the troposphere.

At the end of the summer season, the most active period of photosynthetic activity, the concentration of carbon dioxide is comparatively lower than that in the upper parts of the troposphere.

Brown and Rosenberg (1970) demonstrated that average day and night-time concentration of carbon dioxide over sugar beet had a decreasing trend as the crop developed, and the rate of photosynthetic fixation increased till the crop reached full growth.

The same authors further presented data to show the lowest and highest concentration of carbon dioxide over sugar beet crop. The data showed that during the day when photosynthetic fixation occurred, the minimum concentration was about 275 ppm.

When the crop is still young the variation in the concentration of carbon dioxide over the crop is very small because of little bioactivity. When the crop is actively synthesising the variations increase and are maximised if strong winds blow during the night, as the respired carbon dioxide disappears quickly.

The carbon dioxide concentration in a plant community varies in a 24-hour period. The day-time decrease in the carbon dioxide content of air in the plant community carrying on active photosynthesis may extend up to a height of 150 metres. During the day, the crop is a sink for carbon dioxide received from the ground and the atmosphere. The carbon dioxide concentration within the canopy during day-time is especially low during a calm period. At night, both the crop and the soil are sources of carbon dioxide for the atmosphere. It has been found that minimum carbon dioxide concentration within the crop canopy is usually between 0.025 and 0.029 per cent. However, the minimum value can reach as low as 0.020 per cent. This local deficit of carbon dioxide may cause a decrease of the photosynthetic rate, to the extent of 10 to 20 per cent.

4.4 Water in Relation to Photosynthesis

Irrespective of the fact that only an insignificant part of the water that passes into a plant, is utilised in photosynthesis, water deficiency in a plant seriously retards the rate of photosynthesis. Water stress in the plant directly reduces the rate of photosynthesis because the dehydrated protoplasm has a lower photosynthetic capacity.

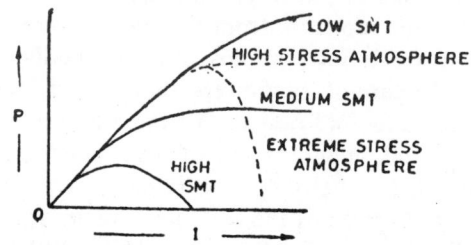

Fig. 4.5 Expected effects of soil moisture stress and atmospheric moisture stress on photosynthesis (P) at different light intensities (I) (Moss, 1965).

Once the leaves lose turgidity, the guard-cells of the stomata close and prevent further intake of carbon dioxide.

Moss (1965) observed that by increasing soil moisture stress, the optimum photosynthetic rate was reached at lower light intensities.

At low soil moisture stress coupled with little atmospheric evaporative demand, the rate of photosynthesis continues to increase with increased light intensities.

High atmospheric stress and particularly the extremely dry conditions of the atmosphere are expected to reduce the rate of photosynthesis. This is probably the result of rapid evaporation from guard cells and closure of the stomata. Figure 4.6 shows photosynthetic response to soil moisture.

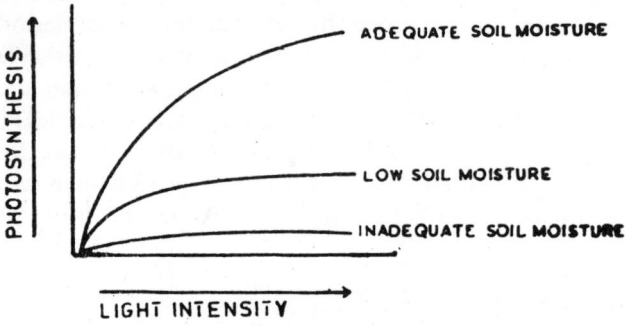

Fig. 4.6 Photosynthesis response to soil moisture.

Plants differ in their ability to withstand a water stress before the photosynthetic rate is seriously reduced. Again, they differ in their ability to redress or recover when the water shortage is over.

In general, the rate of photosynthesis declines after a reduction of 30 per cent of the moisture from the leaves. When about 60 per cent of the moisture is lost, photosynthesis usually stops. It has been found, in the case of sunflowers that turgid leaves carry on photosynthesis at a tenfold rate as compared with wilted leaves.

On the other hand, in another set of experiments on clover, apple and sugar cane, it has been demonstrated that photosynthesis is hardly affected until most of the soil moisture is depleted and the permanent wilting-point is almost reached. Still others have demonstrated that photosynthesis begins to drop when the soil moisture is relatively high. A study of the effects of soil moisture on photosynthesis of sugar cane (Fig. 4.7) shows that this process

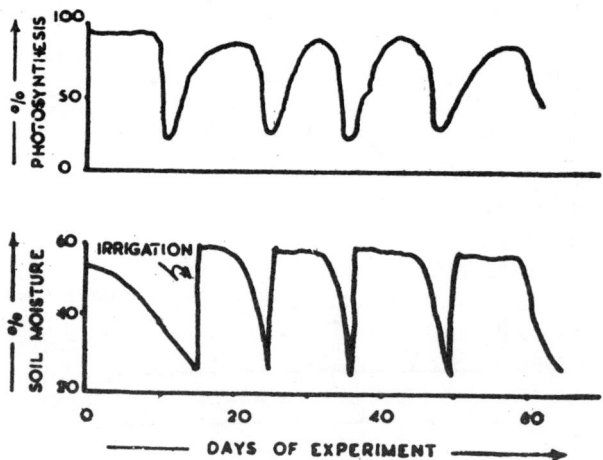

Fig. 4.7 Sugar cane—Photosynthesis response to soil moisture.

does not drop significantly until soil moisture is depleted to less than 40 per cent of field capacity. However, in yet another set of experiments on the same crop, photosynthesis was only 25 per cent of the optimum, when soil-moisture tension reached the permanent wilting point. It has also been found that photosynthesis is slightly reduced at higher moisture levels. This reduction may be attributed to the fact that some of the stomata are hydropassive at higher moisture levels.

4.5 Turbulence

Turbulence in the atmosphere is another environmental factor which strongly affects the intake of carbon dioxide.

The intake of carbon dioxide depends on its concentration in the atmosphere and on its delivery to the leaf. When the atmosphere is calm, carbon dioxide reaches the leaf by the slow process of diffusion. Under these conditions, after a short while, the availability of carbon dioxide to the leaf becomes restricted. When the air is in turbulence, the transfer of carbon dioxide to the leaf is quite rapid (Fig. 4.8, Moss, 1965).

To begin with, it can be said that the rate of photosynthesis is less when it is calm and is greater when the wind is blowing. However, a positive correlation is not always observed between the

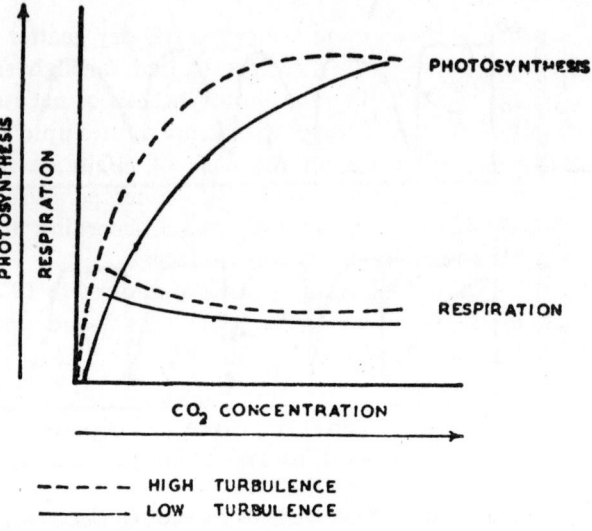

Fig. 4.8   Role of CO_2 concentration and turbulence in photo-synthesis and respiration.

speed of wind and photosynthesis. On the other hand, a decrease in the rate of assimilation has been recorded as the speed of wind increases. This may, however, be attributed to an inadequate water supply to plants growing in sandy soils.

It has been demonstrated that the rate of carbon assimilation is correlated with the speed of the wind only at an extremely low level (Wadsworth, 1959). Different workers have given various values for the maximum wind velocity up to which the rate of assimilation increases. These values range from 0.3 to more than 1 metre per second.

4.6   Pre-conditioning

In addition to the immediate and direct effects of environmental factors, the response of plants to the present environmental conditions which affect photosynthesis may be pre-conditioned. The best example of the pre-conditioning is in maize, in which case it has been observed that if the night temperature falls below 4°C, the photosynthesis during the next two days remains below normal. Again if the maize plants are shaded, tasselling precedes silking and the seeds are sparsely set (Moss and Stinson, 1961).

4.7 Net Photosynthesis

Plant growth depends upon the excess of dry matter produced through photosynthesis, over its loss caused through respiration. The net gain is referred to as net photosynthesis or net assimilation.

The respiration rate increases with temperatures upto the varying maxima for different crops. In the case of alfalfa, a fourfold increase in respiration rate is noticed with a temperature rise from 0° to 20°C. The respiration rate also varies according to the light intensity but the effect is much less significant.

The respiration rate of leaves is usually about 5 to 10 per cent of gross photosynthesis at saturation light intensity and normal wind velocity. The respiration of the whole plant is higher than that of a single leaf. Experiments have shown that the total respiration of alfalfa was between 35 and 49 per cent of its photosynthetic rate, and for sugar beet, the value was 20 to 33 per cent. In temperate climates, the average value for most plants lies between 20 and 30 per cent.

Temperatures during the day and the night exert opposite effects on net photosynthesis. A high night temperature increases the respiration loss and reduces the net photosynthesis, whereas a high day temperature up to about 30°C may increase the net photosynthesis. In the case of barley, it is observed that the net photosynthesis is positively correlated with the day temperature, and is negatively correlated with the night temperature.

Since the ideal condition for net photosynthesis is a high day temperature and a low night temperature, a large diurnal temperature range is desirable. In one of the experiments on clover, it has been proved that as the range of daily temperature rose from 3 to 13°C, the net photosynthesis increased from 50 to 100 per cent.

At a very low light intensity, net photosynthesis is very low, e.g. at the floor of a thick forest. The amount of net photosynthesis is also dependent upon temperature. There is a critical stage at which the net photosynthesis is zero. At this stage, respiration equals gross photosynthesis. This is known as the compensation point. In the case of rice, the compensation point is reached at 150 foot candles at 4.5°C; when the light intensity is 400 foot candles, it is at 15.5°C; and when the light intensity is 1,400 foot candles, the compensation point is reached at 27°C.

Most of the common plants have, however, lower compensation points. At normal room temperatures, the compensation point for the sun species is 100 to 150 foot candles and for shade species it is 50 to 100 foot candles (Ormrod, 1961).

The age of a plant has a great bearing on the net photosynthesis. It declines with age. As the age of leaves increase from the top to the bottom, net photosynthesis rates fall in the same order. In the case of a sugar cane leaf, a young leaf has twice the net photosynthetic rate of a one-year-old leaf.

REFERENCES

Bassham, J. 1977. Synthesis of Organic Compounds from CO_2 in Land Plants. Biological Solar Energy Conversion. Ed. Akhira Mitshi et al. Academic Press: 151–166.

Bierhuizen, J.E. 1973. The effect of temperature on plant growth, development and yield. Proceedings of Uppsala Symposium Plant Response to Climatic Factors. UNESCO: 88–98.

Brown, K.W. and N.J. Rosenberg. 1970. Concentration of CO_2 in the air above a sugar beet field. Monthly Weather Review. 98: 75–82.

Chang, Jen-Hu. 1968. Climate and Agriculture. An Ecological Survey. Aldine Publishing Co: 118–128.

Larcher, W. 1980. Physiological Plant Ecology. Springer-Verlag. Berlin: 73–157.

Lemon, E.R. 1969. Important microclimatic factors in soil-water plant relationships. Modifying the Soils and Water Environment for Approaching the Agricultural Potentials in the Great Plains. Great Plains Agri. Council Publication No. 34: 95–102.

McCree, K.L.. 1981. Photosynthetically Active Radiation. Physiological Plant Ecology. I. Springer-Verlag. Ed. O.L. Lange et al.: 41–53.

Moss, D.N. 1965. Capture of Radiant Energy by Plants Meteorological Monographs. Published by American Meteorological Society. 6: 90–108.

Moss, D.N. and H.T. Stinson. 1961. Differential response of corn to shade. Crop Sci., 1: 416-418.

Nasser Sionit, H. Hellmers and B.R. Strains. 1982. Interaction of Atmospheric CO_2 Enrichment Irradiance in Plant Growth. Agron. J. 74: 721–724.

Ormrod, D.P. 1961. Photosynthesis rates of young rice plants as affected by light intensity and temperature. Agron. J. 53: 93–95.

Rosenberg, N.J. 1974. Microclimate: The Biological Environment. John Wiley, New York: 223–237.

Wadsworth, R.M. 1959. On Optimum Wind Speed. Ann. Bot. No. 23: 195–199.

Chapter 5

ENVIRONMENTAL TEMPERATURE
AND CROP PLANTS

Temperature is a measure of speed (mean kinetic energy) per molecule of the molecules in a body and heat is the energy arising from random motion of all the molecules in a body. Temperature is therefore the intensity aspect of heat energy. Solar radiation is the main source of heat energy to the biosphere. It is transferred from the earth and atmosphere through radiation, convection and conduction and also through evaporation and condensation. The intensity aspect of thermal energy, i.e. temperature, is of paramount importance for organic life because of the following factors:

1) Physical and chemical processes within the plants are governed by temperature and these processes in turn control biological reactions that take place within the plants;

2) The diffusion rate of gases and liquids changes with temperature;

3) Solubility of different substances is dependent upon temperature;

4) The rate of reactions varies with variations in temperature;

5) Equilibrium of various systems and compounds is a function of temperature; and

6) Temperature effects the stability of the enzyme system.

5.1 Soil Temperature

Soil temperature is an important environmental factor in plant growth and distribution. In comparison to air temperature, the amplitude of variations in soil surface temperature is much more pronounced because of the varying characteristics and composition of the soil.

5.1.1 FACTORS AFFECTING SOIL TEMPERATURE

Aspect and slope: These factors are of great importance in determining soil temperature outside the tropics. In the northern hemisphere a south-facing slope is always warmer than a north facing slope or a level plain. This difference exceeds the difference in air temperature.

Tillage: By loosening top soil and creating mulch, tillage reduces the heat flow between the surface and sub-soil. Since mulched surface has greater exposed area and the capillary connection with moist layers below is broken, the cultivated soil has greater temperature amplitude as compared with the uncultivated soil. At noon, the air temperature one inch above the soil is 5 to 10°C higher in cultivated soil as compared to uncultivated soil.

Soil texture: Because of lower heat capacity, sandy soils warm up more rapidly than clay soils, hence are at a higher temperature.

Organic matter: Organic matter reduces the heat capacity and thermal conductivity of soil, increases its water-holding capacity and has a dark colour which increases its absorptivity. In humid climates, because of large water content, peat and marsh are much colder than mineral soils in spring and warmer in winter. But when the organic soils are dry they become warmer than mineral soils in summer and cooler in winter.

5.1.2 THERMAL PROPERTIES OF A SOIL

1) *Specific-heat*: It is the amount of heat required to raise the temperature of one gram of the substance by 1°C. The value for most of minerals present in soil is 0.18–0.20 cal. For humus, it is 0.45 cal.

2) *Heat capacity*: It is the amount of heat required to raise the temperature of 1 cc by 1°C. Most soils have a heat capacity in the range 0.3–0.6 cal/cm^3.

3) *Thermal conductivity*: It is the quantity of heat flowing in a unit time through a 1 cm^2 cross section of the soil in response to a temperature gradient of 1°C cm^{-1} of depth. It varies with porosity, moisture content and organic matter content of the soil.

4) *Thermal diffusivity*: It is the change in °C that occurs in one second when the temperature gradient changes 1° per cc. In other words, it is a ratio between thermal conductivity and heat capacity. Thermal diffusivity rises when the moisture content reaches a certain maximum and then falls.

Table 5.1 Thermal properties of soil components and common soils (Rosenberg, 1974)

Material	Density	Specific heat	Thermal conductivity	Thermal diffusivity
	$(g\ cm^{-3})$	cal. $g^{-1}\ deg^{-1}$	$(cal.\ cm^{-1}\ deg^{-1}\ sec^{-1})$	$cm^2\ sec^{-1}$
Clay	1.8	0.8	0.0028	0.002
Humus soil	0.3	0.3	0.00027	0.003
Wet sandy soil	1.6	0.4	0.0064	0.01
Air	0.0012	0.24	0.00005	0.1667
Water	1.0	1.0	0.0014	0.0014
Ice	0.917	0.505	0.005	0.0108

5.1.3 PHYSICAL LAWS GOVERNING SOIL TEMPERATURE VARIATIONS

Temperature range: Thermal energy at the earth surface is transferred to the lower layers in the form of waves. The amplitude of the waves diminishes rapidly with increasing depth. The soil temperature range at any point below the earth surface is expressed by the equation:

$$R_z = R_0\ e^{-z}\ \sqrt{\frac{\pi}{Kh\ P}}$$

where R_z is temperature range at depth z
R_0 is temperature range at the surface
P is oscillation period in seconds
Kh is thermal diffusivity of the soil

Thus the amplitude or range of each wave decreases exponentially with depth.

Time lag: The time lag of the maximum and minimum soil temperature is expressed as

$$t_2 - t_1 = \frac{z_2 - z_1}{2} \times \sqrt{\frac{P}{Kh\ \pi}}$$

t_2 is time when maximum or minimum temperature is observed at depth z_2
t_1 is time when maximum or minimum temperature is observed at depth z_1.

5.1.4 SOIL TEMPERATURE IN PLANT LIFE

In many instances soil temperature is of greater importance to plant life than air temperature. For example, beech, oak and ash trees can withstand air temperature of −25°C, but the roots cannot withstand a temperature of even up to − 16°C.

Soil temperatures, particularly the extremes, influence the germination of seeds, the functional activity of the root system, the incidence of plant diseases and the rate of plant growth.

Living tissues of many temperate plants are killed when these are exposed to a surface temperature of about 54°C (Baker, 1929). Excessively high soil temperatures are also harmful to the roots and also cause lesions on the stem.

Extremely low temperatures are equally detrimental. Low temperatures impede the intake of nutrients. Soil moisture intake by the plants stops when the later is at a temperature of 1°C.

5.1.5 CARDINAL TEMPERATURES

Three temperatures of vital activity have been recognised which are often termed as cardinal points.

1) A minimum temperature below which no growth occurs. For typical cool season crops, it ranges between 0 and 5°C and for hot season crops between 15 and 18°C.

2) An optimum temperature at which the maximum plant growth occurs. For cool season crops it ranges between 25 and 31°C and for hot season crops between 31 and 37°C.

3) A maximum temperature above which the plant growth stops. For cool season crops it ranges between 31 and 37°C and for hot season crops between 44 and 50°C.

The cardinal temperatures for some of the plants for germination are given in Table 5.2. The cardinal points can be measured only approximately because their position is related to the external conditions, the duration of exposure, the age of the plant and its previous treatment (Parker, 1946).

5.1.6 SOIL TEMPERATURE AND CROP YIELD

Even after germination soil temperature is important for the vegetative growth of crops. This is because for each species, a favourable soil temperature is needed for the ion and water uptake. The soil temperature during the day is more important than the night-time temperature because it is necessary to maintain a favourable internal crop water status in the light of the high evaporation rate.

Table 5 2   Cardinal temperatures for the germination of some important crops (Bierhuizen, 1973)

Plant	Cardinal temperature (°C)		
	Minimum	Optimum	Maximum
Wheat	3–4.5	25	30–32
Barley	3–4.5	20	38–40
Maize	8–10	32–35	40–44
Rice	10–12	30–32	36–38
Tobacco	13–14	28	35
Sugar beet	4–5	25	28–30
Peas	1–2	30	35
Oats	4–5	25	30
Sorghum	8–10	32–35	40
Lentils	4–5	30	36
Carrot	4–5	8	25
Pumpkin	12	32–34	40

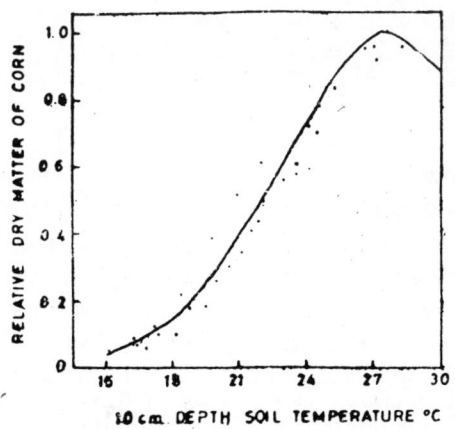

Fig. 5.1   Relative yield of dry matter of young corn plants as affected by soil temperature. (Bierhuizen, 1973)

There are numerous cases where soil temperature is more important than air temperature to plant growth. In the tropics, high temperature of soil causes degeneration of the tuber in potato. Optimum soil temperature for this crop is 17°C, tuber formation is practically absent above a soil temperature of 29°C.

Corn yield is closely related to soil temperature at planting. If at this time soil temperature is low and outlook is for continued moist and cool weather, corn yield is expected to be low (Riley, 1957).

In another set of experiments it has been demonstrated that corn yield increases almost linearly as the 4-inch soil temperature rises from 15 to 27°C. Beyond this temperature, the crop yield decreases (Fig. 5.1). Table 5.3 gives heat units of various agricultural crops for germination.

Table 5.3 Heat units of various agricultural crops for germination and emergence (Bierhuigen, 1973)

Plant	Heat unit	Plant	Heat unit
Spring rye	44	Spring barley	75
Winter rye	46	Winter barley	70
Winter wheat	47	Hemp	96
Spring wheat	52	Flax	98
White mustard	60	Red clover	99
Lentil	67	White clover	134
Peas	90	Oats	90

5.2 Air Temperature

Air temperature is the most important climatic variable which affects plant life. The growth of higher plants is restricted to a temperature between 0 and 60°C and crop plants are further restricted to a narrower range of 10 to 40°C. However, each species and variety of plants and each age-group of plants has its own upper and lower temperature limits. Beyond these limits, a plant gets considerably damaged, and gets even killed. In another range, growth of the plant stops and it becomes dormant, but remains alive. There is also a third range of temperature in which the growth of the plant at a particular stage of development is optimum.

Thus it is the amplitude of variations in temperature, rather than the mean values of it, which is more important to plant growth.

The mid-day high temperature increases the saturation deficit of the plants. It accelerates photosynthesis and ripening of fruits (Papadakis, 1970). The maximum production of dry matter occurs when the temperature ranges between 20 and 30°C, provided moisture is not a limiting factor. The high temperature can devernalise the cryophytes, especially the buds of the sun-exposed deciduous trees. When high temperature occurs in combination with high humidity, it favours the development of many plant diseases. High temperature also affects plant metabolism.

High night temperature increases respiration. It favours the growth of the shoot and leaves at the cost of roots, stolons, cambium and fruits. It governs the distribution of photosynthates among the different organs of the plants, favouring those which are generally not useful. High night temperature also affects plant metabolism. It accelerates the development of non-cryophytes.

Most crop plants are injured and many killed when night temperature is very low. Tender leaves and flowers are very sensitive to low temperature and frost. Plants which are rapidly growing and flowering are easily killed. Low temperature interferes with the respiration of plants. If low temperature coincides with wet soil, it results in the accumulation of harmful products in the plant cells. Frost also interferes with plant metabolism.

5.2.1 SENSIBLE HEAT FLUX AND AIR TEMPERATURE

Very large quantities of energy are transferred from the warm earth surface to the atmosphere and this energy transferred is known as sensible heat. On occasions when the air is warm and the surface is cool, heat gets transferred to the surface. Energy transfer through the laminar sub-layer is similar to that through conduction. The mechanism of the transfer is of course molecular diffusion and not direct conduction. The transfer of energy through the laminar sub-layer is given (Rosenburg, 1974) by the equation

$$A = 60 \, \rho_a \, C_p \, \alpha_h \, \frac{dT}{dz}$$

where A is sensible heat flux in ly/minute, ρ_a is the density of air with a value of 1.13×10^{-3} g cm^{-3} at standard temperature and pressure, C_p is the specific heat of air with a value of 0.24 cal g^{-1} °C^{-1},

ah is the molecular diffusivity of the air for heat and its value is in the range $0.16 - 0.24$ cm^2 sec^{-1}, and $\dfrac{dT}{dz}$ is the temperature gradient between the earth surface and the top of the laminar sub-layer.

Above the laminar sub-layer the molecular diffusion gives way to turbulent diffusion as an agent of energy transport. Assuming no addition or removal of heat in the horizontal direction, heat transfer in the vertical direction can be given by the following equation

$$A = 60 \, \rho_a \, C_p \, K_h \frac{dT}{dz}$$

In this equation K_h is the coefficient of turbulent exchange which increases with height and is a function of turbulence in the atmosphere and its value varies from almost zero to as high as 10,000 cm^2 sec^{-1}.

5.2.2 HEAT TRANSFER FROM PLANT LEAVES

The living organisms including plants dissipate thermal energy through radiation, convection and also by transpiring the water. Thus the measurement of heat transfer from the leaf is a very complex problem. Some of the approaches used in the measurement are as follows:

Convection approach

Gates (Rosenberg, 1974) has given an equation to measure the thermal energy transfer under free convection (caused by only density difference) which is written as:

$$A = 5.86 \times 10^{-3} \left(\frac{T_l - T_a}{D} \right)^{1/4} (T_l - T_a)$$

In the above equation, D is mean width of the leaf in cm and T_l and T_a are the leaf and air temperature respectively.

Under forced convection (when wind is blowing), the heat flux is given by the equation

$$A = 5.93 \times 10^{-3} \, (u/D)^{1/2} \, (T_l - T_a)$$

where u is the wind speed in cm sec^{-1}.

Resistance approach

A simplified equation for the calculation of sensible heat flux from an organic surface through the measurement of air resistance to the flow of heat is proposed by Monteith (1963). The equation is analog to Ohm's law of electric current flow. The equation is:

$$A = \frac{-60\, \rho_a\, C_p\, (T_p - T_a)}{r_a}$$

where A is rate of sensible heat flux

r = resistance of air to the diffusion of heat in sec cm^{-1} which can be estimated from wind speed (Brown and Rosenberg, 1973).

ρ_a is density of air

C_p is specific heat of air

T_l and T_a is leaf and air temperature respectively.

5.2.3 LEAF TEMPERATURE VERSUS AIR TEMPERATURE

Exposed to sun: Thick leaves which are not transpiring actively in still air are several degrees warmer than the air. Under intense radiation and high humidity, some leaves have been found to be 15°C higher than the air.

Likewise, under very hot and low humid conditions leaf temperature can be as much as 10°C higher than the air.

Where plants do not suffer for want of moisture the difference between leaf and air temperature is very small (Chang, 1968).

It has been recorded that at a temperature of 33°C there is a tendency for equality between air and leaf temperature. Below this temperature leaves tend to be warmer than the air and vice versa. Where the temperature exceed 33°C, leaves appear to suffer from water stress.

Shade: Leaves shaded from direct sunlight are usually slightly warmer than air.

At night when the sky is clear, leaf temperature is usually lower than the Stevenson Screen temperature. During a cold and clear night, a leaf is about 2°C cooler than the surrounding air. With cloud cover this difference is minimised. In certain cases the leaf temperature is even higher than air temperature.

5.2.4 LOW AIR TEMPERATURE AND PLANT INJURY

Exposure to extremely low temperature and heavy snowfall damages the plant in several ways like suffocation, desiccation, heaving, chilling and freezing.

1. *Suffocation*

(a) Small plants may suffer from deficient oxygen when covered with densely packed snow.

b) Certain toxic substances accumulate in contact with roots and crowns and tend to inhibit the diffusion of carbon dioxide.

2) *Physiological drought and desiccation*

Spring drought sometimes occurs in coniferous trees in cool temperate climates. This results from excessive transpiration and a lag in absorption of moisture from the soil, caused by a warm period when the soil is still frozen. The result is an internal moisture deficit sufficient to cause death of the twigs. The decreased water absorption by plants at low temperature is the combined effect of the decreased permeability of the root membrane and increased viscosity of water. This results in increased resistance to water movement across the living cells of the roots.

3) *Heaving*

Injury to a plant is caused by lifting upward from the normal position causing the root to stretch or break at a time when the plant is growing. Sometimes the roots are pushed completely above the soil surface.

After thawing, it is difficult for the roots to become firmly established, and the plants may die because of this mechanical damage and desiccation.

4) *Chilling*

Sellschop and Salmon (1928) long ago studied the plant reaction to chilling. They divided the plants in five categories on this basis.

a) Plants killed by exposure to temperatures in the range of $0.5°-5°C$ for 60 hours—rice, cotton, cowpeas.

b) Plants injured by the above conditions but recovered after being placed in favourable conditions—Sudan grass, Spanish and Valencia peanuts.

c) Plants not likely to suffer serious injury—corn, sorghum and pumpkin.

d) Plants injured by prolonged chilling but likely to recover—buck wheat and soybean.

e) Plants not injured by prolonged chilling—sunflower, tomato and potato.

In temperate climates, two types of injuries occur because of low temperature. These are delayed growth and sterility. For example in Japan, rice yield decreases due to insufficient grain maturation caused by low temperatures during the ripening period. When flowering is too delayed by low temperatures at a certain stage before heading, insufficient time is available to the grains to ripen fully before the frost occurs in autumn.

In the sterility type of injury, rice yields decrease due to sterile spikelets caused by low temperature at the booting stage or at anthesis. The observed injury (Satake, 1978) in developmental order is: (1) a stoppage of anther development, (2) pollen unripenness, (3) partial or no dehiscence, (4) pollen grains remaining in anther loculi, (5) little or no shedding of pollen grains on stigma, and (6) failure of germination on stigma.

Freezing injury

Plant parts or an entire plant may be killed or damaged beyond repair as a result of actual freezing of tissues. Freezing damage is caused by the formation of ice crystals first in the intercellular spaces and then within the cells. Ice within the cells cause more injury by mechanical damage disrupting the structure of the protoplasm and plasma membrane.

Freezing of water in intercellular spaces results in withdrawal of water from the cell sap, and increasing dehydration causes the cell to die.

Table 5.4 shows the critical temperatures harmful to crops in different developmental phases.

Table 5.4   Resistance of crops to frost in different development phases (Ventskevich, 1961)

	Temperature (°C) harmful to plant in the phase					
	Germination		Flowering		Fruiting	
1	2	3	4	5	6	7
Highest resistance to frost						
Spring wheat	−9	−10	−1	−2	−2	−4
Oats	−8	−9	−1	−2	−2	−4
Barley	−7	−8	−1	−2	−2	−4
Peas	−7	−8	−2	−3	−2	−4
Lentils	−7	−8	−2	−3	−2	−4
Coriander	−8	−10	−2	−3	−3	−4

Contd.

1	2	3	4	5	6	7
Resistance to frost						
Beans	−5	−6	−2	−3	−3	−4
Sunflower	−5	−6	−2	−3	−2	−3
Safflower	−4	−6	−2	−3	−3	−4
White mustard	−4	−6	−2	−3	−3	−4
Flax	−5	−7	−2	−3	−2	−4
Hemp	−5	−7	−2	−3	−2	−4
Sugar beets	−6	−7	−2	−3	−	−
Carrot	−6	−7	−	−	−	−
Turnip	−6	−7	−	−	−	−
Medium resistance to frost						
Cabbage	−5	−7	−2	−3	−6	−9
Soybeans	−3	−4	−2	−3	−2	−3
Low resistance to frost						
Corn	−2	−3	−1	−2	−2	−3
Millets	−2	−3	−1	−2	−2	−3
Sudan grass	−2	−3	−1	−2	−2	−3
Sorghum	−2	−3	−1	−2	−2	−3
Potatoes	−2	−3	−1	−2	−1	−2
No resistance to frost						
Castor plant	−1	−2	−1	−2	−0.5	−2
Cotton	−1	−1.5	−0.5	−1	−2	−
Melons	−1	−2	−1	−2	−2	−3
Rice	−0.5	−1	−0.5	−1	−1	−
Sesame	−0.5	−1	−0.5	−1	−	−
Peanuts	−0.5	−1	−	−	−	−
Cucumbers	−0.5	−1	−	−	−	−
Tomatoes	0	−1	0	−1	0	−1
Tobacco	0	−1	0	−1	0	−1

Detailed information regarding temperatures which will damage various fruits at different stages of development has been given by Rogers (1970) and is summarized in Table 5.5.

Table 5.5   Low temperature endured for 30 minutes or less by deciduous fruits (Shelter temperature °C)

Fruit	Stages of development		
	Buds closed but showing colour (°C)	Full bloom (°C)	Small green fruits (°C)
Peaches	−4	−2.8	−1.1
Cherries	−2.2	−2.2	−1.1
Plums	−4	−2.2	−1.1
Apricots	−4	−2.2	−0.6
Prunes	−5 to −3	−2.8 to 2.2	−1.1
Grapes	−1	−0.6	−0.6
Walnut	−1	−1.1	−1.1
Almonds	−5 to −3	−4 to −2	−1.7
Pears	−3.3 to −2.5	−2.2	−1.1
Apples	−4.5 to −3.5	−2.8 to −2.2	−1.7

5.2.5 HIGH TEMPERATURE PLANT INJURY

Thermal death point of active cells ranges from 50 to 60°C for most plant species but it varies with the species, the age of tissue and the time of exposure to high temperature.

It has been reported that most plant cells are killed at a temperature of 45 to 55°C, but some tissues withstand a temperature of up to 105°C.

For aquatic and shade plants the lethal limit is 40°C and for most xerophytes, it is 50°C when the plants are exposed to a saturated atmosphere for about half-an-hour.

High temperature results in the desiccation of the plants and disturbs the balance between photosynthesis and respiration (Fig. 5.2). Once the temperature exceeds the maximum up to which growth takes place, the plants then enter a state of quiescence. When the temperature becomes extremely high, a lethal level is reached. At temperatures higher than the optimum cardinal the physiological activity declines as a consequence of inactivation of enzymes and other proteins. Leaf functions are disturbed at about 42°C and lethal effects on active shoot tissues generally occur in the range of 50 to 60°C.

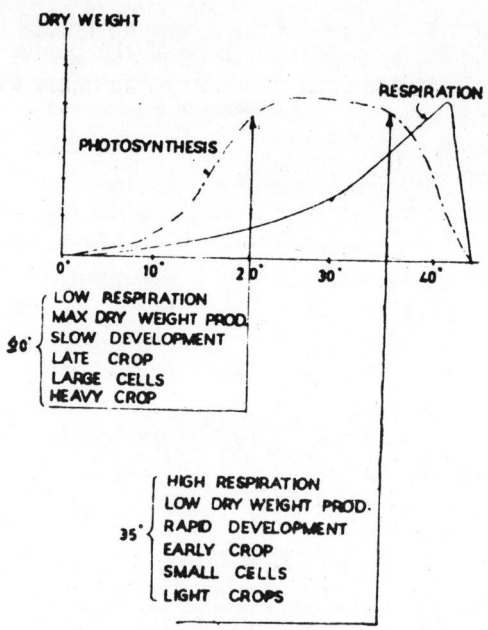

Fig. 5.2   Effect of temperature on photosynthesis and respiration of tomato.
(Bierhuizen, 1973)

Apart from desiccation and disturbed photosynthesis and respiration balance, plants are injured in several ways like excessive respiration from seeds, sun clad and stem girdle.

The higher the temperature the greater is the rate of respiration which results in the rapid exhaustion of food reserves of seeds.

Temperatures on the sunny sides of the bark on stems during hot afternoons and during late night undergo great fluctuations. The injury inflicted because of this short period fluctuation in temperature is known as sun clad.

Stem girdle is another injury associated with high temperature. Exceptionally high temperature at the soil surface and the adjoining laminar sub-layer of the air frequently scorches the short stems. The scorching of the stem is known as stem girdle. This type of injury is most common in young seedlings of cotton in sandy soils where the temperature of the soil surface during summer afternoons may be as high as 60 to 65°C. The stem girdle injury is first noted through a discoloured band a few millimetres wide. This is followed by the shrinkage of the tissues which have been discoloured. It appears that stem girdle causes death of the plants by destroying the conductive and cambial tissues or by an injury which helps the establishment of pathogens.

5.3 Thermoperiodism

The response of living organisms to regular changes in temperatures either day and night or seasonal is defined as thermoperiodism.

Day temperature seldom produces any difference in responses in the flower initiation, size of leaves or rate of leaf production. Night temperature, on the other hand, has in general a pronounced effect on the state of leaf production as well as upon the leaf size. The rate of leaf production remains constant throughout the vegetative development of the plant as long as night temperature remains constant. The effect of fluctuating temperature on growth and development as opposed to constant temperature varies from one species to another. *Lycopus europeaus* (European bugleweed) depends almost completely on fluctuating temperature for germination. It germinates in response to diurnal fluctuations produced by moderate extreme temperature but no germination occurs at constant temperature or as a result of exposure to small (5°C) temperature changes. Germination of *Silene diocia* (Hairy catchfly) is greatly influenced by fluctuating temperature. The maximum germination rate of its seed is at fluctuating temperatures of moderate magnitude rather than at constant temperatures. On the other hand, in case of *Clarkia unquiculata* the germination is highest at constant temperature and it does not increase by fluctuating temperatures.

Low temperature can modify soybean reproductive potential by influencing flower and pod abscission and certain floral aberrancies such as cliestogamy, cliestoflory. It also retards the growth rate (Judith and David, 1981). Under cool day/night temperature combinations of 18/14°C floral development is often disrupted leading to physically malformed parts. The day/night temperature combinations of 14, 18 and 22°C and 10, 14 and 18°C produce 75 to 100 per cent multiple corpellate flowers. Normal floral initiation and pod development occurred when a warm night of 26°C was combined with any of the day temperatures and also at 30/18°C and 30/22°C, while greatest number of pods per plant was obtained at 30/14°C and 26/14°C. In pineapple, flowering is most rapid at a night temperature of 20°C and is slowest at 15° and 25°C. Flower quantities and fruit sizes are greatest for plants grown at a temperature of 15°C. In *Betula papyrifera* (Paper birch) (Downs and Bevingtón, 1981), low night temperature of 14°C was antagonistic to the protective effects of long photoperiods and induced dormancy. In Alaskan birch, high day temperatures partially offset the inhibition effect of cool nights. High night temperatures reduce the effectiveness of short days for inducing dormancy to a lesser degree. In *Plantago lanceolata* (Buck horn plantain) (Allen et al. 1980) most components of growth are affceted by contrasting day/night temperature. The rate of leaf elongation is significantly greater with increasing day temperature than with increasing night temperature. Leaf elongation is reduced more by low night than high day temperature resulting in sharp growth optimum at 26/20°C. The largest rosettes are produced in the 26/20°C thermal regime. Leaf-length was affected by day temperature but it was optimum at intermediate night temperature. High night temperature resulted in shorter leaves than low night temperature. A significantly greater number of leaves were produced when day temperatures were above 26°C and also when night temperatures were around 11°C. Inflorescence quantities in particular greatly increased with increasing temperature; low night temperature significantly reduced the total number of inflorescences produced. Low night temperature also resulted in thicker leaves and increased allocation to the roots. Dry weight allocation into the leaves was significantly increased in 20/11°C temperature regimes. Tomatoes grow faster when the temperature is 26°C by day and 17°C by night than at the constant temperature of 26°C, or any intermediate temperature (Fig. 5.3). For this reason tomatoes do not grow well in warm countries except in those areas where the temperature falls appreciably at night.

Many seeds will grow perfectly well at a constant temperature but there are others like celery which germinate best at a fluctuating temperature. The ecological significance of this response to a diurnal alteration of temperature may be that it promotes germination of those seeds that are close to the soil surface; when such fluctuations do not occur it may suppress germination, especially those of more deeply seated seeds. The emergence of carrot seedlings from soil was faster in fluctuating temperatures than at constant temperature.

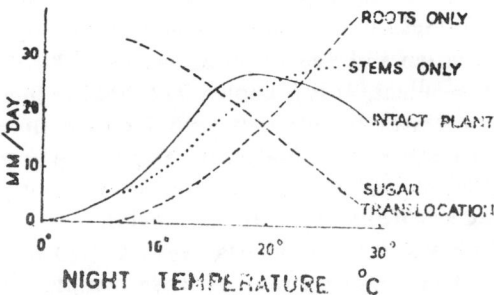

Fig. 5.3 Effect of night temperature on tomato plant. (Chang, 1968)

When germinated seeds of gram (*Cicer arietinum*) were exposed to 13°/11°C of day/night temperature for two days it resulted in increased robosomal protein synthesis followed by a decrease after 5 days at the same temperature.

Apart from the daily fluctuations in the temperature, the long range temperature sequences are important in the development of plants. Annual plants do not need a cold period during their development except plants which germinate in autumn and flower in the spring or summer after a cold winter. The example is that of winter wheat. Peaches cannot flower at high temperature but the vegetative growth phase continues. They need a period of cold weather before flower buds can open. No flower primordia are laid down under conditions of continued high temperature. A dormant bud of *Dicentra* species develop rapidly at 17/12°C. In *Yucca brevifolia* germination and growth of seedlings continue at a fairly rapid rate at 30/23°C and 17/12°C day/night temperature combinations. Sugar-beet plants grown for years at the same thermoperiods (23/17°C) continue vegetative growth and produce thickened stems of 1 m length and never flower. In lobolly pine with 30/17°C temperature average height is 33.2 cm and with 17/17°C temperature growth in height is 10.9 cm. In *Pennisetum americanum* (Pearl millet) high temperatures 38/28°C during all three growth stages lowered grain-yield by reducing basal tillering, the number of grains per inflorescence and the single grain weight. Low temperatures 21/16°C during the vegetative stage increased basal tillering, as a result of which total grain yield per plant increased. Low temperatures during grain development increased the grain filling period and grain yield.

5.4 Vant Hoff's Law or Temperature Coefficient (Q10)

Many physiological processes such as respiration, germination, protein denaturation and the physical process like diffusion, are temperature dependent. It is a known fact that the increase in the rate of these processes corresponds with increase in temperature. In fact the rate of every individual chemical, physical or physiological process increases to certain limits with increasing temperature, i. e. with increasing kinetic energy in the molecules.

Vant Hoff's law which is popularly known as $Q10$ or temperature coefficient is a measure of the rate of these complex physiological and physical processes. According to general usage, $Q10$ is defined as the ratio of the rate of a process at a certain temperature to that at a temperature 10°C lower. The temperature coefficient of a physiological, chemical or physical process is therefore the ratio of the process at any stated temperature to the rate at a temperature usually 10°C lower and is designated as the $Q10$ process (Curtis and Clark, 1950). Thus if a process is 2.3 times as fast at 25°C as at 15°C, the temperature coefficient or $Q10$ is 2.3. Meyer and Anderson (1952) defined $Q10$ of any process as the number of times the rate of the process increases with a 10°C rise in temperature. If the rate of the process is exactly double with a rise of 10°C, then the $Q10$ will be 2.

Calculating the value of $Q10$ is a common method of assessing the effect of temperature on various biological, physical and chemical processes. $Q10$ can be mathematically expressed as

$$Q10 = K_2/K_1 \text{ where } K_2 = \text{rate at } T°C$$
$$K_1 = \text{rate at } T°C - 10°C$$

Most values of $Q10$ reported in the literature are based upon only two data points; however, $Q10$ may be determined graphically or by a linear regression from a plot of log rate (K) vs temperature $(T°C)$ which should yield a straight line of log K. The $Q10$ function assumes an exponential relation of the process to temperature (Berry and Raison, 1981).

It is not always convenient to measure the rate at intervals of exactly 10°C. The approximate values for $Q10$ can, however, be calculated from measurements at any two temperatures using the equation (Sutclifee, 1977),

$$Q10 = \left(\frac{K_2}{K_1}\right)^{\frac{10}{T_2 - T_1}}$$

where $K_2 =$ rate at the higher temperature T_2,

and $K_1 =$ rate at the lower temperature T_1.

By examining the effect of temperature on photosynthesis at different light intensities and CO_2 concentrations, it has been concluded that photosynthesis involves a light phase with a low $Q10$, and a dark phase with a high $Q10$. In living organisms over the physiological range of temperature, enzyme catalysed reactions have a $Q10$ similar to that of chemical reactions. However, at temperatures above 40°C many enzymes become inactivated by denaturation of proteins and there is a progressive reduction in the rate of reaction with time. Thus while the $Q10$ may be high initially it falls rapidly and may eventually reach values lower than unity. The oxygen absorption in respiration increases with temperatures upto 35°C, and $Q10$ is in the range of 2.0 and 2.5. Above this temperature the rate of respiration rises initially but falls markedly with time.

Merits: $Q10$ is a common method of comparing rates of reactions or processes in the biological systems.

As it is already calculated, easily understood and carries no theoretical implications, it remains a useful and favourite tool for recording the temperature relations of complex biological processes (Sutcliffee, 1977).

$Q10$ values of different processes tend to fall within certain limits, and are often used to indicate types of reactions that may occur.

$Q10$ offers an important advantage for analysis of the temperature-dependent complex physiological processes. It can also be used as a plant growth index.

Demerits: Vant Hoff's law or temperature coefficient is valid only in a certain temperature range. Additionally this law is not valid for some processes. For example:

1) The rate of activation of enzymes by heat and denaturation of proteins can increase a 1000 fold over a 10°C rise in temperature.

2) Investigations on the rate of emergence from sand of several vegetable species indicate that $Q10$ values were higher at lower temperature and lower at higher temperatures. Thus it can be seen that this law cannot be attributed to all types of processes.

3) The oxygen absorption increases with temperatures upto 35°C when $Q10$ is in the range of 2.0 and 2.5. Above this temperature the rate of respiration increases initially but falls markedly with time. It is thus evident that this law can only be applied in a certain range of temperatures.

5.5 Growing Degree Days

Growing degree days (GDD), also called heat units, effective heat units or growth units, are a simple means of relating plant growth development and maturity to air temperature (Vittum et al. 1965).

The heat unit or growing degree day concept assumes that there is a direct and linear relationship between growth and temperature (Fig. 5.4). It starts with the assumption that the growth of plants is dependent on the total amount of heat to which it is subjected during its life time. A degree day or a heat unit, is the departure

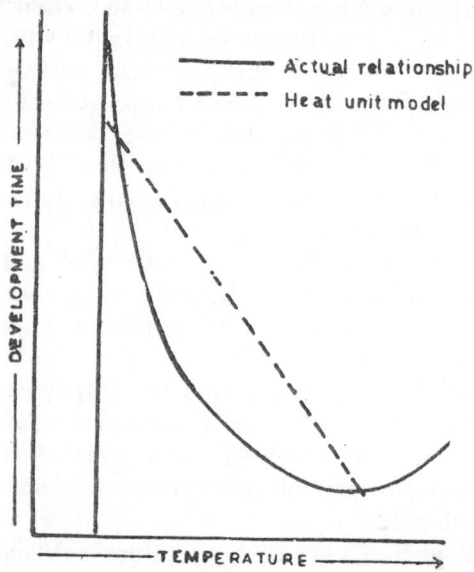

Fig. 5.4   Development time and temperature relationship.

from the mean daily temperature above the minimum threshold temperature. This minimum threshold is the temperature below which no growth takes place. The threshold varies with different plants and for the majority ranges from 4.5 to 12.5°C., there being higher values for tropical plants and lower value for temperate plants. The growing degree days are calculated with an equation written as:

$$\text{Growing Degree Days (GDD)} = \sum_{i=1}^{n} \left(\frac{T \max + T \min}{2.0} - Ti \right)$$

where $\dfrac{T \max + T \min}{2.0}$ is the average daily temperature and Tt is the minimum threshold temperature for a crop.

The simplicity of the degree day method has made it widely popular in guiding agricultural operations and planning land use. Most applications of the growing degree day concept are for the forecast of crop-harvest dates, yield, and quality. It helps in forecasting labour needs for factory and to reduce harvesting and factory cost. The concept is also applied to plants other than crop plants and to the problems of growth and development of insects, plant pathogens, birds and other animals (Hord and Spell, 1962). A potential area of its application lies in estimating the likelihood of the successful growth of a crop in an area in which it has not been grown earlier. The growing degree concept can also be applied to the selection of one variety from several varieties of plants to be grown in a new area. Another application of the concept can be to change or modify the microclimate in such a way as to produce the nearly optimum conditions at each point in the developmental cycle of an organism. This application is, however, still to be evaluated.

Though the degree day concept is very simple and useful, it lacks theoretical soundness and has a number of weaknesses. For example:

1) Except for the modified equations, a lot of weightage is given to high temperature, although temperature above 27°C may have detrimental effects (Brown, 1960).

2) No differentiation can be made among the different combinations of the seasons. For example, the combination of a warm spring and a cool summer cannot be differentiated from a cold spring and a hot summer (Wang, 1962).

3) The daily range of temperature is not taken into consideration and this point is often more significant than the mean daily temperature.

4) No allowance is made for the threshold temperature changes with the advancing stage of crop development.

5) Net responses of plant growth and development are to the temperature of the plant parts themselves, and they may be quite different from temperatures measured in a Stevenson's Screen. Though this difference at a particular time may be small yet the

cumulative effects through an entire growing period can be very large.

6) The effects of topography, altitude and latitude on crop growth cannot be accounted for.

7) Wind, hail, insects and diseases may influence the heat units, but these cannot be accounted for in this concept.

8) Soil fertility may effect the crop maturity. This cannot be explained here (Wilsie, 1974).

In spite of these limitations, the degree day or heat unit concept, with a slight modification, seems to answer a number of questions in forecasting crop growth and maturity.

REFERENCES

Allen H. Teramura., J. Antonovics and Boyd R. Strain. 1980. Experimental ecological genetics in plantago. IV. Effects of temperature on growth rates and reproduction in three populations of *Plantago* lanceolata. L. Amer. J. Bot. 68: 425–434.

Baker, F.S. 1929. Effect of excessively high temperatures on coniferous reproduction. J. For. 6; 922–932.

Berry, J.A., J.K. Raison. 1981. Response of Macrophytes to Temperature. Physiological Plant Ecology I–Response to Physical Environment. (Eds. Lange, Noble, Osmond and Ziegler). Springer-Verlag: 293–294.

Bierhuizen, J.E. 1973. The effect of temperature on plant growth, development and yield. Proceedings of Uppsala Symposium, Plant Response to Climatic Factors. UNESCO: 88–98

Brown, D.M. 1960. Soybean ecology I. Development-temperature relationships from controlled environment studies. Agron. J. 52: 493–496.

Brown, K.W. and N.J. Rosenberg. 1973. A resistance model to predict evapotranspiration and its application to a sugarbeet field. Agron. J. 65: 341–347.

Curtis, O.F. and D.G. Clark. 1950. Introduction to Plant Physiology. N.Y. McGraw Hill: 27-28.

Chang, Jen-Hu. 1968. Climate and Agriculture. An ecological survey. Aldine Publishing Co.: 83–86.

Downs, R.J. and J.M. Bevington. 1981. Effect of temperature and Photoperiod on growth and dormancy of *Betula* papyrifera. Amer. J. Bot. 86: 188–190.

Hord, H H.V. and D.P. Spell. 1962. Temperature as a basis for forecasting banana production. Trop. Agric. 39: 219–223.

Judith F. Thomas and C. David Raper Jr. 1981. Day and night temperature influence on carpel initiation and growth in soybeans. Bot. Gaz. 142: 183–187.

Meyer, B.S. and D.B. Anderson. 1952. Plant Physiology. East-West Press, New Delhi.

Monteith, L.J. 1963. Gas exchange in plant communities. Environmental Control of Plant Growth. L.T. Evans (ed) Academic Press: 95–112.

Papadakis, J. 1970. Fundamentals of Agronomy (Compendium of Crop

Ecology). Av. Cordoba, Buenos Aires: 1–20.

Parker, N.W. 1946. Environmental factors and their control in plant environment. Soil Sci. 62: 109–119.

Riley, J.A. 1957. Soil temperature as related to corn yield in Central Iowa. Mon. Weath. Rev. U.S. Dep. Agric. 85: 393–400.

Rogers, W.J. 1970. Frost and the prevention of frost damage. National Weather Service, NOAA. U.S. Dept. of Commerce: 20–28.

Rosenberg, M.J. 1974. Microclimate: The Biological Environment. John Wiley and Sons. London: 78–85.

Satake, T. 1978. Sterility type cool injury to rice plants in Japan. Climatic Change and Food Production Proceedings of the International Symposium on Recent Climatic Change and Food Production: 245–254.

Sellschop, J.P.F. and S.C. Salmon, 1928. The influence of chilling above the freezing point, on certain crop plants. J. Agric. Res. 37: 315–338.

Sutcliffee, J. 1977. Plants and Temperature, New Delhi. Oxford and I.B.H.: 17–32.

Ventskevich, G.Z. 1961. Agrometeorology. Israel Programme for Seientific Translation. Jerusalem.

Vittum, M.T., B.E. Dethier and R.C. Lesser. 1965. Estimating Growing Degree Days. Proc. Am. Soc. Hort. Sci. 87: 449–452.

Wang, Jen-Hu. 1962. The influence of seasonal temperature range on pea production. Proc. Am. Soc. Hort. Sci. 80: 436–448.

Wilsie, C.P. 1974. Crop Adaptation and Distribution, New Delhi. Eurasia Publishing House: 190–195.

CHAPTER 6

MOISTURE FACTOR IN PLANT GROWTH

The importance of water to plants in paramount for several reasons. It is a constituent part of the protoplasm. On an average, it forms 85–90 per cent of the green weight of actively growing tissues. It is a raw material in photosynthesis. It is a universal solvent and dissolves all plant nutrients present in the soil. It is the medium by which the solutes enter the plant and move about in the tissues. It increases the chemical activity of the compounds in the plants. Its presence in the plants is essential for the normal functioning of the cells and for maintaing their turgidity. The presence of water within the plants and the environment saves them from lethal temperatures.

Plants use moisture from rain, snow, hail and soil. Rain is of tremendous importance to the plant. In general, it provides water to the soil for translocation and for transpiration. Rainy weather is always associated with reduced evapo-transpiration. It favours plant diseases and pests. It also interferes with many farming operations, such as the preparation of seedbed, sowing, harvesting and the threshing of crops. Rain increases soil moisture, but it causes a fall in actual soil fertility. However, the deficiency or absence of rainfall causes the soil horizon to dry up, hampers the supply of moisture to the plants, damages the plants and reduces the yield.

Snow can be beneficial or injurious to the plants in several ways. Certain trees in cold climates have a strong preference to a particular amount of snow-fall. Snow which melts in spring is a big source of moisture for the crops. Heavy snowfall on the other hand, especially when followed by strong winds, breaks off the leaves, twigs and branches of the plants and can reduce th*h* growth for a number of years. Broken trees are often attacked by insects, fungi and other pathogens. The glazing or coating of the leaves and stems causes a lot of damage to the plants by way of suffocation, accumulation of toxic materials and oxygen deficiency. Ice, in contact with the crowns and the roots, inhibits carbon dioxide diffusion.

Hail affects crops *suddenly* and little can be done to prevent it. A hailstorm can decimate foliage, break branches, and shatter the fruit. Cereal crops are more seriously damaged. When the hailstorm is severe, leaves are knocked off and the stalk and heads are broken. When the crop is ripe a hailstorm shatters the grain. Lesions are caused on the plants owing to the mechanical rupture of the mesophyll cells. On many occasions a hailstorm virtually beats a crop to the ground and the damage to it may be a hundred per cent.

Humidity in the air is of considerable importance to the life of plants. It affects the intensity and the quality of solar radiation, evaporation and transpiration. There are certain plants which directly utilize water vapour from the atmosphere without requiring a change in its state into a liquid form. It is also a source of soil moisture.

High air humidity reduces the saturation deficit, but favours many plant diseases and pests. It increases the growth of shoots and leaves at the expense of fruit, stolons, bulbs and cambium. On the other hand, low atmospheric humidity increases the saturation deficit and accelerates transpiration. When transpiration is high, water that reaches the leaves is not sufficient for them even when there is no dearth of moisture in the soil. Due to this excessive transpiration, the stomata closes and photosynthesis is interrupted. When saturation deficit is extreme, most of the plants wilt and some are even killed because of physiological drought.

6.1 Soil Moisture

Almost all the moisture consumed by the plant comes to it from the soil. Therefore the availability of moisture in the soil is a prerequisite for the survival of plants. The capacity of soil for storing available water can be expressed conveniently in terms of maximum available soil moisture in the root zone. The water contained in the soil above field capacity is not available to crops due to quick drainage to lower layers. The water contained below permanent wilting point is also not available to crops as it is tightly held by the soil particles. Thus, it is generally considered that the amount of water held between field capacity and permanent wilting point in the crop root zone is available water for crop use. This is a widely accepted view and is followed by most of the workers for irrigation purposes.

The rate of availability of moisture to crops within field capacity and permanent wilting point, and its effect on crop growth is an important factor in determining crop growth. Veihmeyer and Hendrickson (1955) have made extensive field tests on perennial fruit crops and stated, that water is equally available for plant growth at all levels, between field capacity and permanent wilting point. Their experiments show that favourable conditions of soil moisture extend from the field capacity to about the permanent wilting point. This view has been widely adopted and has had an important influence on irrigation practices.

A logarithmic decrease in the availability of soil water with decrease in water content from field capacity to permanent wilting point is proposed by Jensen et al. (1969). This was not widely used by researchers in irrigation scheduling. On the other hand, Thornthwaite and Mather (1955) proposed a linear decrease in availability of soil water and they have used this approach in their water balance studies. Marlatt et al. (1961) proposed a combination of the Veihmeyer and Hendrickson approach and the linear approach of Thornthwaite and Mather, and they stated that water is available freely at equal rate upto a point between field capacity and permanent wilting point but it decreases linearly after it reaches below that point. Generally 50 per cent depletion level is taken as the point by many of the workers. The 50 per cent level of available water as the minimum amount for successful crop growth was used by several workers for irrigation purposes. But to find out the minimum water requirement the permanent wilting point is usually taken as the minimum threshold level.

6.2 Absorption of Water by Plants

Water enters the plant through the epidermal cells of roots and reaches the intercellular spaces and epidermal cells of leaves from where it is lost to the air. Water flows through plants and is distributed among the various tissues according to the laws of diffusion, cohesion and transpiration. The water content in a plant is not static because there is a continuous process of intake and loss from and to the surrounding environment. The dynamic nature of the plant water balance results in the hydration of the tissues and cells, which in turn governs the activities of processes like photosynthesis, respiration, growth, and supply and distribution of metabolic materials. The degree of hydration of the guard cells in the epidermis also controls the gas exchange.

6.2.1 WATER INTAKE BY ROOTS

The uptake of water by the plants is primarily by the roots, and the structure of the roots is adapted to absorption. Depending upon the species and the intensity of root growth, there is a zone of maximum water absorption, 15 to 200 mm behind the root tip. In this zone the root epidermis produce their membraned extensions, known as root hairs, which increases the absorption surface manyfold. Xylem, the water conducting tissue, is also perfectly developed in this zone.

Water from the soil moves into the root along a potential gradient which is determined by water availability. The availability of water depends upon three factors, viz. (1) the rate of water movement in the soil and towards the absorbing roots; (2) the absolute rate of water absorption; and (3) the size of the absorbing root surface.

With decreasing quantities of water in the soil, the permeability of water decreases. Thus, the lower the quantity of water in the soil, the lower will be the supply of soil water to the roots.

The absolute rate of water absorption depends upon the stress in the water stream due to transpiration from the plants. This ultimately reduces the water potential of epidermal cells, and increases the water potential gradient from soil to roots.

The absolute rate of water absorption also depends upon the size of the absorbing root surface. The extent of the root system in turn determines the volume of the soil occupied by the roots. The horizontal extent of the root system is determined by the competition; and that of the vertical system by the depth of the water supply and aeration. In addition, aerobic conditions, warmth, adequate nutrients and permeable soil are also required for the growth of the roots.

The importance of the root growth lies not only in reaching moist soil but also in maintaining enough absorbing surface. Root hairs play an important role in the absorption of water because they increase the absorbing surface. Root hairs live only for a few days, some for a few weeks and subsequently are destroyed during suberization and lignification of the roots. In aqueous culture root hairs are completely missing, and in moist soils their number is low.

6.2.2 WATER INTAKE BY SHOOTS

Limited quantities of water can be absorbed by the shoots directly from water deposited on the surface: through vertical and horizontal rainfall, from dew or from the water vapour present in the surrounding atmosphere. A prerequisite for this type of liquid water uptake by the plants is a favourable water potential gradient because for water vapour diffusion a decrease of water potential towards the leaf is essential, which is possible only under extremely humid air conditions and possibly when the leaf surface is cooler than the air. Liquid water penetrates the leaves through the stomata and cuticles. However, because of the surface tension of water, its entry through the stomata is very minor. However, the entry of water through the cuticles is directly proportional to its hydration. The beginning of intensive absorption has been observed to take place when a leaf has been immersed in water at least for 90 minutes.

Horizontal precipitation from mist on leaves in the arid coastal areas in South Africa and Peru is a direct source of moisture to the plants.

6.3 Water Flow in Plants

The roots and leaves, the places of water uptake and water loss, are separated from each other by space as well as by a series of tissues which must remain in a state of hydration to maintain an optimum physiological activity. Millions of water paths branch off from the direct transpiration stream towards all living tissues. These are repeatedly multidirected. The changing streams originating from these tissues join the transpiration stream in the direction of the water potential gradient, maintaining a distinct continuity of the direct flow of water, from the soil plant contact to the plant atmosphere contact. The term 'transpiration stream' used to denote this flow of water in plants, is used because this flow ultimately ends in transpiration, which is also the driving force for this flow (Slavik, 1965). This upward flow is often called 'ascent of sap' because it contains water as well as solutes. The direction of the flow is along the potential gradient between the usually moist soil and dry atmosphere.

Three sections can be recognised to grasp the direct path of water from the roots to the leaf surface. The first section is from the root epidermis, across the cortex, the endodermis and finally the vessels of the root. The second section is the specialized tissues of the vascular system, mainly the conducting elements of the xylem. The third section leads from the vessels in the leaf veins through the mesophyll cells, into intercellular spaces and epidermal cells.

6.4   Water Stress and Plant Development

Plant growth and development depends: (1) upon a continuous process of cell division; (2) on the progressive initiation of tissue and organ primordia; and (3) on the differentiation and expansion of the component cells. Along with this is an inter-connected chain of metabolic events which involve the uptake of nutrients from both soil and air, the synthesis of metabolites and structural materials, and also from the flow of substances within the plant body. Because all these plant processes take place in the aqueous medium — and water being a transporting agent as well as a reactant in the majority of these processes — any shortfall in water uptake and dehydration results in negative effects on most of the physiological processes.

The initiation as well as differentiation of the vegetative and reproductive primordia are very sensitive to water stress. Equally sensitive to stress is cell division. However, the fact, that the leaves of plants which have undergone a period of stress have the same number of cells as those which remained unstressed, suggests that they have the capacity for resumed activity when relieved from water stress. Further, unlike the primordial initiation which remains completely suspended during the period of stress, cell division may continue under such situations. The other essential component of growth which is affected by even a slight moisture stress is cell enlargement. It is due to the stoppage of cell enlargement that plants show stunted growth. In some plants, cell enlargement is so sensitive to moisture stress that stem elongation or leaf enlargement is retarded even by diurnal water deficit due to intense radiation, even when the plants are well watered.

Apart from a reduction in the rate of the abovesaid organs' development and cell enlargement, there are several indirect effects on physiological processes. These are because reduced developmental activity of cells and tissues negatively affects the nutrient inflow, protein and carbohydrate synthesis and metabolism.

Reduction in cell expansion results in lower leaf area, and this means reduced photosynthesising surface and ultimately lower biological yield.

The affect of water stress on the continued development of tissues which are either mature or are approaching maturity resembles that of accelerated ͟enescence. The initial indication of this stress is the migration of phosphorus from the older leaves to the stem and meristematic tissues. This is followed by the movement of nitrogen, resulting in progressive protein hydrolysis and breakdown of normal cell functions.

Root development is enhanced in a short stress period. However, progressive reduction in the rate of root elongation is recorded when a serious and prolonged water stress is imposed (Newman, 1966). The roots in relatively moist soil may continue growing even when the plant as a whole suffers from serious internal water stress.

The effect of moisture stress on suberization varies according to the rates of root extension. In some species when the roots are fast-grown, a non-suberized zone may be 10–20 cm, constituting a very active and extensive absorbing surface. With reduced rates of root elongation, the rate of suberization is much greater than the rate of elongation of roots so the non-suberized zone is reduced. With increased water stress it is virtually eliminated in non-elongating roots.

In conclusion, the effects of water stress on plant growth can be summarized as follows (Slatyer, 1973):

Stress affects those tissues most which are in rapid stages of development. Primordial initiation and cell enlargement are inhibited by moisture stress.

Cell enlargement does not compensate after stress is removed; however, initiation is compensated as long as the stress has not been serious. After moisture stress is over, developing tissues are rejuvenated and growth rates of many plants are more rapid than those which remained unstressed. This is due to the continued but slow cell division as well as the availability of nutrients released by the old tissues.

6.4.1 PLANT GROWTH UNDER EXTREME MOISTURE STRESS

The sensitivity of plants to an unfavourable water balance varies from stage to stage during the life cycle of the crop. Young seedlings of plants, especially cereals, can withstand a high degree of drought in the first several days of their growth. As soon as their first leaves bloom they become very sensitive to drought. During active growth different species respond differently to drought. Near maturity they once again lose their sensitivity to drought to some extent.

On the whole, the plant structure is greatly influenced by the moisture status under which it has completed its life cycle. Plants grown in an unfavourable water balance have some marked physiologic and morphologic characteristics when compared with plants grown in an optimum moisture condition (Daubenmire, 1974). Major physiologic and morphologic characteristics of plants grown in moisture stress environments are:

1) the protoplasmic viscosity is decreased, but
2) its permeability is increased;
3) resistance to wilting is increased;
4) phenologic events like flowering and fruiting are accelerated;
5) the size of the shoots is decreased whereas that of roots is increased;
6) the cell size in leaves is smaller, thus resulting in reduced size of blades, stomata and vain islets;
7) the cuticle and cell walls are thickened;
8) the size of the intercellular spaces is reduced.

Soil moisture stress and grain yield

There are three key stages when water stress affects the grain yield in cereals and these are:

1) Stage of floral initiation and inflorescence development.
2) Stage of anthesis and fertilisation.
3) Grain-filling stage.

Inflorescence development

For most cereal crops even a slight water stress can reduce the rate of appearance of floral primordia. If the stress period at this stage is severe and prolonged, the total number of spikelets are substantially reduced.

Fertilisation

Stress at anthesis can markedly reduce fertilisation in most cereals. The best example is that of corn (Table 6.1) in which a reduction of 50% yield is caused by wilting at this period (Robins and Domingo, 1953).

Table 6.1 Effect of water regime on grain yield of corn
(Robins and Domingo, 1953)

Treatment	Yield (bushels/acre)	Shelling %
1. Irrigated at anthesis + 3 subsequent irrigations	138.3	82.9
2. Irrigated at anthesis + 2 subsequent irrigations	132.9	81.9
3. Wilted at anthesis + 2 subsequent irrigations	79.1	76.7
Wilted at anthesis + 1 subsequent irrigation	66.7	77.6

Scientists are of the opinion that stress at this stage is likely to interfere with germination of pollen or growth of pollen tubes from the stigma to the ovules. This type of the injury is, however, more pronounced in the case of corn as compared with other cereal crops.

For wheat, it has been observed (Fischer, 1974) that grain yield is reduced to a great extent when stress developed about ten days before the emergence of wheat ears, due to pronounced effects on the number of grains formed per spikelet.

Grain filling

The weight per grain is influenced by pre-flowering and post-flowering conditions. However, the post-flowering stage is the most important. In case of wheat, virtually all the increase in dry weight after anthesis is by grain filling. Thus water stress by reducing photosynthesis during this period can lead to a large yield decrease.

6.5 Drought

Over the years there has come to exist a long list of definitions for drought. These indicate that drought has varied meaning for different people. To a farmer drought means a shortage of moisture in the root zone of his crops. To a hydrologist it is the below-average water level in lakes, reservoirs and streams. To an economist it is a water shortage which adversely affects the stability of the economy. Drought causes a number of problems. Moderate drought during crop growth periods can result in stunted growth of the crop and reduced crop yield. When the situation is more severe drought becomes a natural calamity and is typified by the drying-up of wells, springs, small streams and depletion of water stored in lakes and reservoirs, causing shortages of drinking water and power supply to all sectors of the economy. In many areas a prolonged drought can result in starvation and death to thousands of humans and animals.

Since drought has varied meaning to different people, it is difficult to give a complete and adequate definition for drought. Palmer (1965) has enumerated various definitions, his own being a prolonged and abnormal moisture deficiency. In general drought may be defined as a complex phenomenon which results from the prolonged absence of precipitation, in conjunction with high rates of evaporation. This causes abnormal loss of water from water bodies, lowering of the water table, and dehydration of the root zone of the soil, thus upsetting water supply to plants.

Drought can result not only from precipitation deficiency, but also from excessive evapotranspiration. In foggy coastal areas of Peru and Chile, a dry spell is not particularly harmful to vegetation, although there may be serious hydrological consequences.

6.5.1 CLASSIFICATION OF DROUGHT

Droughts can broadly be divided into three categories (Van Bavel, and Verlinden, 1956).

1) *Meteorological drought*: Meteorological drought is a situation when the actual rainfall is significantly lower than the climatologically expected rainfall over a wide area.

2) *Hydrological drought*: Hydrological drought is associated with marked depletion of surface water and consequent drying up of lakes, rivers, reservoirs etc. Hydrological drought results if meteorological drought is sufficiently prolonged.

3) *Agricultural drought*: Agricultural drought is a condition in which there is insufficient soil moisture available to a crop.

6.5.2 DROUGHT ANALYSIS

In the early part of this century, a drought was considered to be just the lack of rainfall over a certain period. Many of the drought definitions were based on this lack of rainfall. Thus only rainfall data were taken into consideration in analysing drought.

Climatologists have long realized that rainfall data alone is insufficient to quantify drought. Air temperature considerations play a significant role and have been used by several workers in their attempts to analyse the dryness of climate. These studies gave rise to various classifications of climate like the ones proposed by Koppen as well as Thornthwaite (1931).

Subsequently for the purpose of analysing agricultural drought, the loss of moisture from the soil reservoir was given much attention. Scientists used precipitation, evapotranspiration and available soil moisture in the root zone as inputs to quantify the occurrence of agricultural drought. The water balance approach of Thornthwaite, using the same data, was successfully used to quantify droughts in various parts of the world. Papadakis (1975) proposed an index using rainfall, evaporation and available soil moisture as inputs. This index was used successfully by many workers to study agricultural drought in various parts of the world.

More complex models were developed by several authors using other climatic variables in all parts of the world to study the frequency of drought and its effect on crop plants. These models, however, need exhaustive data and calculation procedures. The most popular among them is that of Palmer (1965). The underlying concept of the Palmer Index is : that the amount of precipitation required for the near normal operation of the economy of an area during certain specific periods, depends upon the average climate of the area, and on the prevailing meteorological conditions both during and preceding the period in question. He developed a method of computation for required precipitation. The difference between the actual precipitation and required precipitation gives a fair and direct measure of the variance from the normal of moisture. The variances have been properly weighted, thus resulting in index numbers for reasonable comparison both in time and space.

Early investigators used annual data to analyse aridity and drought. This was mainly due to the ready availability of this data and easy computations.

As the annual variation in any climatic parameter is marginal and the crop growing season is generally lower than an year, it was recognised that periods of less than an year should be studied to analyse agricultural drought. Thus a part of the year, like the crop season, was utilized frequently by investigators in their analyses. In India climatologists utilized the monsoon rainfall to analyse droughts in the various states of the country. Thornthwaite's $P - E$ index has also been used for various durations of the season.

Subsequently monthly periods were taken into consideration. Thornthwaite (1931) used monthly averages of precipitation and evaporation to delineate arid climates. Palmer (1965) used monthly weather data to analyse meteorological drought in North America. Several other workers also used monthly data to analyse drought periods (Stelia, 1972; Subrahmanyam and Sastri, 1971).

Monthly data were found suitable in analysing the drought condition with respect to climatic aridity, agricultural production and stream flow, but the data were found inadequate to represent the soil moisture deficiencies occurring at various stages of crop growth. In a month, the total rainfall may be more than the average but in a week of that month, the crops in that region might suffer due to deficiency of rainfall. There was therefore a need to study drought on a weekly or daily basis.

Most of the workers interested in agricultural drought analysis now use either weekly periods or daily periods. Daily values tend to vary a great deal and are difficult to analyse on a larger scale. Weekly periods are therefore found to be more suitable in analysing drought, and scheduling irrigation.

6.5.3 DROUGHTS IN INDIA

For the entire country, weather information is inadequate to build a historical series of droughts prior to the year 1875. However since drought is invariably the immediate cause of famine in this country, useful information regarding its recurrence can be inferred from the accounts of famine reported in historical records. From the beginning of the 11th century to the end of the 17th century, there were 14 famines. In a period of about 90 years, commencing 1765, the country experienced 12 famines and four severe scarcities, while between 1860–1908 famine or scarcity prevailed continually in some part of the country.

Reliable rainfall data from a good network of stations are available with the India Meteorology Department from 1875 onwards. For determining the drought years, areas of those meteorological sub-divisions which received rainfall of less than 75 per cent of the normal during the monsoon are added. The area so obtained was expressed as a percentage of the total area of the country. The year in which the area exceeded 20 per cent is termed as a drought year. Between 1875 and 1974, 19 years of drought were observed. Of course, 1877, 1899, 1904 and 1918 were the worst drought years the country has experienced. In each of these years more than 50 per cent of the country reeled under severe drought conditions. Among these, 1918 stands out as the worst year in the history of recorded rainfall observation in this country; the area affected being 70 per cent of the total (Sarker, 1979).

6.5.4 PROPENSITY FOR DROUGHT IN INDIA

According to the definition proposed by the India Meteorological Department when the rainfall variance from the normal is 26 to 50 per cent, it is termed "moderate drought", and when the deficiency exceeds 50 per cent it is called as "severe drought". The recurrence of drought in various parts of India is given in Table 6.2.

Table 6.2   Recurrence of drought in India

Recurrence	Regions
Once in 4–5 years	Rajasthan, Punjab, Gujarat and Telengana.
Once in 6–8 years	Haryana, Jammu and Kashmir, Uttar Pradesh (east), Sub-Himalyan West Bengal, Vidarbha (interior), Karnataka (south) and Coastal Andhra Pradesh.
Once in 10 years	Himachal Pradesh, Uttar Pradesh (west), Madhya Pradesh, Bihar (plains), Marathwada, Konkan, Rayalseema and Kerala.
Once in 15 to 20 years	Madhya Maharashtra, South Assam, Tamilnadu (interior), Karnataka (north) and Orissa.
Very rare	Coastal Karnataka, Bihar Plateau, Bengal.

The areas prone to moderate droughts are Rajasthan, Saurashtra-Kutch, parts of Gujarat, Haryana, Punjab, western U.P., Maharashtra and Central Karnataka. The areas where the recurrence of severe drought is frequent are western Rajasthan and Kutch.

REFERENCES

Daubenmire, R. F. 1974. Plants and Environments. A Text Book of Plant Autocology. John Wiley and Sons: 74–154.

Fischer, R. A. 1974. The effect of water stress at various stages of development on yield processes in wheat. Plant Response to Climatic Factors. Proc. of Uppasala Symp. UNESCO: 233–141.

Jensan, M. C., J. E. Middleston and W.O. Pruitt. 1969. Scheduling irrigation from pan evaporation. Wash. Agril. Expt. Sta. Circ. 386.

Marlatt, W. E., A.V. Havens, N. A. Willets and G. D. Bull. 1961. A Comparison of computed and measured soil moisture under snap beans. J.Geo phys. Res.. 66: 535–541.

Newman, E. L. 1966. Relationship between root growth of flex (*Linum Usitatissimum*) and soil water potential. New Phytol. 65: 273–283.

Palmer, W. C. 1965. Meteorological Drought. Res. Paper No. 45. U. S. Deptt. of Commerce, Weather Bureau: 1–8.

Papadakis, J. 1975. Climates of the world and their potentials. Buenes Aires: 1–15.

Robins, J. S., C. E. Domingo. 1953. Some effects of severe soil moisture deficit at specific growth stages in corn. Agron. J. 45: 612–621.

Sarker, R. P. 1979. Droughts in India and their Predictability. International Symposium on Hydrological Aspects of Droughts. Souvenir: 33–40.

Slatyer, R. O. 1973. The effects of internal water status on plant growth, development and yield. Plant Response to Climatic Factors. Proc. of the Uppasala Symp. UNESCO: 177–191.

Slavik. Bondan, 1965. Supply of water to plants. Monograph. Vol. 6. American Meteorological Society : 149–162.

Stelia D. 1972. Drought analysis in four Southern States by a new index. Dist. Abat. Int. A. 32.

Subrahmanyam, V. P. and C. V. S. Sastri. 1971. New techniques in drought analysis. Ann. Arid. Zone. 10: 21–44.

Thornthwaite, C. W. 1931. The Climate of North America according to a new Classification. Geographical Rev. 21: 633–655.

Thornthwaite, C. W. and J. R. Mathar. 1955. The water budget and its use in irrigation. Water. USDA Year Book of Agriculture: 346–357.

Van Bavel, C. H. M. and F. J. Verlinden. 1956. Agricultural drought in North Carolina. North Carolina Agrl. Expt. Station. Tech. Bull. No. 122.

Veihmeyer, F. J. and A. H. Handrickson. 1955. Does transpiration decrease as the soil moisture decreases. Trans. Amer. Geophys. Union. 36: 425–428.

CHAPTER 7

WATER LOSS AND ITS MEASUREMENT

7.1 Evaporation

The change of state of water from solid and liquid to the vapour and its diffusion into the atmosphere is referred to as evaporation. It plays a major role in the redistribution of thermal energy between the earth and the atmosphere, and is an essential part of the hydrological cycle

The process of evaporation involves supply of energy for the latent heat of vaporization and transfer process. This transfer process is governed by turbulence. Evaporation is a continuous process as long as there is a supply of energy, availability of moisture and vapour pressure gradient between the water surface and the atmosphere.

Water vapour diffuses into the atmosphere from different surfaces like lakes, rivers, ponds, cloud droplets, rain drops, moist soil, animals and plants, but there is no fundamental difference in the physics of the process. Evaporation also occurs directly from the solid state, that is, from snow and ice, provided there exists an appropriate vapour pressure gradient.

Over the land surface which is covered with vegetation, evaporation involves the following processes:

1) the movement of water within the soil towards the soil surface, or towards the active root system of the plants;

2) movement of water into the roots, and then throughout the plant tissues to leaf surfaces;

3) the change of water into vapour at the soil surface, or at the stomata of plants, with a large conversion of thermal energy into the latent heat;

4) change of rain water or snow from the outer surface of plants into the vapour; and

5) the physical removal of the water vapour from the boundary layer.

The process that involves these activities is termed *evapotrans-piration.*

7.1.1   MEASUREMENT OF EVAPORATION

There are several simple devices and empirical methods of estimating evaporation. Small containers of different kinds can measure evaporation quite accurately. However, for practical purposes, the measurement of evaporation—from the surface of large water bodies, crop fields, bare soil, or catchment areas—has greater significance and is therefore required. The relationship between the size of the evaporating surface and the rate of water loss has been described in Fig. 7.1. The rate of evaporation is fairly independent of the

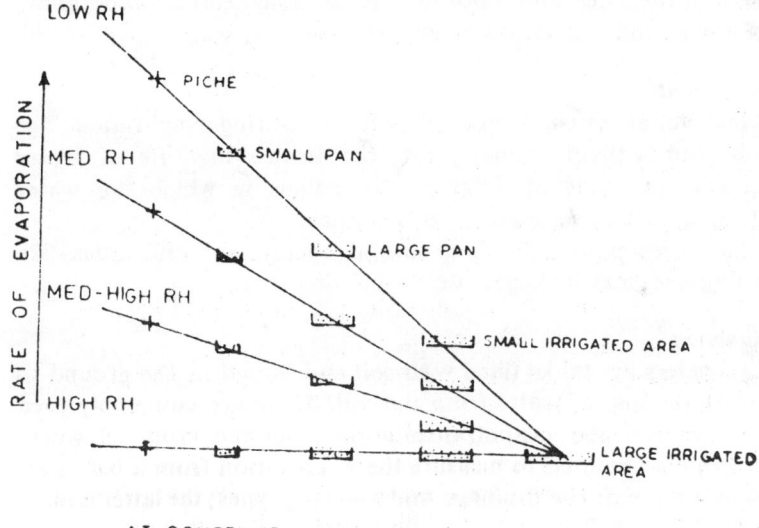

Fig. 7.1   Rate of evaporation and size of evaporating surface.

size of the measuring pan under high humidity conditions. However when the air is dry, the size of the pan greatly influences the rate of evaporation. Therefore in order to make use of measurements taken from these pans and the other bodies a relationship between them needs to be established. There are four main types of evaporimeters or pans, used for measuring evaporation. There are floating pans;

pans placed above the ground; pans sunk in the soil; and devices with special evaporation surfaces.

Floating pans

These pans are made to float in water bodies with suitable rafts. Water loss from these pans is similar to the water loss from the surrounding water surface.

The installation and operations of these pans in the water bodies are costly. Moreover, their operation becomes difficult when the wind is strong.

Pans placed above the ground

The US Weather Bureau A Class pan is now widely used in many countries. The major drawback of this pan is that the sensible heat flux from the sides and bottom results in increased evaporation, and it gives inflated values of evaporation.

Sunken pans

Many countries use sunken pans for measuring evaporation. The US Bureau of Plant Industry and the British Institute of Water Engineers use pans of different dimensions in which the water surface is kept close to the earth's surface.

The sunken pans suffer from several operational difficulties like cleaning and heat leakage.

Lysimeters

Lysimeters are tanks filled with soil and buried in the ground to measure the loss of water from the soil. These are commonly used for measuring the evapotranspiration from the crop. However they can also be used to measure the evaporation from a bare soil. Lysimeters are of the drainage and weighing types; the latter is most commonly used.

The weighing lysimeter can measure evaporation and evapotranspiration for very short intervals of time. Apart from the measurement of evaporation and evapotranspiration, the weighing lysimeters can also give additional informtaion like the diurnal patterns of evaporation, variations in energy partitioning and the relationships between transpiration and soil moisture tension.

The biggest drawback of lysimeters is the high cost of their installation and their immobility.

Special devices

The most common special device to measure evaporation is the pich evaporimeter which consists of an inverted graduated tube filled with water, with filter paper clamped over its mouth. The instrument is kept in the Stevenson Screen. Similarly, black Bellane atmometers commonly used in Canada consist of a black porous disc, 7.5 cm in diameter fixed to the end of a ceramic funnel into which water is fed from a burette.

These instruments are not very reliable. Both overestimate the effects of wind while underestimating the effects of solar radiation.

7.2 Transpiration

Most of the water absorbed by plants is lost to the atmosphere. This loss of water from living plants is called transpiration. It can be stomatal, cuticular or lenticular. The transpiration which takes place through stomata is called stomatal transpiration. The maximum stomatal transpiration takes place through leaves.

Outside the epidermal cells of a leaf there is a thin layer called the cuticle. Sometimes gaps or pores in the cuticle are present and water loss through these gaps is called cuticular transpiration.

Pores or gaps in roots or stems are called lenticules and loss of water through lenticules is called lenticular transpiration.

7.2.1 FACTORS AFFECTING TRANSPIRATION

The rate of transpiration depends both upon meteorological factors and crop characteristics.

Light: Stomata open in light and close in the dark, hence the opening of stomata during the day leads to transpiration.

Humidity: Lowered humidity results in higher transpiration. That is, increased difference between atmospheric and leaf humidity leads to increased transpiration.

Temperature: Humidity or vapour pressure is a function of temperature. A decrease in temperature increases vapour pressure in the environment, reducing the saturation deficit. The reverse is the case at higher temperatures. Thus it follows, that at higher temperatures there will be an increase in transpiration.

Wind: In windy conditions, fresh dry air will replace the saturated air around the plant, leading to increased transpiration. The wind also has a cooling effect on leaves, thus decreasing the vapour pressure between leaves and the atmosphere.

Root/Shoot ratio: If the root/shoot ratio is greater, there will be more absorption and less transpiration; and vice versa.

Availability of water to plant: With greater availability of water to plants, transpiration will rise, and vice versa.

Leaf characteristics: If the leaf area is large, transpiration will be high. A thicker cuticle will result in lowered cuticular transpiration. The presence of epidermal hair on leaves restricts the loss of water vapours to the atmosphere.

7.2.2 SIGNIFICANCE OF TRANSPIRATION

Transpiration is often termed as a necessary evil. Necessary because it is essential for all translocations; evil because it results in water loss, and ultimately, water stress in plants.

The loss of water may have several effects on the plant, some of which are direct and some indirect. The most important effect is through vaporization which, as a change from liquid to vapour will result in cooling at the surface where vaporization takes place. This cooling process saves the plants from excessively high temperatures, which otherwise could have a lethal effect on many plants.

7.3 Evaporation versus Transpiration

The fundamental difference between evaporation from a free water surface and transpiration from plants is, that while in the case of transpiration a diffusive resistance occurs due to the internal leaf geometry including the stomata, there exists no such resistance in evaporation from a free water surface.

Since the stomata closes at night, the rate of transpiration drops to 5 to 10 per cent of that during the day. On the other hand the rate of evaporation remains relatively high because of the availability of energy stored at night. The potential evapotranspiration from short grass is less than the evaporation from free water, due to greater reflection of energy from the vegetative surface, closure of stomata during the night, and resistance to diffusion imposed by the stomata.

7.4 Evapotranspiration

Evapotranspiration (ET) is the combined loss of water from vegetation — both as evaporation from soil and transpiration from plants. Both the processes are basically the same and involve a change of state — from liquid to vapour. When water is adequately available at the site of transformation (i.e. soil or plant surfaces) the rate of evapotranspiration is primarily controlled by meteorological factors, like solar radiation, wind, temperature and the evaporating power of the atmosphere.

The dependence of evapotranspiration on meteorological factors at a given place has led to the concept of *potential evapotranspiration* (PET) in which the contribution of plant and soil factors are ignored. It is the upper limit of evapotranspiration. Potential evapotranspiration is the water transpired from a uniform, short, green, actively growing vegetation when water is unlimited. The concept assumes that there is ample supply of water at the site of evaporation and the rate is governed by evaporating capacity of the atmosphere. Soil and plant factors have practically no role to play in potential evapotranspiration. However, the radiation and aerodynamic properties of crop surfaces may modify the effect of meteorological factors on evapotranspiration.

Recent researches have demonstrated that over a relatively longer period—at least one month,—the potential evapotranspiration is constant for a given area. The fluctuations between years or monthly potential evapotranspiration are low. This is also true for variables of climate.

The concept of potential evapotranspiration and its conservative nature has helped researchers in simpler modelling of this complicated phenomena. As a result many empirical formulae have been developed depending on climatic factors only.

When empirical methods of determining potential evapotranspiration are calibrated under condition of unlimited water supply, they provide reasonable quantitative estimates. This is due to the conservativeness of potential evapotranspiration; additionally because the variance from average values of potential evapotranspiration are correlated with variances of many climatic variables from their means.

In general, empirical formulae correlate evapotranspiration with air temperatures, incident solar radiation, atmospheric humidity or a combination of these (McGuinness and Bordne, 1972).

The measurement of evapotranspiration under natural conditions is of great importance in the estimation and management of present and future water resources, and for solving many theoretical problems in the field of hydrology and meteorology. In the planning of irrigation, evapotranspiration data are used: as a basis for estimating the acreage of various crops, or combination of crops, that can be irrigated with a given water supply; or as a basis for estimating the amount of water that will be required to irrigate a given acreage. Evapotranspiration data are therefore being increasingly used for scheduling irrigation. Evapotranspiration data are also used as a basis for evaluating the overall efficiency of irrigation in the field. As agroclimatic index it has been widely used to assess the effect of the water supply on both the growth and yield of the crops.

7.5 Estimation of Potential Evapotranspiration

The actual evapotranspiration is a function of potential evapotranspiration. The determination of potential evapotranspiration is therefore, the first step towards the measurement of actual evapotranspiration. Numerous formulae and methods for calculating potential evapotranspiration have been proposed over the years. Some of these are purely empirical, while others exist in which the basis is the physics of evaporation phenomena. Though the list of all such formulae is very big, an attempt has been made here to enumerate and describe some of the universally popular ones, without discussing their merits and demerits. These formulae will be of interest to many students and research workers who may like to test and use some of them in their studies, using the input of local climatological data.

The formulae described here are grouped into three broad categories. In the first category are those in which the input is only air temperature; in the second category are those formulae in which the input are air temperature, humidity or solar radiation. The third category are formulae which use the combination method, i.e. in which the inputs are all the pertinent climatic elements. With each formula an example of computation has been given to make the task of the users as simple as possible.

1. METHODS USING ONLY ONE WEATHER PARAMETER AS INPUT

Thornthwaite method

Thornthwaite (1948) gave the following formula for computing monthly potential evapotranspiration:

$$e = 1.7 \, (10T/I)^a$$

where e = unadjusted *PET* in cm per month

(a month consisting of 30 days each and 12 hours a day)

$T =$ Mean air temperature (°C)

$I =$ Annual or seasonal heat index.
It is the summation of 12 values of monthly heat indices i.

$i = (T/5)^{1.514}$

$a =$ An empirical exponent computed by the following expression:

$a = 0.000000675\ I^3 - 0.0000771\ I^2 + 0.01792\ I + 0.49239$

For daily computation, the formula is modified as under:

$$PET = \frac{k \times e \times 10}{\text{no. of days in month}} \text{ mm day}^{-1}$$

where $k =$ adjustment factor for which table values are given by Michael (1978)

Sample calculation for February 8, 1984
Mean air temperature $= 13°C$

$\left. \begin{array}{l} I = 125.5 \text{ for Ludhiana} \\ a = 2.85 \end{array} \right\}$ Mavi and Chaurasia (1980)

Putting these values in the Thornthwaite equation...

$$e = 1.7 \left(\frac{10 \times 13}{125.5} \right)^{2.85} = 1.77 \text{ cm}$$

Correction factor for 30°N latitude $= 0.90$, therefore

$$PET = \frac{0.90 \times 1.77 \times 10}{30} = 0.53 \text{ mm day}^{-1}$$

2. METHODS USING TWO WEATHER PARAMETERS AS INPUT

(a) *Papadakis method*

Papadakis formula (1965) for computation of daily PET can be written as

$$PET = \frac{0.5625\ (e_{max} - e_{min-2}) \times 10}{\text{no. of days in month}}$$

where $PET =$ Potential evapotranspiration in mm/day

$e_{max} =$ Saturation vapour pressure corresponding to daily maximum temperature (*mb*)

$e_{min-2} =$ Saturation vapour pressure corresponding to dew point temperature (*mb*). Papadakis concluded that dew point temperature is roughly equal to daily minimum temperature minus 2 degree.

0.5625 is the Papadakis constant.

Sample calculation for February 8, 1984
Data

Max. air temperature = 19.7°C

Min. air temperature = 6.3°C

Therefore

Dew point temperature = 4.3°C

e_{max} = 22.92 *mb*
e_{min-2} = 8.26 *mb* $\bigg\}$ From table

Putting these values in equation

$$PET = \frac{0.5625\,(22.92 - 8.26) \times 10}{28} = 2.94 \text{ mm day}^{-1}$$

(b) *Hamon method*

For estimation of daily *PET*, Hamon (1963) method is given as

$$PET = 0.0055 \left(\frac{DL}{12}\right)^2 (AH \times 2.88) \times 25.4$$

where *PET* = Daily potential evapotranspiration in mm
DL = Day length
AH = Absolute humidity in gm^{-3}

$$= 217\,\frac{ed}{T}$$

where *ed* = Actual vapour pressure in *mb*
T = Mean air temperature in degree absolute

Sample calculation for February 8, 1984
Data

Mean air temperature = 13°C = 286°A

Day length   = 10.98

ed = 9.5 mm = 12.66 *mb*

$$AH = \frac{217 \times 12.66}{286} = 9.61$$

Putting these values in the Hamon equation,

$$PET = 0.0055 \left(\frac{10.98}{12}\right)^2 (9.61 \times 2.881) \times 25.4$$

$= 3.24$ mm day^{-1}.

(c) *Makkink method*
Makkink (1957) proposed the following method for computation of *PET*:

$$PET = 0.61 \times 0.0171 \; RI \times \left(\frac{\Delta/\gamma}{\Delta/\gamma + 1} \right) - 0.12$$

where   *PET* = Daily potential evapotranspiration in mm
$\qquad$ *RI* = Solar radiation in langleys (Ly).
Factor 0.0171 coverts Ly to mm of water evaporation equivalent.
$\qquad \Delta$ = Slope of saturation vapour pressure vs temperature curve
$\qquad \gamma$ = Psychrometric constant (0.27)

Sample calculation for February 8, 1984
$\qquad\qquad$ *Data*
Mean air temperature $= 13°C$
$\quad RI = 276$ Ly
Values of Δ/γ at 13°C $= 1.462$
Putting these values in the Makkink equation,

$$PET = 0.61 \times 0.01710 \times 276 \times \frac{1.462}{2.462} - 0.12$$

$$= 1.59 \text{ mm day}^{-1}.$$

(d) *Jensen and Haise method*
Jensen and Haise (1963) proposed the following method for calculation of *PET*:

$\qquad PET = (0.014TA - 0.37) \; RI$ mm day^{-1}
where   *TA* = Temperature in °F (Air)
$\qquad$ *RI* = Solar radiation in water equivalent (inches day^{-1})
$\qquad$ Computing formula $PET = (0.014 \; TA - 0.37)(0.000675 \times Rs)$ inches day^{-1}
$\qquad\qquad$ *Rs* = Solar radiation Ly day^{-1} and
0.000675 converts Ly into inches.

Sample calculation for February 8, 1984
$\qquad\qquad$ *Data*
Air temperature *(TA)* $= 55.4°F$

Solar radiation (Rs) = 276 Ly

Putting these values in the equation,

$$PET = (0.014 \times 55.4 - 0.37) \times 0.000675 \times 276 \times 25.4$$

(25.4 converts inches into mm)

$$= 1.91 \text{ mm day}^{-1}.$$

(e) Modified Jensen and Haise method

Clyma and Chaudhary (1975) gave the following modified version of Jensen and Haise (1963) method for computation of PET:

$$PET = 0.012 (T - 15.4) Rs$$

where T = Mean temperature in °F

Rs = Solar radiation in water equivalent (mm day^{-1})

Sample calculation for February 8, 1984

Data

Air temperature (T) = 55.4°F

Solar radiation (Rs) = 276 Ly

$$= 276 \times 0.0171 \text{ mm day}^{-1}.$$

Putting these values in above equation,

$$PET = 0.012 (55.4 - 15.4) 276 \times 0.0171$$

$$= 2.27 \text{ mm day}^{-1}.$$

(f) Blaney-Criddle method

Blaney-Criddle (1950) proposed the following method for the estimation of daily PET:

$$PET = (0.0173 TA - 0.314) Kc. TA (DL/4465.6) \times 25.4 \text{ mm day}^{-1}$$

where TA = Mean air temperature in °F

Kc = Crop coefficient for which they gave table values

DL = Day length

Sample calculation for February 8, 1984

Data

Air temperature (TA) = 55.4°F

Day length (DL) = 10.95 by interpretation from Marvin's table

Kc = 0.71 from table for alfalfa

$$PET = (0.0173 \times 55.4 - 0.314)0.71 \times 55.4 (10.95/4465.6) \times 25.4$$
$$= 1.44 \text{ mm day}^{-1}$$

(g) Turc method

Turc proposed the following method (McGuinness and Bordne, 1972) for the calculation of daily potential evapotranspiration:

$$PET = \frac{0.40 \, Tc \, (RI + 50)}{(Tc + 15) \text{ no. of days in month}} \text{ mm day}^{-1}$$

where Tc = Air temperature in °C (Mean)

RI = Solar radiation in Ly

Sample calculation for February 8, 1984
                 Data

Mean air temperature = 13°C

Solar radiation (RI) = 276 Ly

There are 28 days in February. Putting these values in the above equation,

$$PET = \frac{0.40 \times 13 \, (276 + 50)}{(13 + 15) \, 28}$$
$$= 2.16 \text{ mm day}^{-1}$$

(h) Stephens and Stewart method

Stephens and Stewart (1963) gave the following formula for the computation of PET:

$$PET = (0.0082 \, TA - 0.19) \, (RI/1500) \times 25.4 \text{ mm day}^{-1}$$

where TA = Mean air temperature in °F

RI = Solar radiation in Ly day^{-1}

Sample calculation for February 8, 1984
                 Data

Mean air temperature (TA) = 55.4°F

Solar radiation (RI) = 276 Ly

Putting these values in the above equation,

$$PET = (0.0082 \times 55.4 - 0.19) \, (276/1500) \times 25.4$$
$$= 1.24 \text{ mm day}^{-1}$$

(i) Grassi method

Grassi (1964) proposed the following formula for the estimation of daily potential evapotranspiration:

$$PET = k \, C_{Rs} \, CT \, C_{crc} \, F \times 25.4$$

where $k = $ Constant $= 0.537$

         $C_{Rs} = $ Coefficient for radiation $= 0.000675 \, RI$

where $RI = $ Radiation in Ly

         $CT = 0.620 + 0.00559 \, TA$

where $TA = $ Mean air temperature in °F

         $C_{crc} = $ Coefficient representing plant cover set at 1.0 for meadow

         $F = 1.09$ for alfalfa

Putting these values in above equation,

$$PET = 0.537 \times 0.000675 \times RI \, (0.620 + 0.00559 \, TA)$$
$$\times 1.09 \times 25.4 \text{ mm day}^{-1}$$

Sample calculation for February 8, 1984

Data

Air temperature $(TA) = 55.4°F$

Solar radiation $(RI) = 276$ Ly

Putting these values in the above equation, the computing formula can be written as under:

$$PET = 0.537 \times 0.000675 \times 276 \, (0.620 + 0.00559 \times 55.4)$$
$$\times 1.09 \times 25.4$$

$$= 2.58 \text{ mm day}^{-1}$$

3. COMBINATION METHOD

Penman method

Penman (1948) gave the following formula for estimation of potential evapotranspiration from free water evaporation:

$$PET = KE_o$$

where $PET = $ Daily potential evapotranspiration in mm

        $K = $ Constant, for which Penman gave values

        $E_o = $ Evaporation from open water surface in mm day^{-1}

$$E_o = \frac{\Delta \, Q_n + \gamma \, E_a}{\Delta + \gamma}$$

where $Q_n = $ Net radiation in mm of water

$$= QA \, (1 - r) \, (0.18 + 0.55 \, n/N)$$
$$- \sigma Ta^4 \, (0.55 - 0.092\sqrt{ed}) \, (0.10 + 0.90 \, n/N)$$

r = Reflection coefficient of surface

QA = Angot's value of mean monthly radiation in mm of water day^{-1}

T_a = Mean air temperature in °A

Δ = Slope of saturation vapour pressure vs temperature curve

γ = Psychrometric constant (0.27)

ea = Saturation vapour pressure at mean air temperature

n/N = Ratio of actual to possible sunshine hours

σ = Stefan-Boltzman constant

ed = Saturation vapour pressure of the atmosphere in mm of Hg at dew point temperature

$$= \frac{R.H. \text{ mean} \times ea}{100}$$

Ea = An aerodynamic component

$Ea = 0.35 \, (ea - ed) \, (1 + 0.0098 U_2)$

U_2 = Wind speed in miles/day at 2 m height

$$= \frac{\log 6.6}{\log h} \times U_h \text{ in which } U_h \text{ is wind speed in}$$

miles day^{-1}

at any other height h in feet.

Sample calculation for February 8, 1984

(A)   *Data*

1. Mean air temperature = 13°C
2. Mean R.H. = 82%
3. Actual sunshine hours = 10.9
   (n)
4. Possible sunshine hours = 11.1
   (N)
5. n/N = 0.98
6. Wind speed at 3 metre height U_h = 72 miles/day

$$U_2 = 72 \times \frac{\log 6.6}{\log 9.6} = 59.76 \text{ miles day}^{-1}$$

7. QA (Extraterrestrial radiation) = 10.7 mm day^{-1}
8. r (reflection coefficient) = 0.25

(B) Solving $QA (1 - r) (a + b\,n/N)$

9. $(1 - r) = (1 - 0.25) = 0.75$

10. $(a + b\,n/N) = 0.18 + 0.55 \times 0.98 = 0.76$

11. $QA (1 - r) (a + b\,n/N) =$ item $7 \times 9 \times 10 = 6.10$

(C) Solving expression $\sigma Ta^4 (0.55 - 0.092 \sqrt{ed})$

$$(0.10 + 0.90\,n/N)$$

12. (i) $ea = 11.2$

    (ii) $ed\ \dfrac{82 \times 11.2}{100} = 9.2$

    (iii) $\sqrt{ed} = 3.03$

13. σTa^4 from tables $= 13.4$ mm day^{-1}

14. $(0.55 - 0.092\sqrt{ed}) = (0.55 - 0.092 \times 3.03) = 0.28$

15. $(0.10 + 0.90\,n/N) = (0.10 + 0.90 \times 0.98) = 0.98$

16. Items $13 \times 14 \times 15 = 3.68$

(D) $Qn =$ item $11 - 16 = (6.10 - 3.68) = 2.42$

(E) $E_a = 0.35 (ea - ed)(1 + 0.0098\,U_2)$

$\qquad = 0.35(11.2 - 9.2)(1 + 0.0098 \times 59.76) = 1.11$

$\Delta = 0.80$ and $\gamma = 0.49$ (constant)

$$E_0 = \frac{0.8 \times 2.42 + 0.49 \times 1.11}{0.8 + 0.49}$$

$\qquad = 1.92$

$PET = k \times E_0,$

$\qquad = 0.6 \times 1.92 = 1.15$ mm day^{-1}.

The measurement of evaporation and evapotranspiration with the empirical formulae has a great appeal, because majority of these formulae are simple and use commonly recorded standard climatological data as input.

The major limitation of the empirical formulae is that they hold good in the respective localities where they were developed. Mavi and Chaurasia (1980) evaluated these empirical formulae under the climatic conditions of the Punjab. They found that all the formulae underestimated the potential evapotranspiration. This may be because of the fact that in none of these formulae the role of advective energy has been taken into account, which is, however, an important meteorological phenomena in Punjab during the summer season.

REFERENCES

Blaney, H.F. and W.D. Criddle. 1950. Determining Water Requirements in irrigated areas from climatological and irrigati onal data USDA. Soil Conserve. Serv. ScS—T 96:48.

Clyma, W. and M.R. Chaudhary. 1975. Calibration and application of the Jensen-Haise evapotranspiration equation. Colorado State University Water Manage. Tech. Rep. : 40.

Grassi, C.J. 1964. Estimation of evapotranspiration from climatic formulas. M S. Thesis. College of Eng. Utah State Univ. Logan: 101.

Hamon, W.R. 1963. Estimating potential evapotranspiration. Amer. Soc. Civ. Engin. Trans. 128 : 324–342.

Jensen, M.E. and H.R. Haise. 1963. Estimating evapotranspiration from solar radiation. J. Irrig. and Drain. Div. Amer. Soc. Civ. Engin. Proc. 89:15–41.

Makkink, G.F. 1957. Testing the Penman formula by means of lysimeters J. Inst. Water Engin. 11: 277–288.

Mavi, H.S. and R. Chaurasia. 1980. A Comparison of open pan evaporation with computed values under Punjab conditions. National Seminar on Agroclimatology, Coimbatore : 70–78.

McGuinness. J. L. and E.F. Bordne. 1972. A comparison of lysimeter derived potential evapotranspiration with computed values. USDA. Tech. Bull. 1452.

Michael, A.M. 1978. Irrigation: Theory and Practice. Vikas. Pub.

Papadakis, J. 1965. Potential evapotranspiration. Buenos Aires: 54.

Penman, H.L. 1948. Natural evaporation from open water, bare soil and grass. Proc. Roy. Soc. (London) A. 193: 120–145.

Stephens, J.C. and F.H. Stewart. 1963. A comparison of procedures for computing evaporation and evapotranspiration publ. No. 62. Int. Assn. Sci. Hydrol. I.U.G.C. Barkeley: 123–133.

Thornthwaite, C.W. 1948. An approach towards a rational classification of climate. Geographical review 38: 55–94.

CHAPTER 8

RAINFALL CHARACTERISTICS AND SOIL WATER BALANCE

A central problem for research in agrometeorology is as how to convert the knowledge of the physical environment into a reliable means for making decisions, with respect to crop management. The two universal environmental risks in agricultural production are, adverse temperature and inadequate variable water-supply. In tropical, subtropical, semi-arid and arid climates, the management of inadequate water supply for crop production needs more attention than other factors of the environment. Several studies have been undertaken and procedures submitted to determine rainfall characteristics and the water balance of the soil, in order to make maximum use of rainfall and to supply irrigation water at the critical stages of crop growth. Some of the methods are briefly reviewed in this chapter.

8.1 Rainfall Characteristics

A knowledge of the probable dates of commencement and end of the rainy season and the duration of intermittent dry and wet spells, can be very useful for planning various agronomic operations like preparation of seedbed, manuring, sowing, weeding, transplanting, harvesting, threshing, drying etc. This results in minimised risk to crops, and to optimum utilization of limited resources like labour, fertilizer, herbicides and insecticides. There are critical periods in the life history of each crop, from sowing to harvesting. Thus with a knowledge of dry spells, a farmer can adjust sowing periods in such a way, that moisture sensitive stages do not fall during dry spells (Ramdas, 1966).

Under irrigated farming, irrigation can be planned using data regarding consecutive periods of rainfall, to satisfy the demands for critical periods. The knowledge of wet and dry spells can also help a great deal in improving the efficiency of irrigation-water utilisation. To study these characteristics of rainfall it is assumed that each year provides one observation for an event of characteristic interest, and the total observations are then analysed assuming that they are a simple random sample from a single distribution. The estimates of the probability of an event could then be made by fitting a suitable distribution (Stern and Coe, 1982). Several studies have been made in India and abroad, to identify the rainfall characteristics which can be used for planning agricultural operations like sowing dates, harvesting dates and periods and frequency of irrigation.

8.1.1 ONSET OF EFFECTIVE RAINS

To define the commencement of effective rains in tropical climates is not easy due to the intermittent and patchy nature of rainfall. The event may be defined in various ways for varied purposes.

India Meteorological Department (1943) prepared a chart showing normal dates for the onset of the southwest monsoon over India, taking longterm averages of 5-day accumulated rainfall in 180 stations. The period characterising an abrupt rise in the normal rainfall curve was taken to define the onset of monsoon. This chart assists in overall indication of the arrival and progress of monsoon over the entire country. However for agricultural planning over small areas, this chart has serious limitations. This criteria has no relation to the building up of a moisture reserve in the soil, which alone is vital for commencement of sowing operation.

Kowal and Krabe (1972) defined the start of the rains as the first ten-day period with more than 25 mm precipitation provided that rainfall in the next ten days exceeded half the potential evapotranspiration.

In deciding on a criterion of rainfall occurrence favourable for commencement of sowing operations, two basic requirements have to be satisfied. First, that a sustained rainspell, which more or less represents the transition from premonsoon to monsoon conditions, should be identified. Secondly, in the spell so chosen, the rain that falls should be such as to percolate into the soil upto a reasonable depth and also build a moisture profile therein after loss through evaporation. Keeping in view the above requirements, Raman

(1974) selected a criterion for rainfall occurrence favourable for the commencement of sowing operations as: a spell of at least 25 mm of rain in a period of seven days, with 1 mm or more on any five of these seven days, assuming an evaporative loss of 18 mm at the end of five days in the spell. The weekly spell taken was compatible with the average life cycle of monsoon depression in the area. Based on this criteria the dates of commencement of the first spell were chosen for each year and their mean, median, standard deviation and semi-intersquartile range calculated, and these were mapped. These were used to study the spatial distribution of the dates of commencement of sowing rains in the black cotton soils of Maharashtra.

Benoit (1977) defined the start of growing season in Northern Nigeria as the date when rainfall exceeded evaporation and remained greater than zero for the remainder of the growing season; provided that a dry spell of five days or more did not begin in the week after this date. Based on this he determined the start of the growing season in Northern Nigeria.

The planting date of millet in Niger are observed to coincide with the first occurrence of 20 mm of rain over a two-day period (Davy et al., 1976).

Reddy (1977) has done a trend analysis on the dates of the onset of the monsoon over Kerala, to give longrange forecasts. He discovered that the trend suggested a cycle variation with a period of about 54 years. By taking the median date for the onset of southwest monsoon over Kerala (i.e. 31st May) as normal, he observed that the trend was below normal from 1900 to 1926, above normal from 1927 to 1953 and again below normal from 1954 onwards. To complete the cycle he forecast a below normal trend to continue upto 1980, and from 1981 onwards an above normal trend will commence.

Ashok Raj (1979) prepared a comprehensive computer based technique for forecasting rainfall characteristics like the onset of effective monsoon, based on the following criterion:

1) The first day's rain in the 7-day spell, signifying the onset of effective monsoon, should not be less than 'e' mm where 'e' was the average daily evaporation.

2) The total rain during the 7-day spell should not be less than $5e + 10$ mm.

3) Atleast four of these seven days should have rainfall, with

not less than 2.5 mm of rain on each day.

Using this criterion Ashok Raj determined the onset of effective monsoon for each year; and by assuming they would follow a normal distribution, he determined the onset of effective monsoon at 60 and 50 per cent probability levels, in Kerala, Andhra Pradesh, Maharashtra, Rajasthan and Meghalaya, by taking one district from each state.

Stern et al. (1982a) assumed planting to take place in the first decade, after May 1, in which there was more than 30 mm of rain and three or more rainy days. He thus prepared the crop water model for sorghum in the Hyderabad region.

Stern et al (1982b) computed the probability distribution for the start of the rains from a Markov chain model, for Samaru of Northern Nigeria. The event which signals the start of the rains was defined as the first day, or two-day, rain spell in which the total precipitation has greater than a given amount 'x', where 'x' was taken as 20 mm.

Stern and Coe (1982) used a general definition for the start of the rains with three components. Therefore:

1) The event making the start of the season was not considered until after a stated date 'D'.

2) An event 'E' then indicates a potential start date, defined as the first occurrence of atleast 'x' mm rainfall totalled over 't' consecutive days.

3) The potential start could be a false start if an event 'F', occurs afterwards, where 'F' was defined as a dry spell of 'n' or more days in the next 'm' days.

For finding out the start of rains at Kano (Africa), Stern and Coe (1982) took 'D' as 1st May, 'x' as 20 mm in two consecutive days and 'F' as a ten-day spell in the next 30 days. By using frequency distribution, he determined the potential start and false starts at different probability levels.

In all the abovementioned criteria, workers defined the event signifying the start of rains as a particular amount of rainfall received over a period of days. They however neglected the soil moisture characteristics, which decide the availability of water and workable condition of the soil. A potential start of rains must make the soil sufficiently moist to support the germination of seeds. Thus, while deciding the start of rains or the onset of monsoon, it is important to bring into consideration the soil moisture characteristics; this has been done in this study.

8.1.2 WITHDRAWAL OF EFFECTIVE RAINS

Walter (1967) defined the end of rainy seasons as the last date on which a threshold amount was exceeded. Ashok Raj (1979) called the last rainy day of the season the date of withdrawl of effective monsoon. Another means of finding out the end of rains was to use the first occurrence of a long dry spell after a specific date.

The above mentioned criteria are based solely on rainfall, but a measure of soil water storage would be needed to define the end of the period of crop growth more realistically. Stern and Coe (1982) used a simple daily water balance for this purpose. They had chosen two constants: a soil moisture storage capacity W and the daily evapotranspiration, 'E'. A notional daily water budget for the soil, Wn was then evaluated taking the value of 'S' and zero respectively as upper and lower limits, rainfall (R) as input and evapotranspiration (E) as output. Thus on day 'n'

$$W_n = W_{n-1} + R_n - E$$

i.e. the value of W_n on day 'n' was evaluated by taking its value on the previous day, adding the rainfall on day 'n' and substracting the evaporation. If the result was less than zero, it was set to zero, while if it was greater than 'S', it was set to S. The end of rains was defined as the first date after the date 'D' on which the value drops to zero. This was recorded for each year of the records and from their frequency distribution the end of rains was found at different probability levels.

8.1.3 DRY SPELLS

Dry spells, like the drought, mean different things to different people. From the agronomic point 'a dry spell' is not a drought of climatic magnitude but a period of a few days or weeks.

Neuman (1955) calculated the mean length of dry spells with the equation

$$ud = \frac{1}{p_o}$$

where ud is the mean length of the dry spell and p_o is the probability of a wet day given that the previous day was dry. The above equation was based on the assumption that the lengths of wet and dry spells were independent and obey a geometric distribution, which generally arise under the Markov chain model.

Medhi (1976) used the Markov chain model for the occurrence of dry and wet days in Gauhati.

A dry spell is the interval between two wet spells of seven-day magnitude, with atleast 25 mm of rain. Five of these seven days must have rainfall of more than 1 mm, or the next realisation of rainfall of 25 mm or more (Raman, 1974). Using this criteria Raman calculated the average length of the dry spell after the onset of the monsoon for black cotton soil of Maharashtra.

Ashok Raj (1979) defined the dry spell as the interval between the end of a seven-day spell, which begins with the onset of effective monsoon, and another rainy day with $5e$ mm or more of rain or the commencement of another 7 day rainy spell with 4 of these as rainy days and with a total rain of $5e$ mm or more during this spell. If the duration of this dry spell exceeded a certain value, depending on the crop soil complex of the region, this dry spell was called a critical dry spell.

Stern and Coe (1982) calculated the probability of a dry spell of length 'd' days occurring in the next 'n' days by using the recurrence relations.

Stern et al. (1982a) found the dry spells by recording the daily observations of rainfall as sequences of wet and dry spells. The largest positive number in the period of interest was extracted for each year. The proportion of years with a dry spell greater than any given length could be found directly. If a long dry spell overlapped two periods of interest, it could contribute to both periods. The method described above took a period as its basis and examined each year whether or not a particular spell length had been exceeded in that period. The next analysis was based on the spell length itself. Each spell was defined by its length and was counted only once; this necessitated a convention for spells which overlapped the periods. Here a dry spell was arbitrarily classified as belonging to the period in which it came to an end.

Stern et al. (1982b) used recurring relations to evaluate the probability distribution of dry spells. The method evaluates the probability for each successive day by calculating the probability of a three-day dry spell in the seven days following an initial rainy day. If there had not been a three-day dry spell till then the current day (today) must be rainy with probability either p_D and p_{DD} respectively.

The following recurrence relations were used:

$$p_{cum} \text{ (tomorrow)} = p_{DD} \text{ (today)} \times q + p_{cum} \text{ (today)}$$
$$\text{where } p_{cum} = \text{Cumulative probability}$$

$$p_{DD} \text{ (tomorrow)} = p_D \text{ (today)} \times q$$

$$p_D \text{ (tomorrow)} = p_R \text{ (today)} \times q$$

$$p_R \text{ (tomorrow)} = 1 - [\, p_D \text{ (tomorrow)} + p_{DD} \text{ (tomorrow)} + \\ p_{cum} \text{ (tomorrow)}]$$

$$= p_D \text{ (today)} \times p + p_{DD} \text{ today} \times p$$

where, p = probability of rain in any day in a month

$$q = 1 - p$$

Even though the abovementioned model is accurate in the statistical sense, but the dry spells can be of any length, within any period and totals can also be valid over any period. Thus, calculating the probability of a dry spell to length 'd' days, in the next 'm' days, is of no great value in direct agricultural planning.

Reddy (1985) used the following criteria to study the monsoon characteristics in Punjab.

8.1.4 ONSET OF EFFECTIVE MONSOON IN PUNJAB

The commencement of a seven-day rainy spell was defined as the date of onset of the effective monsoon, if the following conditions were satisfied:

1) The first day's rain in the seven-day rainy spell should not be less than 'e' mm, where 'e' is the average daily evaporation of June and July months.

2) The total rain during the seven-day rainy spell should not be less than 'x' mm, where 'x' is the amount of rainfall which brings the top 30 cm soil layer to the field capacity. Here 'x' is equal to the total soil moisture content (in terms of depth) at field capacity in the top 30 cm soil layer.

3) At least three out of these seven days must be rainy days with not less than 2.5 mm of rain on each day.

The significance of choosing the seven-day spell is purely from the meteorological stand point; that it is compatible with the average life-cycle of depression in the monsoon season (Raman, 1974). The first day's rainfall was taken as more than average daily evaporation, because rain only in excess of this will contribute to soil moisture after meeting that day's evaporative demand.

8.1.5 Withdrawal of Effective Monsoon in Punjab

The end of the last wet spell of the monsoon was taken as the withdrawal of monsoon. However to define the withdrawal of effective monsoon, the criterion of 'end of rains', proposed by Stern and Coe (1982), was used with suitable modifications. According to the modified criterion, the withdrawal of effective monsoon was defined as the date after the last wet spell of the season on which the available moisture content in the top 50 cm of the soil falls to zero. To calculate this, a simple water-balance method was used:

$$W_n = W_{n-1} - E_n$$

where W_n = Water balance on nth day after the last spell of rain

E_n = Crop evapotranspiration on nth day (mm/day)

W_{n-1} = Water balance of $(n - 1)$th day

$$W_{n-1} = M - \sum_{i=1}^{n-1} E$$

where M = Available soil moisture content in the top 50 cm soil layer

$\sum_{i=1}^{n-1} E$ = Total evapotranspiration upto $(n - 1)$th day after the last wet spell

As the evapotranspiration values are different for different crops, these values change but in this study all the selected kharif crops had similar evapotranspiration values, therefore the author got similar dates of withdrawal of effective monsoon with respect to all the selected crops.

8.1.6 Wet Spell

A *wet spell* is defined as a rainy day with 'x' mm of rainfall; or a seven-day spell where the total amount of rainfall equals 'x' mm or more, and the condition that three out of these seven days must be rainy with rainfall more than 2.5 mm on each day. In this criterion 'x' is the amount of rainfall which brings the top 50 cm soil layer to field capacity. The water-holding capacity varies with the type of soil, as also the value of 'x'. This value of 'x' is equal to 83 cm for light soils, 125 mm for medium soils and 166 mm for heavy soils of Punjab. Based on the predominant soil type of the regions, 'x' value was chosen for all the selected stations of Punjab.

Table 8.1 Monsoon Rainfall Characteristics in Punjab

Station	Onset of effective monsoon	Wet Spell Duration			Critical Dry Spell Duration		Withdrawal of effective monsoon
		1st spell	2nd spell	3rd spell	1st spell	2nd spell	
Ropar	June 27	11	19	16	14	21	September 26
Hosbiarpur	July 1	10	20	15	15	21	September 23
Gurdaspur	June 29	10	21	15	13	21	September 22
Amritsar	July 3	8	13	8	15	21	September 12
Ludhiana	July 3	8	16	15	15	21	September 22
Sangrur	July 3	8	14	13	15	21	September 19
Moga	July 5	7	9	8	16	22	September 13
Bhatinda	July 5	7	9	8	16	22	September 12
Ferozepur	July 8	7	7	7	16	22	September 10
Muktasar	July 10	7	7	7	16	22	September 10

8.1.7 CRITICAL DRY SPELL

A *critical dry spell* is defined as the duration between the end of a wet spell and the start of another wet spell; during which a 50 per cent depletion of available soil moisture occurs in the top 50 cm soil layer. It is calculated by using the following formula:

$$CDS = \frac{AMD}{ET}$$

where CDS = Critical dry spell (days)

       AMD = 50 per cent of the available soil moisture in the top 50 cm soil layer, expressed in terms of depth (mm)

       ET = Average maximum daily evapotranspiration of a crop (mm/day).

Average maximum daily evapotranspiration values has been used by many workers in making evaluations at the irrigation interval of many crops. Therefore it was also taken in evaluating the length of dry spells for different crops at all the selected stations of Punjab.

Based upon these criteria, the monsoon characteristics observed at various stations in Punjab are presented in Table 8.1.

8.2 Soil Water-Balance Models

Water-balance models can be used in a number of ways. A water-balance model is a simple method to calculate crop water-use. It can be used in intelligent planning of long range water-resource management. This knowledge can be used to modify the components of water-balance so that water can be best utilized in crop production (Shockley, 1966).

Agroclimatic models using soil water-balance data are usually framed on the basis of a water budget in which precipitation (plus irrigation) minus run-off is added to the soil water-store which is then depleted by deep drainage and evapotranspiration. By knowing all the components of the water-balance equation, an agroclimatologist can predict the length and characteristics of the growing period in any region. To improve rainfall efficiencies and to better understand the crop responses to moisture variation, a detailed quantitative description is needed of all components of the water-balance equation and their changes during the season.

8.3 Water-Balance Equation

The soil water-balance equation is generally written (Slatyer, 1968) in the form

$$P - O - U - E + \Delta W = O \qquad (1)$$

where P = Precipitation
   O = Run-off
   U = Deep drainage
   E = Evaporation or evapotranspiration
   ΔW = Change in soil water storage (initial minus final) during
         a period, and for the depth of measurement.

All symbols have dimensions of length, e.g., cm.
The above equation can be more specifically written as:

$$\int_{t_1}^{t_2} [(P-O) - E - V_z] \, dt = \int_{t_1}^{t_2} \int_{0}^{z} \frac{dQ}{dt} \, dz \, dt \qquad (2)$$

where $t_2 - t_1$, is the time interval in sec.
   V_z is net downward flux of water at depth z in cm sec^{-1}
   z is lowest point of measurement in cm.
   Q is volumetric water content in cm^3 water cm^{-3} of soil.
   P, O and E are in cm sec^{-1} units.

These equations can be used on any scale, ranging from continental land masses and hydrological catchments, down to individual plants.

8.4 Measurement of Components of Hydrological Cycle

a) *Precipitation*: The measurement of rainfall is easier than that of other components. However, a marked difference in the pattern of precipitation actually reaching the ground may develop in plant communities due to the interception of precipitation by vegetation. The significance of these phenomena depends on the scale of the study. For catchment studies these may be neglected, but for ecological studies they can be of considerable influence. The precipitation which remains on the leaf or stem is always depleted to some degree by evaporation. Interception losses are greater in the rainy season when the trees are in full leaf.

b) *Surface run-off*: Run-off occurs whenever the rate of precipitation exceeds the rate of infiltration and the resultant accumulation of surface water exceeds the pondage capacity at the point of measurement. Run-off also varies with the amount and intensity of precipitation and surface characteristics like slope, texture and structure of the soil surface.

In natural situations, the slope is seldom constant, and while run-off tends to reduce soil water storage at the top of a place and increases it at the bottom, minor changes of slope generally modify the slope run-off relationship. It is rather difficult to measure run-off directly. It is frequently estimated by using the basic water balance equation, and by estimating evaporation and deep drainage.

c) *Deep drainage*: Generally the loss of water from or to the zone below maximum root depth is considered to be negligible. However, there is evidence that this is not negligible; Rose and Stern (1965) have suggested a method for calculating it with hydraulic conductivity and soil moisture profile data. The formula is:

$$Vz = K + K \, (d_h/d_z) \tag{3}$$

where Vz = Rate of downward flow of water in cm sec^{-1}

K = Hydraulic conductivity in cm sec^{-1}

d_h/d_z = Rate of change of soil water suction (h) with depth (z) in cm.

The soil water suction (h) is calculated from soil water potential ϕ in dynes cm^{-2} with the equation

$$h = - \, \phi/\rho wg$$

where ϕ = Soil water potential

ρw = Density of water

g = Acceleration due to gravity

unless 'h' is very small, d_h/d_z is much greater than unity so that the K term in the equation is almost negligible. Thus the through drainage term 'U' in first equation is given by

$$U = \int_{t_1}^{t_2} V_z \, dt$$

In the above equation $t_2 - t_1$ is the time period between observations.

d) *Measurement of change in water storage*: Change in water storage $\triangle W$ is most accurately measured with lysimeters. But due to difficulties in the installation and maintenance of lysimeters, this is not practicable. Soil water-sensing equipment like gypsum blocks, tensiometers and neutron probes are used to measure changes in soil water storage.

e) *Evapotranspiration*: Evapotranspiration E is determined either with evaporimeters or with emperical formulae with meteorological inputs. The values obtained with evaporimeters and emperical formulae are corrected to represent evapotranspiration.

A number of studies have been published in which the book-keeping procedures of water-balance computation have been adopted. A few examples of these methods are given here.

The first one is the Thornthwaite method, a pioneering work on water-balance. The second example is a two-layer model which adopts a better approach by combining several studies. The third example is one in which comprehensive corrections have been applied to keep track of the depletion of water from the soil in a standing crop.

8.5 Thornthwaite's Method of Water-Balance Computation

An example of Thornthwaite's method of water-balance computation is given in Table 8.2. To facilitate the use of this method, a step by step description to estimate the various components and book-keeping procedures follows:

The requirements are the data of mean monthly temperature, the latitude of the station, the monthly precipitation and tables and charts prepared by the author (Thornthwaite and Mather, 1957).

Step 1. Unadjusted potential evapotranspiration (Unadj *PE*), to be ascertained from the nomogram and tables given by Thornthwaite (Thornthwaite and Mather, 1957).

Step 2. Adjusted potential evapotranspiration (*PE*). Correct the unadjusted *PE* values according to the latitude of the station and to the month of the year (Thornthwaite and Mather, 1957).

Step 3. *P* is the rainfall and can be snowfall.

Step 4. *P* — *PE*.

This is the difference between precipitation, and the adjusted potential evapotranspiration.

If *P* is less than *PE*, the value is negative.

If *P* is more than *PE*, the value is positive.

Step 5. Accumulated Potential Water Loss (Acc Pot WL).

In wet climate

where *P* > *PE* (annual values)

Start with 0 in the month just before the one where negative value of *P*—*PE* has started.

In dry climate

where *P* < *PE* (annual values)

Find the potential value of water deficiency with which to start accumulating negative value for *PE*.

The starting value can be found out as follows:

Table 8.2.   Water Balance (All values except T & I are in mm. The water-holding capacity in the root zone of the soil is 100 mm)

Month	J	F	M	A	M	J	J	A	S	O	N	D	Y
T°C	-6.0	-5.2	0	6.7	13.3	18.0	20.9	19.5	15.5	9.6	2.9	-3.4	
I	0	0	0	1.56	4.4	6.95	8.72	7.85	5.55	2.69	0.44	0	38.16
Unadj PE	0	0	0	1.0	2.1	3.0	3.5	3.2	2.5	1.5	0.4	0	
PE	0	0	0	34	79	115	135	115	78	43	10	0	609
P	68	63	75	74	75	80	90	81	76	76	86	66	910
P−PE	68	63	75	40	-4	-35	-45	-34	-2	33	76	65	301
Acc Pot WL					-4	-39	-84	-118	-120				
ST	234	297	100	100	96	67	42	30	29	62	100	166	
ΔST	0	0	0	0	-4	-29	-25	-12	-1	33	38	0	
AE	0	0	0	34	79	109	115	93	77	43	10	0	560
D	0	0	0	0	0	6	20	22	1	0	0	0	49
S	0	0	75	40	0	0	0	0	0	0	0	0	153
RO	4	3	39	39	20	10	5	2	1	1	19	10	153
SMRO	0	0	20	89	44	22	11	5	3	1	1	0	197
Tot Ru	4	3	59	128	64	42	16	8	4	2	20	10	350
DT	239	299	315	228	160	99	58	38	33	64	120	176	

(Thornthwaite and Mather, 1957)

a) Sum up all the negative $P-PE$ values
b) Sum up all the positive $P-PE$ values
c) Locate the value arrived in 'a' (Thornthwaite and Mather, 1957) and locate corresponding value of actual retention.
d) Locate the value arrived in step c on the vertical scale on the left side of the figure 1.2 (Thornthwaite and Mather, 1957).
e) Follow horizontally across on this line until it intersects the sloping line whose value equals the sum of the positive $P - PE$ (step b). Read the value of the potential deficiency with which to start accumulation.

Step 6. Storage (*St*)
For the negative values of $P - PE$, locate the storage figures, using table 1.3 (Thornthwaite and Mather, 1957).
For the positive $P - PE$ values, proceed as
a) Locate the last negative value in column $P - PE$
b) Note the storage value of '*a*'
c) Add to the value of (b) the first positive (i.e. the positive value next to the negative value).
d) Complete the procedure for the rest of the months.

Step 7. Change in Soil Moisture (ΔSt)
It is the difference in the storage value of two consecutive months. No difference is recorded when the values are above 300.

Step 8. Actual Evapotranspiration (*AE*)

When $P > PE$

then $PE = AE$

When $P < PE$

then $AE = P + St^*$ (Soil Moisture Storage)

It means that *AE* is the sum of *P* and *St* without considering the sign of *St*.

Step 9. Moisture deficit (*D*)
It is the difference between $PE - AE$
or $$D = PE - AE$$

Step 10. Moisture Surplus (*S*)
1) Surplus exists when storage (*St*) is 300 and more and $P - PE$ is positive.
2) When storage values are moving up towards 300, the first

---

*The negative sign of *S* is not considered.

surplus will be $(P - PE) - St$.

Step 11. Water Run-Off (RO)

RO is one-half of the surplus (S), the rest half goes to the next month. This should be added to the surplus of that month. Again, one-half of that month will be the run-off. Add the remaining one-half to the S of the next month, and the procedure continues, as given in the following example:

J	F	M	A	M	J	J	A	S	O	N	D	(months)

S 0 0 75 40 0 0 0 0 and so on
RO 0 0 38 39 19 10 5 2

Step 12. Snow-Melt Run Off $(SMRO)$

It is computed in areas of snow fall.

Step 13. Total Run-Off $(Tot. RO)$

It is the sum of the water surplus run-off and the snow-melt run-off.

Step 14. Total Moisture Detention (DT)

It is the sum of storage St and total run-off.

8.6 A Two-Layer Water Balance Model

This study (Ligon et al., 1967) employs a soil-moisture balance or bookkeeping procedure which utilizes the available climatological data and produces daily estimates of the soil moisture storage. From these estimates, the occurrence of various levels of soil moisture deficiency is determined. This information can be used as an estimate of the frequency with which such conditions will occur in the future.

In developing this moisture-balance, an attempt is made to incorporate the best procedures reported in literature with due consideration of the data available. Some portions are essentially the same as used in earlier studies of drought or moisture deficiency. At other points, modifications and adaptations are made to meet the particular requirement of this study. The steps followed in the original study are given below:

Step 1. A portion of a typical procedure is shown in Table 8.3. The total available moisture-holding capacity is divided into two volumes—48.50 mm of moisture (Mp column) which is held in the uppermost layer and is considered readily avilable for plant use and evaporation, and the remainder (Mu column) which is held in the lower horizon and is less readily available. Actually two balances are maintained—one for each of these two reservoirs. The actual

Table 8.3 Water-Balance
Wheat Crop at the PAU Farm, Ludhiana

Date		P	PT (corrected)	ET	Mp 48.5	Mu 92.0	Mt 140.5	Excess
		(mm)	(mm)	(mm)	(mm)	(mm)	(mm)	
25	Nov. 1983	—	2.2	2.2	46.2	91.0	138.2	—
26	Nov. 1983	—	4.6	4.6	41.2	92.0	133.2	—
27	,, ,,	—	2.9	2.9	38.3	92.0	130.3	—
28	,, ,,	—	2.7	2.7	35.6	92.0	127.6	—
29	,, ,,	—	2.8	2.8	32.8	92.0	124.8	—
30	., ,,	—	2.3	2.3	30.5	92.0	122.5	—
1	Dec. 1983	—	2.3	2.3	28.2	92.0	120.2	—
2	Dec. 1983	—	2.2	2.3	26.0	92.0	118.0	—
3	,, ,,	—	2.4	2.4	23.6	92.0	115.6	—
4	,, ,,	—	2.8	2.8	20.8	92.0	112.8	—
5	,, ,,	—	3.1	3.1	17.7	92.0	109.7	—
6	,, ,,	—	3.1	3.1	14.6	92.0	106.6	—
7	,, ,,	—	3.4	3.4	11.2	92.0	103.2	—
8	,, ,,	—	2.3	2.3	8.9	92.0	100.9	—
9	,, ,,	—	4.4	4.4	4.5	92.0	96.5	—
10	,, ,,	—	2.3	2.3	2.2	92.0	94.2	—
11	,, ,,	—	0.6	0.6	1.6	92.0	93.6	—
12	,, ,,	—	4.8	4.8	0.0	88.8	88.8	—
13	,, ,,	—	1.7	1.6	0.0	87.2	87.2	—
14	,, ,,	—	1.9	1.8	0.0	85.4	85.4	—

P is daily precipitation
PE is daily potential evapotranspiration (open pan values)
ET is evapotranspiration (corrected)
Mp is moisture in upper layer (30 cm depth)
Mu is moisture in lower layer (60 cm depth)
Mt is moisture in the root zone

thickness of the upper soil layer is variable and dependent upon the soil characteristics—it may vary from 15 cm for a silt-loam soil, to nearly 30 cm for sandy soil. The thickness of the underlying soil layer is likewise variable.

Step 2. Potential evapotranspiration (*PE*) is computed with some locally appropriate method, possibly an open pan.

Step 3. Estimated daily evapotranspiration (*ET*) is the potential evapotranspiration reduced by factors for precipitation and for soil dryness. On days when measurable precipitation (*P*) occurred, the actual evapotranspiration was taken as one-half of the potential value. This takes into account the higher humidities, lower temperatures and decreased solar radiation usually associated with rainy days.

On days without precipitation, estimated evapotranspiration (*ET*) was equal to the potential evapotranspiration if the moisture value was carried over in the readily available (*Mp*) column from the previous day. If no moisture was carried over in the *Mu* column, the estimated evapotranspiration was the potential evapotranspiration times, the ratio of the amount of available moisture carried in the *Mu* column to the total amount of available moisture in this column at field capacity. Expressed in mathematical form:

$$ET = \frac{PE}{2} \text{ (When } P > 1 \text{ mm)}$$

$$ET = PE \text{(When } P < 1 \text{ mm, } 0 < Mp < 48.5 \text{ mm) i.e. when } P$$
is less than 0.0 and *Mp* lies between 0 and 48.5 mm.

$$ET = (PE) \frac{Mu}{Mu \text{ (max.)}} \text{ (When } P < 1 \text{ mm, } Mp = 0) \text{ i.e. when}$$

P is less than 1 mm and *Mp* is zero.

When *ET* is the estimated evapotranspiration for the day

PE is the daily potential evapotranspiration.

P is the precipitation of the day.

Mu is the quantity of moisture brought forward from the previous day in the lower soil layer.

Mp is the quantity of moisture brought forward from the previous day in the upper soil layer.

The daily moisture change

$$\Delta M = P - ET$$

Although the moisture held between the wilting-point and the field capacity is available to plants, it is now generally accepted that this moisture is not all equally available. In other words, as the soil dries, the remaining moisture is held more tightly and is more difficult for the plants to obtain. This point is taken into account in the moisture-balance when the estimated evapotranspiration rate is reduced as the soil moisture content decreased.

Step 4. Δ*M* is taken out or added algebraically to the readily available (*Mp*) column. *Mp* is not allowed to drop below zero or to exceed 48.5 mm. Any portion of *Mp* which could not be taken care of within these limits is transferred to the less readily available (*Mu*) column. If *Mu* is thus raised above its maximum capacity, the overflow is transferred to the soil-moisture excess column. *Mu* is never allowed to drop below zero. The *Mt* column represents the total available moisture (the sum of *Mp* and *Mu*) on any day.

The bookkeeping procedure for water-balance estimation with this method is given in Table 8.3.

8.7 Estimation of Soil Moisture Deficiency

Pierce (1966) put forward a method for daily and short-range estimates of water-balance for different crops, using the mean temperature and rainfall as the sole meteorological data. Starting with a tentative determination of potential evapotranspiration from the mean temperature, four percentage correction factors are applied to accomplish the needed downward adjustments for the day length, crop stage, soil dryness and the rainy day. After applying these corrections, the evapotranspiration losses are balanced against measured rainfall to give daily estimates of the crop moisture deficit. The procedure is expressed in symbolic form with the equation:

$$ET = PE \times L \times C \times D \times R$$

where ET = evapotranspiration
PE = potential evapotranspiration
L = day length correction
C = crop stage correction
D = soil dryness correction
R = rainy day correction

The bookkeeping procedure for computing the values of soil moisture deficiency (CMD) under wheat crop with this method is given in Table 8.4.

Table 8.4 Soil Moisture Deficiency Under Wheat (hypothetical)

Month	PE	Day-length correction	Crop-stage correction	Rainy day correction	Soil dryness correction	$ET = 1 \times 2 \times 3 \times 4 \times 5$	Rainfall	Rainfall/run-off	Corrected rainfall	CMD without any excess holding	CMD without allowance to percolation	CMD after percolation	CMD (lower limit) up to −.75"
	1	2	3	4	5	6	7	8	9	10	11	12	13
April 1	.058	1.06	.80	.60	—	0.029	1.14	—	—	—	—	—	−.75
2	.072	1.06	.82	.50	—	0.031	0.17	—	—	—	—	—	−.75
3	.045	1.07	.84	—	—	0.040	—	—	—	—	—	—	−.70
4	.034	1.07	.86	—	—	0.032	—	—	—	—	—	—	−.658
5	.034	1.07	.88	—	—	0.032	—	—	—	—	—	—	−.616
6	.034	1.08	.90	.60	—	0.032	0.24	—	—	—	—	—	−.075
7	.058	1.08	.91	—	—	0.057	—	—	—	—	—	—	−.683
8	.107	1.09	.93	—	—	0.108	—	—	—	—	—	—	−.565
9	.092	1.09	.94	—	—	0.094	—	—	—	—	—	—	−.461
10	.040	1.09	.95	—	—	0.041	—	—	—	—	—	—	−.410
11	.016	1.10	.95	.60	—	0.010	0.08	—	—	—	—	—	−.470
12	.088	1.10	.96	—	—	0.092	—	—	—	—	—	—	−.368

(Contd.)

Table 8.4 (Contd.)

April	1	2	3	4	5	6	7	8	9	10	11	12	13
13	.103	1·11	.96	.60	—	0.109	0.53	—	—	—	—	—	−.750
14	.070	1.11	.97	.50	—	0.037	0.17	—	—	—	—	—	−.750
15	.092	1.11	.98	—	—	0.100	—	—	—	—	—	—	−.640
16	.096	1·12	.98	—	—	0.105	—	—	—	—	—	—	−.525
17	.120	1.12	.99	—	—	0.133	—	—	—	—	—	—	−.382
18	.068	1.12	.99	.60	—	0.045	0.34	—	—	—	—	—	−.667
19	.072	1.13	.99	.50	—	0.042	0.75	—	—	—	—	—	−.750
20	.134	1.13	1.00	.40	—	0.060	0.04	—	—	—	—	—	−.720
21	.094	1.13	1.00	—	—	0.106	—	—	—	—	—	—	−.604
22	.115	1.13	1.00	.60	—	0.077	1.22	—	—	—	—	—	−.750
23	.157	1.14	1.00	.50	—	0.089	0.81	—	—	—	—	—	−.750
24	.120	1.14	1.00	.40	—	0.054	0.03	—	—	—	—	—	−.716
25	.120	1.14	1.00	—	—	0.136	—	—	—	—	—	—	−.670
26	.148	1.15	1.00	—	—	0.170	—	—	—	—	—	—	−.490
27	.167	1.15	1.00	.60	—	0.192	—	—	—	—	—	—	−.288
28	.174	1.15	1.00	—	—	0.120	0.04	—	—	—	—	—	−.218
29	.208	1.16	1.00	—	—	0.241	—	—	—	—	—	—	+.023
30	.219	1.16	1.00	—	—	0.254	—	—	—	—	—	—	+.277

8 8 A Soil Moisture Index for Irrigation Planning

An index for soil moisture-balance has been used for determining water requirements and scheduling irrigation for various crops in different agroclimatic regions of Punjab (Mavi and Mahi, 1978). The index is calculated as follows:

$$I = \frac{R + SM}{PE}$$

where *I* is the weekly moisture index

       R is the weekly rainfall

       SM is the available soil moisture in the beginning of the week, and

       PE is the weekly open pan evaporation.

The soil moisture adequacy for optimum crop growth for the summer (kharif) crops has been taken at the following threshold value of the index:

Maize   : soil moisture index > 1.0 for 13 weeks
Groundnut: ,,   ,,   ,,   > 1.0 for 18 weeks
Bajra   : ,,   ,,   ,,   > 0.75 for 12 weeks
Sugarcane : ,,   ,,   ,,   > 0.75 up to end November
Rice   : ,,   ,,   ,,   > field capacity for 13 to 17 weeks depending upon short, medium or long duration variety.

Based upon this method, the actual moisture indices to be maintained by the kharif crops for optimum yield—sown early, normal and late in the season—are shown in comparison with the probability of occurrence of these conditions, and presented in Fig. 8.1. An example of the bookkeeping procedure is given in Table 8.5.

The following assumptions are made in calculating the soil moisture index in this model:

1) Areas situated at the same latitude and/or having identical amount of rainfall have identical amounts of evaporation.

2) The moisture storage capacities of the predominant soil groups of Punjab, for which the index has been developed, are not variable in different parts of the State.

For irrigation scheduling the following presumptions are made:

1) The crop root zone extends up to 75 cm.

2) The soil moisture in the root zone must not exceed the storage capacity, except for rice. The excessive moisture from

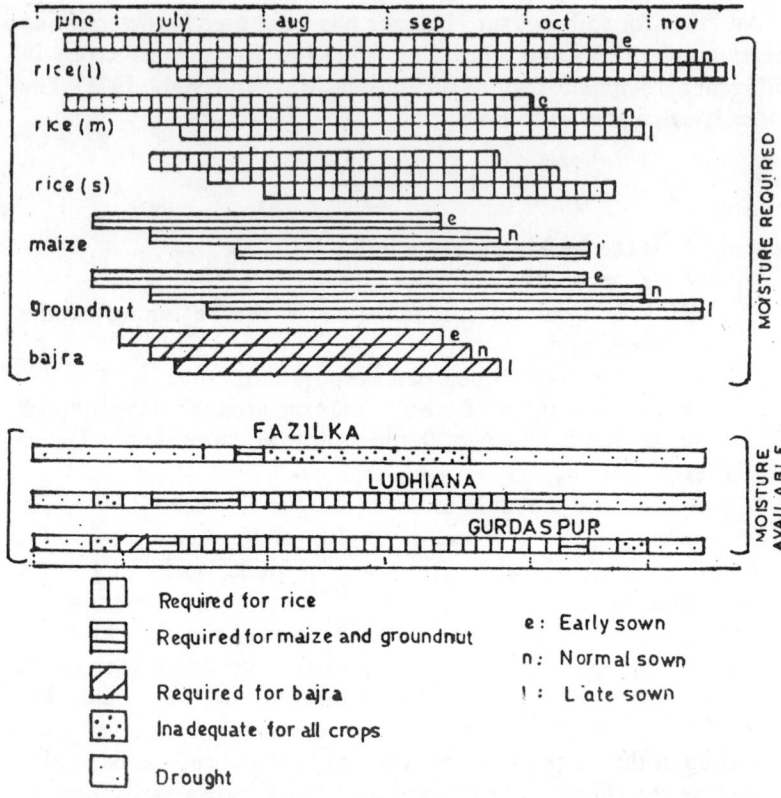

Fig. 8.1 Soil moisture Status for Summer Crops in three Agroclimatic Regions of Punjab.

rainfall is disposed of either as seepage to lower layers or as run-off by the end of week. For rice, the moisture must remain above field capacity during the crop period. Irrigation (75 mm of water) is commenced when the index value drops below the optimum defined for the crop.

3) The moisture stored in the soil is zero at the beginning of June, because evaporation in the month of May far exceeds rainfall.

4) The moisture index, to assess the additional water requirements in terms of irrigation, has been worked out with probability of rainfall at 25 per cent. The irrigation needed at this probability level is fairly certain.

Table 8.5 Soil Moisture Index for Scheduling Irrigation for Groundnut Crop at Ludhiana

Standard Met. Week	Rainfall R (mm)	Res. Moisture (brought forward) R_{AM} (mm)	Irrigation I (mm)	Available Soil Moisture $R + R_{AM} + I$ (mm)	Pot Evaporation (PE) (mm)	Moisture Index uncorrected $\frac{R + R_{AM}}{PE}$	Moisture Index Irri. corrected $\frac{R + R_{AM} + I}{PE}$	Res. Moisture (to be carried forward) $R + R_{AM} + I - PE$ (mm)
5	50	0	—	50	53	0.95	0.95	0
6	58	0	—	58	46	1.26	1.26	12
7	41	12	—	53	34	1.58	1.58	19
8	54	19	—	73	30	2.43	2.43	43
9	51	43	—	94	29	3.24	3.24	65
10	58	65	—	123	24	5.13	5.13	93
11	59	93	—	152	28	5.42	5.42	93
12	57	93	—	150	32	4.75	4.75	93
13	50	93	—	143	33	4.33	4.33	93
14	45	93	—	138	31	4.45	4.45	93
15	15	93	—	108	35	3.09	3.09	73
16	12	73	—	85	36	2.36	2.36	49
17	9	49	—	58	34	1.71	1.71	24
18	0	24	75	99	36	0.67	2.75	63
19	0	63	—	63	35	1.80	1.80	28
20	0	28	75	103	35	0.80	3.12	68
21	0	68	—	68	33	2.06	2.06	35

Rao (1982) further improved this method using the evapotranspiration variable instead of pan evaporation, and adding a crop coefficient factor. The equation used is

$$I = \frac{R + SM}{ET}$$

where I is the soil moisture index
R is weekly rainfall in mm
SM is soil moisture stored from previous week in mm
ET is evapotranspiration in mm

where $ET = PE \times Kc$

PE is pan evaporation and
Kc is crop coefficient.

The crop coefficients were selected for the major crops of Punjab. The coefficients published by F.A.O. (Dorrenbos and Pruitt, 1975) were used in this investigation to modify the pan evaporation values, which in turn were used in the water-balance computation to calculate the index.

Assuming this modified pan evaporation to be actual evapotranspiration from crops, an index value of 0.8 was chosen as the threshold limit of the Modified Papadakis Index (MPI) to irrigate a crop (Dorrenbos and Pruitt, 1975). One time irrigation was assumed to add 70 mm of water to the root zone depth of soil. At the beginning of the planting or sowing of a crop, the soil root zone was assumed to be at field capacity either, by rainfall or by presowing irrigation.

Depending on the area and distribution of crops in different agroclimatic regions of Punjab, six crops were selected in this investigation. These were rice, bajra, maize, groundnut, sugarcane and wheat. The water-balance computations were carried out for these crops and the number of times irrigation needed was worked out.

For paddy the field was assumed to be at saturation and it had 50 mm standing water at the time of planting. For this crop soil moisture was never less than saturation. Whenever soil moisture level fell below the limit at which water availability was less than 80 per cent of water need, the field was irrigated.

For other crops, the soil moisture was assumed to be at field capacity before sowing, either by irrigation or by rain. For these crops, the soil moisture did not go below PWP plus 0.8 MPI level. If it fell below, then an irrigation was affected.

The number of times irrigation needed by maize crop, as determined with this method, is presented in Table 8.6.

Table 8.6 Number of Times Irrigation Required for Maize at 70 to 30 per cent Risk Levels, in 3 Different Soil Types, in Various Agroclimatic Regions of Punjab.

AGROCLIMATIC REGIONS

Risk levels	AWC*	Ludhiana	Gurdaspur	Ferozepur	Ropar	Amritsar	Fazilka	Bhatinda
70%	200	0	0	0	0	0	1	0
	125	0	0	0	0	0	1	1
	75	0	0	1	0	0	2	1
60%	200	0	0	1	0	0	1	1
	125	0	0	2	0	0	2	2
	75	1	0	2	1	0	3	3
50%	200	1	0	2	0	0	3	1
	125	2	0	3	1	0	4	4
	75	3	1	4	2	1	5	4
40%	200	3	0	3	1	0	3	3
	125	3	0	4	2	1	4	4
	75	4	1	4	2	2	5	4
30%	200	3	1	3	3	1	4	4
	125	4	1	4	3	2	5	5
	75	5	2	4	4	3	5	5

*Maximum available water capacity of soil

REFERENCES

Ashok Raj, P. C. 1979. Onset of effective monsoon and critical dry spells. IARI Res. Bull. No, 11 (New series).

Benoit, P. 1977. The start of growing season in Northern Nigeria. Agric. Meteorol. 18: 91–99.

Davy, E. G., Mattei, F. and Solomon, S. I. 1976. Special environmental report, No. 9 World Meteorological Organization, 289.

Dorrenbos, J. and W. O. Pruitt. 1975. A guideline for predicting crop water requirements. FAO irrigation and Drainage paper 24. FAO, Rome.

India Meteorological Department. 1943. "Climatological Atlas for Airmen", Poona.

Kowal, J. M. and Krabe, D. T. 1972. An agroclimatological Atlas of the Northern States of Nigeria. Ahmadu Bello University Press, Zarie.

Ligon, J. T., A. B. Elan and D. G. Dickson. 1967. Occurrence of Soil moisture deficiency in Kentucky. UKAES Bulletin 706.

Mavi, H. S. and Gian Singh Mahi. 1978. A study of agricultural droughts and irrigation planning in the Punjab. Proceedings of the International Symposium in Hydrological Aspects of Droughts, New Delhi, 577-586.

Medhi, J. 1976. A Markov chain model for the occurrence of dry and wet days. Indian J. Met., Hydrol. and Geophys.; 27: 431-35.

Neuman, J. 1955. On the frequency distribution of dry and wet spells in Tel Aviv. Bull. Res. Coun. Israel. Sect. A. 5A (i) : 28-39.

Pierce, L. T. 1966 A method of estimating soil moisture under corn, meadows and wheat. DARDC, Wooster, Res. Bull. 988.

Raman, C. R. V. 1974. Analysis of commencement of monsoon rains over Maharashtra State for agricultural planning. Published scientific report No. 216, IMD, Poona.

Ramdas, L. A. 1966. Crops and weather in India, ICAR. 10-30.

Rao, K. Koteswara. 1982. A study of agricultural droughts and irrigation needs of important crops in different agroclimatic regions of the Punjab. (Unpublished) M. Sc. Thesis, PAU, Ludhiana.

Reddy, C. Sita Rama. 1985. A study of the pattern of rainfall distribution in the Punjab during monsoon season with special reference to the onset and withdrawal of effective monsoon season and the nature and magnitude of dry spells. (Unpublished) M. Sc., Thesis, PAU, Ludhiana.

Reddy, S. J. 1977. Forecasting the onset of southwest monsoon over Kerela. Indian J. Met., Hydrology and Geophysics 28 (1): 113-114.

Rose, C. W. and W. R. Stern. 1965. The drainage components e water balance equation. Aust. J. Soil Res, 3 : 95-100.

Shockley, Dell G. 1966. Evapotranspiration and farm irrigation planning and management. Evapotranspiration and its role in Water Resource Management. Conference Proceedings Am. Soc. Agri. Eng.: 3-6.

Stern, R. D, and R. Coe. 1982. The use of rainfall models in agricultural planning. Agril., Met., 26 : 35-50.

Stern, R. D., M. D. Dennet and I. C. Dale. 1982a. Analysis of daily rainfall measurements to give agronomically useful results. I. Direct Methods. Expt. Agril. 18 : 223-226.

Stern, R. D., M. D. Dennett and I. C. Dale. 1982b. Analysis of daily rainfall measurement to give agronomically useful results. II, A modelling approach. Expl. Agric. 18 : 237-53.

Slatyer, R. O, 1968. The use of soil water balance relationships in agroclimatology. Agroclimatological Methods. Proceedings of the Reading Symposium, UNESCO : 73-84.

Thornthwaite, C. W. and J. R. Mather. 1957. Instructions and tables for computing potential evapotranspiration and water balance. Publ. in Climatology Drexel Inst. of Tech., Lab. of Climatology. 10 : 185–311.

Walter, M. W. 1967. Length of the rainy season in Nigeria. Nigerian Geographical Jour., 10 : 123–28.

CHAPTER 9

CLIMATIC NORMALS FOR CROP AND LIVESTOCK PRODUCTION

Living systems are influenced by the environment which includes both external and internal elements. The internal environment is stable and its effects are slow and subtle. The external environment is the climate which regulates and determines the growth and development of crop plants and animals. The excess or deficiency of climatic elements exerts a negative influence on organic life. Because of their complex effects it is difficult to determine optimal values of these elements for the maximum growth and production of crops and animals. The data discussed in this chapter is therefore to be treated as informational material. Climatic normals mean the degrees of temperature, amount of rainfall, humidity etc. which distinguish optimal conditions from those defined as abnormal, both because of excess and insufficiency.

9.1 Climatic Normals for Crop Plants

9.1.1 RICE

Rice is a heat-loving plant and it originated somewhere between the areas extending from Southern India to Indo-China. It requires high temperatures, an ample water supply, and high atmospheric humidity during the growth period.

Temperature: Most of the latest high-yielding rice varieties are thermosensitive, and their growth duration and development phases are greatly influenced by environmental temperature. For sprouting, a minimum of 10°C temperature is required. The optimum temperature required for flowering is 22 to 23°C and for grain formation, 20 to 21°C (Thomas, 1957). At temperatures above 22°C the respiration rate is accelerated and the grain filling period is reduced. The crop tolerates day temperatures upto 40°C, provided water is not a limiting factor. A mean temperature around 22°C is required for the entire growing period of the crop. If night temperatures drop lower than 15°C towards the end of vegetative phase, even the flower primodia initiation fails to take place.

It is a well known fact that the rice yield is greatly reduced by formation of sterile spikelets, which are induced by low temperatures (Shahi, 1978). The period during which low temperatures are most critical is about ten to eleven days before heading occurs. When low temperatures do not occur during this critical period, sterility is not induced—even when a low temperature of 12°C prevails for as long as six days. However, the degree of sterility varies with the type of crop and the season. On an average, the critical low temperature for inducing sterility is a constant (day and night) 15–17°C for the highly cool tolerant varieties and 17–19°C for the cool sensitive varieties. The diurnal temperature changes however, have a modified effect on the rate of sterility. It has been demonstrated that sterility is not induced when the day temperature is high enough to compensate for low night temperatures.

Moisture: Rice has heavy moisture requirements. It can be classified as a hydrophyte. A heavy rainfall of 125 cm is required during its vegetative period. There should be a monthly rainfall of 200 mm to grow lowland rice and 100 mm to grow upland rice, successfully. The feet of the plant should remain submerged in water from the time of sprouting to the milk stage of the grain. At waxy ripeness no standing water in the field is required.

9.1.2 MAIZE

The crop is best adapted to intermediate climates of the earth to which the bulk of its acreage is confined.

Temperature: Maize produces good results where the growing season is more than 140 days, with a mean temperature of around 24°C and a night temperature above 15°C (Martin and Leonard, 1967). No maize cultivation is possible in areas where the mean summer temperature is below 19°C, or where the average night temperature during the three summer months falls below 21°C. However, high night temperatures also result in less yield (Chang, 1981). In a controlled experiment, the crop gave 40 per cent lesser yield at 29°C night temperature as compared with 18°C. The maize seed can germinate at 7°C. An air temperature of − 1°C is sufficient to adversely affect the plant. A temperature of − 2 to − 3°C prevailing for a few days, during tasseling and the milk stage of the crop destroys it. Excessively high temperatures are also harmful at this stage. If the temperature remains above 35°C during noon hours for several days pollen is destroyed and the yield is drastically reduced.

Moisture: Maize is adapted to humid climates and has high water requirements. It needs about 75 cm of rainfall during its life period. It expends the water economically and tends to be a relatively drought-resisting crop. During the germination period and subsequently upto the earing stage, maize plants can develop with very little moisture. However, the crop requires heavy doses of water during its inflorescence. Its water requirements are again small, when it is developing towards maturity. On an average, the range of consumptive use of water by maize is estimated between 41 and 64 cms (Neild and Richman, 1981).

9.1.3 MILLETS

Millets are heat-loving plants, mostly distributed in sub-humid and semi-arid climates.

Temperature: For germination, the minimum temperature required is 8 to 10°C. The plants are not frost-resistant; when temperatures fall below 1°C, the young leaves of plant are damaged and growth is retarded. A temperature of 35 to 40°C is normally tolerated by them. The optimum temperature for the growth of millets is difficult to define. However, best yields have been obtained where the mean temperature during the growth period is 26 to 29°C. High yields are rarely obtained below a mean air temperature of 24°C.

Moisture: Millets have low moisture requirements and are highly drought-resistant. The transpiration coefficient of millets is very small and is about one-half to one-third that of wheat. They have an exceptionally high capacity for soil water uptake through their root system. Plants become dormant during drought periods, but revert to normalcy subsequently. A minimum of 28 to 35 cm rainfall is needed for the crop to be successful. With less rainfall, the crop is almost always a failure. During a 5-week period, from flowering to seed setting, a minimum of 2.5 mm of water a day for normal growth and 3.7 mm for higher yields, is required (Martin, 1941).

9.1.4 SUGAR CANE

Sugar extracted from cane is produced mainly in tropical climates, whereas sugar from beets is produced in temperate climates.

Temperature: Sugar cane takes 12 to 24 months for maturity and requires a uniform but high temperature. For the best crop, the mean monthly temperature should remain above 22°C. The optimum temperature for the best growth is known to be around 30°C (Subbaramayya and Rupa Kumar, 1980). Growth and yield are drastically reduced in sub-tropical areas, such as North-western India where temperature often falls below 0°C during winter nights. A soil temperature of 27°C is optimum for plant growth. Below 21°C, the growth of crop is retarded, when the soil temperature falls below 10°C, the growth of the crop stops; and when the air temperature falls below 12°C harmful effects can be noticed on plants (Burr et al, 1957).

The yield of the crop is reduced to one-half if the sunshine is cut down to half the normal. Low temperatures greatly interfere with the deposition of sugar in the plant.

Moisture: The crop requires 125 to 165 cm of rainfall in a year. Torrential rainfall followed by bright sunshine are ideal. For harvesting and handling it requires comparatively dry conditions.

9.1.5 COTTON

Cotton is also a heat-loving plant, and is the most important fibre crop of the world.

Temperature: Cotton is best adapted to sub-tropical climates. The latitudinal limit of commercial production of the cotton crop coincides with areas having an average summer temperature of 21°C. Below this production is rarely economical. It needs 200 frost-free days. At a temperature of 15°C it sprouts within ten to fifteen days, and at a temperature of 20°C it sprouts within six days. The development rate is maximized at a temperature range of 25 to 30°C. High temperatures beyond 40°C have negative effects on the growth of plants. Temperatures below 15°C retard growth and reduce the number of fruits. Frost does a great deal of damage to the plant.

Moisture: The minimum rainfall limit for cotton is 50 to 65 cm. Heavy rainfalls, during sowing and the early stage, are undesirable. Dry autumn months are desirable for good quality produce.

Excessive rainfall at later stage may cause the shedding of leaves, squares, blooms and bolls. It also stimulates top growth, delays maturity, interferes with picking and discolours lint. High humidity favours many pests and diseases. The ideal rainfall for cotton is of the thunder-shower variety, with bright sunny days between the rains. Cotton yield reduces when the weather remains cloudy frequently; or if the plants are too close to one another.

9.1.6 GROUNDNUT

Groundnut is a tropical plant. The latitudinal extent of the crop is from 45°N latitude to 30°S latitude.

Temperature: It can be raised under a wide range of temperatures. However both very high temperatures and frost, adversely effect it. A temperature range of 14 to 16°C is necessary for the seed to germinate. Low temperatures retard germination of seeds and growth of plants, and lengthens flowering. Higher temperatures on the other hand, result in the best performance in terms of length of the stem, number of flowers and number of pods. The maximum number of pods have been harvested at a mean soil temperature of 23°C. The number of pods decreases as soil temperatures increase.

Rainfall: Best results are obtained with about 60 cm rainfall. Good crops are also harvested in areas where the rainfall is 125–150 cm. On the other hand, fair yields have been obtained in areas where the amount of rainfall is 37–50 cm which is well distributed during the crop season. An ideal rainfall for a successful groundnut crop is 7.5 to 12.5 cm during the summer months, preceding sowing; 12.5 to 17.5 cm during the fortnight after sowing, and 37–60 cm well distributed during the growth of the crop (Seshadri, 1962). It needs dry conditions at the time of harvesting. Rains at the time of sowing help in good germination and good stand. Well distributed rainfall during growth ensures normal vegetative growth and development of the pods. High atmospheric humidity stimulates greater rates of flowering, resulting in increased peg setting. During the vegetative period the soil moisture stress delays flowering, fruit setting and ultimately results in poor yield.

9.1.7 WHEAT

This crop has a wide latitudinal distribution. The best adaptation of the crop is in areas with moderate temperature and sub-humid to semi-arid conditions.

Temperature: Wheat can withstand temperatures from extremely low to fairly high. It is grown near the equator as well as 60° North and 40° South latitudes. In the Northern hemisphere the poleward limit of economic wheat production corresponds with May isotherm of 10°C.

There exist two types of wheat; spring and winter wheat. Spring wheat is grown in areas where the winter is prolonged and severe; and the winter wheat is grown in those areas where winters are short and mild. However, irrespective of the fact that wheat is grown in India during winter, the varieties grown are of spring wheat. Minimum, optimum and maximum cardinal temperatures for the germination of the wheat crop are 3 to 4.5°C, 25 and 30–32°C respectively (Peterson, 1965). A mean daily temperature of 15 to 20°C is the optimum for growth and development. Higher temperatures of about 30 to 35°C have generally detrimental effects on growth (Azzi, 1956). It can survive a temperature of −8 to −10°C in the spring during the early periods of its vegetative growth.

The optimal range of temperature for the germination of winter wheat and, for its vegetative growth is 15 to 20°C. If mean temperatures surpass 25°C during the vegetative period, the crop is adversely affected. High temperatures, beyond 30°C, when synchronizing with low relative humidity at maturity, result in reduced yields.

Moisture: Spring wheat plants use 50 to 1000 grams of water during their vegetative period. One hectare of wheat consumes about 2500 to 3000 tonnes of water. For swelling, the moisture required by the seed is 40 to 60 per cent of dry weight of the seed. The non-availability of moisture inhibits the formation of side shoots. Dry soil can completely arrest the lateral shoots during the tillering period Water deficiency at the heading stage results in shrivelled grains and low yield. In Punjab, experiments have shown that 35 to 40 cm of well distributed rainfall in the entire crop season or four irrigations—one at crown initiation and subsequently three at 40 days interval each—produce the best yields for the crop.

9.1.8 BARLEY

The climatic requirements of barley are similar to those of wheat. It can withstand dry heat but not hot humid weather. The yield of the crop is determined mainly by the temperature. Seeds can germinate at 1.7°C. However, the optimum for emergence is between 15-20°C. During the early growth period a mean temperature of approximately 15°C is optimum for growth. Higher temperatures coupled with drought reduce the yield considerably. From inflorescence onwards, dry weather is best for barley.

As compared to wheat, barley is more economical in the use of water. Its transpiration coefficient is about two-thirds that of wheat.

9.1.9 OATS

The best climate for oats is when the climate is cool and humid. Oats require comparatively cool temperatures during germination, shooting, booting and heading stages, else the yield will decrease regardless of how favourable all other factors may be. Oats can germinate at a temperature of 2 to 3°C. The crop gives best results when mean air temperatures during period do not exceed 11°C.

The crop requires a minimum of 20 cm of precipitation during its growth period. Insufficient moisture during heading cause great reduction in the crop yields. Drought during the early growth stages stunts culm growth; whereas late in the cycle too much moisture decreases yield, and after the blooming stage it retards growth.

9.1.10 SUGAR BEET

The vegetative period of sugar beet is of 150-170 days. It is estimated that from planting to maturity it accumulates 2200 to 2400°C growing degree days above 10°C.

Sugar beet is highly sensitive to solar radiation conditions. Sunny days with sufficient water supply encourage the accumulation of sugar. Solar radiation is especially significant in the second half of summer when the sugar content of the roots is increasing. Sugar beet seeds commence sprouting at about 3-4°C. At 5°C the sprouts appear after twenty to twenty-five days; at 10°C within ten to twenty days; and at 20°C within a period of five to eight days.

Sugar beet is comparatively frost-resistant. At −2 to −3°C only the cotyledons are killed. Growing plants are damaged only at temperature at −6° to −7°C. When ripening, beets are resistant to even heavy frost. Their resistance increases with the sugar content. The water requirements of the crop are comparatively moderate and it can withstand droughts for several days. Strong, dry winds in spring are unfavourable to beets since the sand carried by them injures the delicate leaves or buries the plant. Hail is harmful only in the early developmental stages of the plant. Its climatic requirements may be summarised as follows:

1) Warm weather and sufficiently warm soil during the sowing-to-sprouting period.

2) Adequate soil moisture during the sowing period.

3) Moderate weather with temperatures within the range of 18–20°C, and considerable precipitation in the period of vegetative development.

4) Warm but not hot weather, with a sufficient amount of light intermittent precipitation during the period when sugar is produced.

9.1.11 GRAM

Gram is grown in all climates which are sufficiently cool and humid for wheat cultivation. It has, however, much greater resistance to drought, but less resistance to humid weather when compared with wheat.

Temperature: Gram can germinate over a wide range of temperatures, from 10 to 45°C. For rapid germination a constant temperature of 20°C or a fluctuating temperature between 15–20°C is considered to be the optimum. Different cultivars of gram differ in frost-tolerance. Seedlings emerge within four to six days after sowing at 20°C, as compared with six and a half to nine days when sown at 14.5°C. Young seedlings can withstand temperatures as low as −8 to −10°C (Anon., 1979). At subsequent stages low temperatures and frost are injurious to the crop.

The optimum temperature for early vegetative growth ranges from 21 to 32°C (night and day). Over the entire growth period somewhat lower temperature (18–29°C) are optimum (Anon., 1979).

The nodulation of roots in tropical gram legume is adversely affected when the root temperature exceeds 30°C. Where gram is grown without nitrogenous fertilizers, high temperatures hamper nodule formation, irrespective of the fact that temperatures exceeding 30°C maintain good plant growth. Optimum temperatures for nodule formation vary from 15 to 18°C in sub-tropical areas like Punjab.

Gram thrives best in scanty or low rainfall areas. It is estimated that rainfall of 15–20 cm, well distributed in the crop season is best for raising a good crop. It gives good yield under irrigated conditions and one to two irrigations are sufficient for raising a good crop in the absence of rain. Excessive rainfall immediately after sowing, at flowering, and fruiting stages cause heavy losses. Excessive atmospheric humidity appears to be a major limiting factor for seed setting in gram crops. The highest pod formation has been recorded at relative humidity ranging from 21–41 per cent.

However, extremely low atmospheric humidity at flowering and pod formation stages results in reduced yield.

9.1.12 SOYBEAN

The climatic requirements of soybean are similar to those of maize. Therefore soybeans can be grown wherever maize is produced.

Temperature: The optimum temperature for germination of soybean seed is 30°C, but this temperature is usually not reached in temperate zone soils during stand establishment. The minimum and maximum temperatures for seed germination are estimated at about 5° and 40°C respectively (Sibba et al, 1982). Survival rate, dry matter accumulation and plant height of seedlings decrease when seeds containing low moisture (about 6%) are imbibed at 5°C. Seeds containing higher moisture levels behave normally under the same conditions. Both high and low moisture-containing seeds develop normally when imbibed at 25°C. A moisture level of 13–14% is the lowest which gives adequate protection from low (5°C) temperature during the imbibing process.

The freezing temperature can result in an almost complete damage of leaves, up to the pod filling stage, and in low seed yield when exposed before pod filling. The high temperature during flowering and ripening, increases fat but reduces proteins. Nodulation and nitrogen fixation in soybeans is greatly affected by soil temperature. Soybean growth is limited by temperatures in excess of 33°C. At 27°C, nodule formation, nodule development and nitrogen fixation was found to be most rapid. Nodulation is slow and leaves remain yellow when the soil temperature remained below 21°C for a period of 30 days. Nodules were formed at 33°C but at slower rates than at 27°C.

No emergence of soybean is observed at 20 per cent soil moisture. At lower moisture levels, the small and medium sized seed give more rapid emergence and greater root development than large seeds. Water requirement of soybean varies with climatic conditions, management practices and length of growing season. The maximum water-use estimates of 64–75 cm are reported in desert areas. In sub-tropical climates, a rainfall of about 65 cm during the growing season is sufficient for a successful crop.

Moisture deficiency during vegetative stages of soybean development reduces the rate of plant growth. Leaf enlargement decreases rapidly as leaf water potential increases. Yield of soybean is adversely effected by moisture stress during the pod filling period and may result in 20–50 per cent reduction in grain yields. Stress during the pod filling period also reduces seed size. The late season moisture stress may result in premature loss of leaf area and shortening of the pod filling period. An excess of soil moisture inhibits nitrogen fixation. The yield of soybeans grown with adequate supplies of soil moisture can, however, be affected adversely by low atmospheric humidity. A significant reduction in yield occurs when the actively growing soybean crop is subjected to comparatively dry air.

9.1.13 SUNFLOWER

The ecological requirements of sunflowers are similar to those of maize. The crop is however, somewhat more resistant to drought and frost than maize. Since the yield of sunflowers is considerably less than other oilseed crops, and is susceptible to diseases, it is not a popular crop in those areas where oilseed crops like groundnut are profitably grown.

Temperature: Sunflower cannot withstand extremes of temperatures. Seedlings can tolerate moderate frosts until they reach the four to six leaf stage. During the remaining period of vegetative growth and flowering the plants are sensitive to low temperatures. The crop can once again tolerate frost without significant damage during the seed ripening period.

Crops grown at day/night temperature of 24–26°C/18–20°C and relative humidity 60–70% in a controlled environment, or from the third stage of organigenesis at 30–40°C/18–20°C and relative humidity 70–80 per cent revealed that high day temperatures decrease the number and weight of seeds per plant, and seed yield and oil content (Klyuka and Tsurkani, 1976).

The root temperature also affects its growth. Increased root temperatures generate a greater growth of leaves; resulting in higher production of photosynthates.

High relative humidity has a marked positive effect on growth of the crop. Water stress is found to be a factor responsible for limiting the growth of lateral buds.

Water requirements: The crop has moderate water requirements.

It can mobilise water from quite deep layers of the soil. Under the climatic conditions of Northwestern India, no irrigation is required for winter season sunflower provided two good showers are received in the season. In the absence of rain, two irrigations are sufficient for a successful crop. In areas where the crop is grown during summer, it requires about 380 mm of water. On sandy loam soils it requires about 550 mm of water. A good shower or an irrigation before flowering increases plant height. Excessive soil moisture leads to vegetative growth and adversely effects the seed yield, while water stress reduces seed setting, seed yield and oil content.

Light : Sunflower has a specific response to light. In the morning, the head of the plant faces east towards the rising sun. The head follows the path of the sun during the day and at sunset, it faces the west. During the night, the head rotates towards east and the cycle is repeated. The heliotropic response of the sunflower is different from the other phototropic reactions of plants, in that sunflowers anticipate the appearance of the sun. If the leaves are removed the head no longer follows the sun. The plant ceases its heliotropic behaviour at, or shortly after, anthesis. As a result as much as 90 per cent of the plant heads are facing east at the time of maturity. Reduction in light intensity has a marked effect on the rate of photosynthesis. In early stages shading reduces vegetative growth, while during flowering and seed formation reduced light intensity has adverse effects on seed yield.

9.1.14 MUSTARD

Mustard is a crop of subtropical and temperate climates. It requires relatively cool temperatures, a fair supply of moisture during the growing season and a dry harvest period. It grows well in area having 25–35 cm annual rainfall. Raya has a deep root system with an equally extensive lateral spread, being therefore suited to both irrigated and unirrigated conditions.

Experiments have shown that higher temperatures during shorter days (nine hours day light) markedly reduced the height of plants, developed a large number of leaves on the main stem, and supressed flowering (Bose, 1973).

High temperatures and absence of rain during flowering periods decrease seed yields. This combination also disrupts the biosynthesis of fat and fatty acid content in the seeds.

Rainfall affects the emergence of seedlings. It was found that sprouting of the mustard seed was maximum when there was no rainfall after sowing. The crop produces the best results in areas where rainfall during the growth period is 10 to 15 cm (Bose, 1973).

9.2   Vegetable Crops

The majority of winter vegetable crops produce best results when grown within the temperature range of 16–21°C. Okra is the only crop which prefers high temperatures and is intolerant to lower temperature (Hartmann et al., 1981). Some vegetable crops like beans, tomatoes, onions and cucumber deliver the best yields in the temperature range of 13 to 27°C. Vegetables except beans, require high water amounts in the soil throughout the growing season. Commercial production is therefore chiefly confined to regions having annual rainfall between 75 and 100 cm. Instead of annual, the growing season rainfall ranging between 50 and 60 cm is more representative of the ideal moisture for the growth and production of the vegetable crops.

9.2.1   CABBAGE AND CAULIFLOWER

Cabbage is grown commercially to some extent in every country in the sub-tropical and temperate areas of the world.

Temperature: Cabbage grows best when monthly mean temperatures are between 15.5 and 21°C. It approaches the head stage slowly at a mean temperature of 13 to 15.5°C, and can stand market supply for many days at a mean temperature of about 10ºC. This permits a long harvest period of good quality cabbage. It will withstand frost in the fall or winter in the head stage, but freezing is generally destructive. When the monthly mean temperature exceeds 21°C, growth becomes slow and abnormal and the quality is usually poor (Boswell and Jones, 1941). Cabbage is biennial and requires a dormant period at cool temperature. In plants that have formed heads, exposure to a mean temperature of about 4.4ºC. for six to eight weeks will induce seed stalks, while in immature plants as little as two weeks of this same temperature will suffice if the stems are appreciably larger than a lead pencil.

Cauliflower, like cabbage, grows best in the temprature range of 15.5 and 21°C. However, this crop is less tolerant to extremes of temperatures. The crop is also adversely affected by strong winds and low atmospheric humidity.

9.2.2 TURNIPS

The weather requirements of this vegetable crop are similar to that of cabbage. But when immature the plants will tolerate short periods of chilling, at a temperature of about 4.4°C, better than cabbage. When turnips reach marketable size, mild freezing temperatures are less damaging to them than to cabbage. The optimum temperature for turnips is 13–15°C (Ventskevich, 1961).

Mean temperatures above 24°C cause serious damage to the leaves of turnip plants, depressing growth or even ruining them. As mean monthly temperatures rise much above 21°C, they retard growth and affect the appearance, colour and taste of turnips unfavourably.

9.2.3 PEAS

This is a less hardy crop as compared with cabbage and turnips. The optimum mean temperature for peas of about 13 to 18°C are probably somewhat lower than that of cabbage but peas are more seriously damaged by frost. Slight freezing may injure or destroy the blossoms and pods although the leaves and the stem may not be damaged. Temperatures as high as 27°C for even a day or two are damaging to peas through premature ripening, adversely affecting the quality and yield (Ann. 1979).

9.2.4 POTATOES

The climate plays a vital role in production of potatoes. Regions with mean July temperatures below 21°C produce higher yields than the warmer areas. Optimum soil temperatures for the potato crop vary for different stages of the plant. Young sprouts in the soil make rapid development at a constant temperature of about 24°C; however the later growth will be better at approximately 18°C. Soil temperatures above 24°C cause excessive branching of the young sprouts, shortening of the internodes, and decrease in fragmentation of the leaves. The progressively lower tuber yields at higher temperature are due to a reduction in the synthesis of surplus carbohydrates over that consumed in respiration. A decrease in the tuber formation and production at a constant temperature above 25°C and complete inhibition at 29°C has been demonstrated (Burton, 1972). It is further suggested that, under field conditions, the temperature producing complete inhibition may be somewhat higher. Mild frost to the extent of −1°C partially damages the potato leaves but when temperature falls below −2°C the exposed parts of most of the varieties are damaged.

Rainfall: The water requirements of the potato crop during its· vegetative period are not very high. It has been estimated that a rainfall of 15 to 20 cm or an equivalent amount of irrigation is sufficient for a normal crop. At the time of germination, it requires little external moisture, because the potato tubers themselves contain adequate amounts of water However, as the leaves grow after sprouting, the water requirements of the crop increase. The optimum soil moisture for the potato crop is 65 to 80 per cent of the field capacity. Immediately after sowing and before sprouting, heavy rain will adversely affect the crop. Alternate dry and rainy weather leads to an excessive growth of the potato plant and encourages the formation of the off-shoots on the young tubers.

9.2.5   ONIONS
The onion sprouts appear at 2.4°C and the optimum temperature for their growth is 19–20°C. When frost is very light, it has no harmful effect on the plants but when temperatures fall to −3 to −4°C, the ends of leaves begin to die. High temperatures (in the range of 34–40°C) hamper its growth. The water requirements of onions are high, therefore drought is a check on their development. A decrease in air and soil humidity is preferable when the onion bulb matures (20–40 days before harvest time).

9.2.6   CUCUMBER
The cucumber is a heat-loving plant. A total of 1800 to 2000 growing degree days above a threshold of 10°C are required in the vegetative period for a good crop.

Below 12°C cucumber seeds do not sprout; at 18°C sprouts appear slowly (within eight to ten days) and at 25–30°C they appear within three to five days. Seeds sown very early, in a cold and humid soil, will not germinate. The optimum temperature for its growth is around 25°C. Cucumbers also require a high atmospheric humidity and a fairly humid soil. When air temperature falls below 14°C the plants turn yellow and growth stops.

9.2.7   TOMATOES
The temperature requirement of tomatoes differs at different stages of its growth. Germination of tomato seeds commences when the soil temperature is 14–16°C. Went (1957) reported that a day/

night temperature of 26.5°/20°C is optimum for vegetative growth. Reduced growth rate of plants is observed at a soil temperature below 17°C and air temperature below 20°C. The growth stops when the air temperature drops to about 8°C. High temperatures (of 30–35°C) especially when accompanied by low relative humidity cause large scale flower dropping. This phenomenon was often observed in drought areas. Fruit setting is higher and fruit size larger at a temperature approximately. 18°C. Below 10°C no fruit setting takes place. The optimum temperature for ripening of tomatoes is 20–25°C. Tomato plants require large amounts of light. Shaded and poorly lighted plants produce low yields.

9.3 Fodder Crops

9.3.1 CLOVER

Clover is a plant of humid temperate climates. It stands up very well at low temperatures provided there is a sufficient supply of moisture. Depending on the season, winter hardiness and a number of other properties, clover is of two types. Winter 'one cut' and the spring 'twice cut'. The winter crop ripens early, successfully withstands severe cold and has a longer duration. The spring crop is less resistant to frost. Germination usually begins at 1° to 2°C, although sprouting may be retarded due to drying up of the upper layer of the soil.

Red clover is not resistant to prolonged heat spells and soil moisture deficits. A fully developed stand of pure clover, and of clover mixed with timothy, can be lodged by a heavy rain. When lodging takes place before flowering, pollination conditions deteriorate. Even two centimeters of rainfall on each of two consecutive days may be sufficient to fully lodge the crop. High temperatures also damage this crop. Leaves wilt when the temperature is 30°C and atmospheric humidity is comparatively low.

When atmospheric humidity is extremely low during the ripening period, the seeds produced are of very poor quality and the pods may break and shed their contents.

9.3.2 LUCERNE

Lucerne is a more heat-demanding crop than clover. Lucerne germinates in spring at a temperature of 7–9°C. It sprouts like clover and is frost resistant. It suffers no particular damage even at temperature as low as − 4° to − 5°C. Lucerne sowing is not adversely affected by high temperatures provided there is sufficient availability of moisture. It is better frost-resistant than wheat and clover. It can germinate at relatively low temperatures. When the temperature is 10–12°C and the humidity is sufficiently high, sprouts appear on the seventh or eighth day.

The water requirements of lucerne are quite high during germination, and later again during the flowering phase. Owing to its rapidly growing root system and deeply penetrating roots (to a depth of about 5 m) it is a drought resistant plant and withstands quite long spells of dry weather.

9.4 Fruit Trees

9.4.1 CITRUS FRUITS

Citrus fruits include sweet orange, grape fruit, lemon and lime. These are raised both in humid and sub-humid regions.

Temperature: The lowest temperature at which seed germination and tree growth can take place is 13°C and the maximum temperature upto which growth takes place is 38°C. The optimum temperature for growth ranges between about 23 and 33°C for sweet orange, and 26 to 33°C for sour orange (Magness and Traub, 1941). The hardiest types of citrus can withstand a temperature of −8°C. Others more sensitive, like the lime are injured when the day temperature drops to 28°C, indicating thereby that their limits are confined to the tropics. Younger trees of less than six years are comparatively more seriously damaged by low temperatures.

Moisture: For normal fruit production, about 90 cm rainfall per year is needed. In humid climates there is sufficient rainfall for the production of these fruits. In many areas, during the winter season, the rainfall is however inadequate, and the application of irrigation water is very beneficial when trees are in bloom.

The shape, skin texture and colour of citrus fruits are affected by climatic factors of which relative humidity is the most dominating factor. It has been observed that in areas where relative humidity is high, citrus fruits tend to be smoother, thin skinned, better in quality and are more juicy.

Hot dry desiccating winds are a major contributing factor in poor yields. Such winds, in addition to mechanical damage, cause defoliation, death of twigs and loss of fruits through excessive transpiration.

9.4.2 DECIDUOUS FRUITS

Apple, pears, peaches, cherries, plums and apricot belong to the deciduous group of fruit trees This entire group requires a winter dormant period for proper development and fruit production. Because of this specific requirement these fruit trees are limited to temperate regions having sufficiently severe winters. An exposure to 600 to 900 hours rest period below 7°C is necessary for peaches and apples. Pears of Asiatic species have relatively short cold requirements. Varieties of European origin, however, require about the same amount of cold as required by peaches. Although the deciduous fruit trees require a certain degree of cold, extremely low temperatures are destructive to the fruits, specially if these low temperatures occur before a previous period of hardening. For example, apples are not damaged if the temperature does not go below −2.5°C. However, below this temperature, the flowers and seeds are killed. Deciduous fruits as a group, are not adapted to extremely high temperatures. The best quality cherries in the USA are produced where the mean temperature during the summers are around 18°C; and apples where it ranges between 18 and 26°C. Where the mean temperature for the three summer months exceeds 26°C apple yields are very poor. At higher temperatures apple buds fail to open. Peaches on the other hand, require a summer temperature considerably higher than that for apples and cherries.

Moisture: The deciduous fruit trees require ample available moisture in their root zone throughout the growing season. A minimum of 75 cm of well distributed precipitation or a combination of snowfall, rainfall and irrigation should be available for best production. The exact water requirements however, vary from one climatic region to another.

9.5 Climatic Normals for Animal and Poultry Production

Like crop plants and fruit trees, livestock and poultry production is greatly influenced by meteorological conditions. Food production from animals and poultry can, therefore, be greatly increased and improved in quality if proper environmental conditions are provided to them in animal houses and poultry sheds.

9.5.1 CATTLE

Cattle belong to the warm-blooded group of animals having a physiological system called 'thermoregulation', since the body temperature of these animals in cold weather is maintained by an internal combustion system; and in hot weather, they bring the body temperature down by various cooling mechanisms. These mechanisms consist of an increased vascularity of the subcutanious area, and the evaporation of certain amounts of water either from the surface of the body (perspiration), or from inside the body, more particularly in the respiratory organs. In both the cases the energy, required to transform the water from liquid to the gaseous state, is removed from the body to be released into the environment. However it is also necessary that the air in the environment be capable of absorbing that additional moisture. If the ambient temperature is higher than the ideal body temperature and the atmospheric humidity is very high, these cooling mechanisms cannot function satisfactorily, and the body of the animal becomes warmer and ultimately death may follow. Different breeds of cattle have, however, varying adaptations to different environment. European cattle have a comfort zone between $-1°$ and $15°C$ while Indian cattle are comfortable between $10°$ and $27°C$ (Mather, 1974).

All domestic animals have adapted to variations in heat and cold. The range of tolerance and comfort for adult animals is quite wide, when compared to new born animals who have more narrowly defined ranges of comfort, and are generally at levels considerably higher than those for their parents. Scientific breeding must, therefore, provide the animals with temperature and humidity levels corresponding to their range of comfort.

In the case of calves for slaughter, weight is inversely proportional to environmental temperatures. For example, a 50 kg calf will feel comfortable at $15°C$ while a 200 kg calf will begin to pant at the same temperature showing signs of heat stress. For this age group temperatures of approximately $12°C$ will be best. When cattle are gaining weight, the ideal temperature for them falls further. For example, a 500 kg animal will feel most comfortable at a temperature of $10°C$.

The desired environment also varies with different breeds of beef cattle. Short horn cattle gain much more weight at $10°$ than at $27°C$. Hereford steers, when kept at a temperature $7°C$ below the ambient gain more weight per day, when compared to those kept at ambient temperatures. Moderate winds are desirable as compared to calm for gaining more weight. This also improves the feed utilization by the animals.

Table 9.1. Optimum Combination of Temperature and Humidity for Livestock Production
(Seeman, Chirkov, Lomas and Primault, 1979)

Type of livestock	Temperature range (°C)	Humidity range (%)
Calves for breeding	5–20	50–80
Calves while fattening	18–20	50–60
Young breeding cattle	5–20	50–80
Young cattle while fattening	10–20	50–80
Milk cows	0–15	15–80
Suckling pigs	33–22	50–80
Pigs for slaughter	22–15	50–80
Sows	5–15	50–80
Sheep	5–15	50–80
Chicks	34–21	50–70
Egglaying hens	15–22	50–80

9.5.2 MILK CATTLE

Low temperature is favourable for higher milk production of good quality. The optimum temperature range of milk production is 0 to 15°C, irrespective of the weight of the cattle. Beyond 15°C the fat content of cow's milk begins to decline. However variation in ideal temperatures are recorded from breed to breed. In case of Holsteen cows there is no adverse effect on the milk yield of animals even at a temperature of −12°C; while the milk yield of Jersey cows begin to decline when the temperature drops to −1°C. A 20 per cent reduction in milk yield of Jersey cows, has been recorded at a temperature of −12°C. On the warmer side, milk yield of the Jersey cows is unaffected at a temperature of 27°C while production from Holsteen drops rapidly when the temperature exceeds 24°C. In case of Brahman cows milk production does not fall until 35°C temperature is reached. When the temperatures are within the ideal range, changes in relative humidity produce no significant change in milk production; but at temperature beyond 24°C, high relative humidity amplifies the effect of high temperature towards reduced production.

The adverse effects of high temperatures (exceeding 33°C) are minimised to some extent by winds blowing between 8 and 16 km p.b. However, at lower temperatures, no positive results of wind are recorded (John, 1965).

9.5.3 Goat and Sheep

These animals live in diverse climates. It is, therefore, not surprising to find breeds of goat well adapted to extremes of temperature. Thus it is very difficult to set ideal temperature limits for breeding goat. Sheep are also one of the most tolerant of domestic animals to increased air temperature. The environmental requirements of goat are, therefore, applicable to sheep as well. Like goat, sheep originated in different areas, therefore the zone of thermal indifference varies enormously from breed to breed. The most critical period in a sheep's life is the day it is born. It has been estimated that in United States 20 to 25 per cent of the lambs die within 5 days of their birth. Thus the proper environment for lambs from birth to weaning, and weaning to slaughter are very critical (Glimp and David, 1974). Sheep of European origin have a zone of thermal indifference between 16° and 12°C for lambs, and between 15° and 5°C for sheep used in the production of meat or wool. In the case of sheep for milk a lower temperature results in higher fat content. Sheep kept at a temperature of 32°C and relative humidity between 60 and 65 per cent showed an increase in body temperature, respiration rate and pulse rate as compared to those kept within the range of 3 to 13°C.

9.5.4 Pigs

Independent of the weight, the optimum temperature for sows is between 8 to 15°C. This temperature range is to be maintained after giving birth and for the entire duration of lactation. In cool and humid climates, it has been recorded (Smith and Allen, 1976) that death rates of pigs during transportation and after, increases rapidly above 18°C. Strong sunshine appears to add to the death rate. However, the young animals require quite different enviromental conditions to develop properly. It is therefore essential to have separate stalls for suckling pigs and their mothers. The two groups will only meet at the temperature boundary for suckling pigs and their mothers.

Suckling pigs

At birth, pigs require a temperature around 33°C. As the suckling pigs gain weight, they begin to tolerate lower temperatures. For example, when a pig attains 20 kg weight, the ideal temperature for the animal is 22°C. For pigs intended for fattening or breeding, the range of ideal temperatures become lower and lower as they gain weight. Whereas a 20 kg pig is most comfortable at 22°C, a 60 kg pig will prefer a temperature closer to 15°C. Fattening pigs are very sensitive to the humidity levels in the environment. They do well within a narrow humidity range of 50 to 70 per cent. Keeping pigs quite dry under hot and dry weather can lead to their death through hyperthermia. In hot climates where temperature exceed 30°C in addition to shade, sprays of water and wet mud are provided to compensate for their limited ability to evaporate water from respiratory tracts (Mount, 1979).

9.5.5 POULTRY

In order to survive, chicks require a relatively high temperature. At hatching the ideal temperature is 34°C, which gradually decreases by approximately 2°C each week of the life of chicks. When the chicken reaches a weight of 300 g, its ideal ambient temperature is 21°C. To develop properly chicks require a rather low relative humidity, between 55 and 60 per cent. These figures show the importance of micro-climate in which poultry can be raised. Chicks struggle against temperature fluctuations with great difficulty. For instance, a 300 g chick, kept at 30°C will mostly die of exhaustion from loss of breath. On the other hand, very young chicks if raised at about 25°C will not grow at all, because all the food taken by them is used to keep up the body temperature.

Optimum temperatures for egg production are in the range of 10 to 16°C. At higher temperatures the egg production is more drastically reduced when compared to variances at the lower level of temperature in the range. If nutrition is not limiting, there is no depression in egg production even upto 25°C (Emmans and Charles, 1977). At higher temperatures the egg weight also falls. It has been established that the optimum temperature for egg-laying hens is approximately 13°C. The upper limiting temperature is 29°C while the lower limiting temperature is 6°C. Although the efficiency of all breeds of egg-laying hens fall with increased temperature, there is a breed difference to cold tolerance. Some breeds of hens have been found to lay as many eggs at 8°C as they did at the optimum temperature. On the other hand in some breeds there is a marked decrease in eggs at lower temperatures. The optimum relative humidity for laying-hens is around 50 per cent. Excessive humidity is the worst enemy of poultry birds.

REFERENCES

Anonymous. 1979. Crop Production—Rabi Crops. Deptt of Agronomy, PAU, Ludhiana.

Anonymous. 1979. Proceedings of the International Workshop on Chick Pea Improvement. Hyderabad. 121–149.

Azzi, Girolamo. 1956. Agricultural Ecology. Constable & Co. 82–101.

Bose, T.K. 1973. Effect of temperature and photoperiod on growth, flowering and seed formation in mustard (Brassica juncea cross). Indian Agriculture. 17 : 75–80.

Boswell, V.R. and H.A. Jones. 1941. Climate and Vegetable Crops. Climate and Man. Year Book of Agriculture. US Dept. of Agriculture : 373–399.

Burr, G.D., C.E. Hart, H.W. Brodie., T. Tanimoto., H.P. Kortschak, D. Tokahashi, F. Ashbon and R.E. Coleman. 1957. The sugarcane plant. Ann. Rev. Plant Phys. 8 : 275–308.

Burton, W.G. 1972. The response of potato plant and tuber to temperature. Crop Processes in Controlled Environments. Proceedings of the International Symposium held at Glass House, Crops Research Institute, Little Hampton: 217–233.

Chang, Jen–Hu. 1981. Corn yield in relation to photoperiod, night temperature and solar radiation. Agric. Meteorol. 24 : 253–262.

Emmans, G.C. and D.R. Charles. 1977. Climatic environment and poultry feeding in practice. Nutrition and Climatic Environment. Eds. W. Haresign, Henary Swan and Dyfed Lewis : 31–49.

Glimp, Hudson and David Ames. 1974. Sheep and Their Environment—New Knowledge Needed. Proc. Int. Livestock Environment Symposium: 425–426.

Hartmann, H.T., W.J. Flocker and A.M. Kofranek, 1981. Growth, development and utilization of cultivated plants. Plant Science. Prentice-Hall, Inc., 227–237.

John, H.D. 1965. Response of Animals to Heat. Agricultural Meteorology. Meteorological Monographs. American Meteorological Society. 6 : 109–122.

Klyuka, V.I. and S.N. Tsurkani. 1976. Effect of temperature on growth and productivity of sunflower in controlled environment. FCA. 3192–284.

Magness, J.R. and H.P. Traub. 1941 Climate adaptation of fruit and nut crops. Climate and Man. Year Book of Agriculture. US Dept. of Agriculture: 400–420.

Martin, J.H. 1941. Climate and Sorghum. Climate and Man. Year Book of Agriculture. US Department of Agriculture: 343–347.

Martin, J.H. and W.H. Leonard. 1967. Principles of Crop Production. The Macmillan Company: 291–345.

Mather, J.R. 1974. Climatology. Fundamentals and Applications. McGraw-Hill Company : 180–198.

Mount, L.E. 1979. Adaptation to Thermal Environment. Edward Arnold : 182-207.

Neild, R.E. and N.H. Richman. 1981. Agroclimatic normals for maize. Agric. Meteorol. 24 : 83-95.

Peterson, R.F. 1965. Wheat—botany, cultivation and utilization. Interscience Publishers Inc. : 17-33.

Seeman, J., Y.I. Chirkov, J. Lomas and B. Primault. 1979. Agrometeorology. Springer Verlag : 182-199.

Seshadri, C.R. 1962. Groundnut Monograph. The Indian Central Oilseed Committee : 130-134.

Shahi, H.N. 1978. Effect of time of transplanting and age of seedlings on the performance of dwarf high-yielding varieties of rice in Punjab. Indian J. Genet and Pl. Breeding. 39 : 75-82.

Sibba, M.R., L.E. Sehradev, S.S. Hirana and C.D. Upper. 1982. Effects of freezing temperature on field grown soybean plant at various stages of pod fill, yield and seed quality. Crop Sci. 22 : 73-78.

Smith, L.P. and W.M. Allen. 1976. A study of weather conditions related to death of pigs during and after their transportation in England. Agril. Meteorol. 16: 115-124.

Subbaramayya, I. and K. Rupa Kumar. 1980. Crop weather relationships of sugarcane and yield predicting in north-west Andhra Pradesh, India. Agric. Meteorol. 21 : 265-279.

Thomas, J.E. 1957. Rice in Spain. World Crops. 9 : 247-250.

Ventskevich G.Z. 1961. Agrometeorology. Israel Programme for scientific translation. Jerusalem : 90-125.

Went, F.W. 1957. Climate and Agriculture. Plant Agriculture. Readings from Scientific American. W.H. Freeman and Company : 108-118.

CHAPTER 10

WEATHER AND CLIMATE MODIFICATION

10.1 Weather Modification

From the food gathering stage to the last quarter of the twentieth century, man's needs for water have been increasing. However the vagaries of rainfall have not changed. Adequate availability of water through rainfall has, therefore, always been the major worry of man, making him amenable to any activity that could bring him rain. Just as the present heads of governments are concerned and plan for the adequate supply of water to their people and farms, so also primitive tribal chiefs were responsible for bringing rain to their people. Like the clever politicians of today, the wise tribal chiefs, as a hedge against failure, delegated the responsibility of rain-making to somebody else. Then, if there was no rain, it was the luckless assistant who was punished rather than the chief. The early rainmakers, fore-runners of the present day meteorologists, were perhaps among the most intelligent primitive men who had to guess at the scientific reasons of the phenomenon of rain. That these gentlemen often succeeded in duping their chiefs and tribes to preserve their lives is itself a tribute to their intelligence. Again, it was these people who set the stage for scientific enquiry into the causes of weather and rainfall (Halacy, 1968).

10.1.1 MAGIC IN RAIN-MAKING

The initial attempts for making artificial rain started with magic. During the intermediate stages between magic and science, religion and psuedoscience gained importance in rain-making. At different times, in different countries, rainmakers have performed strange ceremonies: invoking the spirits of the dead, mock ploughing, even hurling curses on gods if they failed them.

The pioneer rainmakers were magicians who used the imitation, appeal, supplication and intimidation approaches to make it rain. They sprinkled water on the soil hoping the heavens would do the same. They beat drums to imitate thunder, used firebrands to simulate lightening and blew mouthfuls of water into the air like rain. Women were made to carry water to pour in fields in order to make the heavens to do the same. Water was blown in the air through special pipes, and blood was sprinkled on the soil to bring rain. Bathing in the rivers, even ploughing rivers was resorted to in attempts to bring rain. Frogs were hung from trees to induce the heavens to make it rain over them.

When imitation failed, magicians often turned to supplication. Children were buried neck-deep in the soil to cry for rain, shedding tears to imitate it. Where supplication too failed, intimidation was resorted to. Magicians would run in various directions flailing at the sky with a stick or a sword, shouting for it to rain. Even today there are many variations of this weather magic in many parts of the world practised for rain-making.

10.1.2 RELIGION IN RAIN-MAKING

It is difficult to pin point the exact time when the rain-makers turned from magic to gods. Imitative magic gave way to supplication, a sympathy-inducing approach directed, not towards clouds and the heavens, but gods representing these phenomena. During the earlier stages, tribal chiefs or appointed rainmakers were regarded the source of rain. This respect later shifted to the dead persons. Thus supplications were first directed at the tomb of a departed ancestor. Men prayed for rain to the dead and then to gods. Praying for rain is firmly rooted in Indian culture till this date.

It was believed that prayer itself could bring rain. But as an insurance, presenting non-living gifts to the rain god was added to the prayer (Anonymous, 1976). In the next stage of its evolution the idea was of gifts making sacrificial offerings. Initially these were in the form of animals, and subsequently involved live human sacrifice. Often the sacrifice was of a captured enemy. North American tribals roasted young women from enemy tribes, killed them with arrows and then buried them in fields which needed rainfall. Intimidation was also a big tool in religion. In China, huge paper dragons were part of religious festivals and when the rains failed these dragons were angrily torn apart. In several European countries statues of saints were uprooted and made to stand on their heads when prayers before them failed to bring rain (Halacy, 1968). As late as 1893, Italians suffering from long drought, banished statues of saints from their country. On occasions the statues were stripped of wings and chained when rains failed. Among other religious attempts to change the weather, one prevalent in Europe was to erect bells and crosses to protect the vineyards. The bells were thought to prevent hail, lightening and windstorm. When the gods failed to bring rain through prayer or intimidation then neighbours were approached. In Bengal when there was no end to drought, people threw filth and dirt on the houses of neighbours who in turn abused them; this was considered auspicious for rainfall. In the Shahpur district of Pakistan, people would throw a pot of filth on the thresh-old of a notorious old shrew of the area during a drought. This not surprisingly, resulted in a fluent stream of foul language which will accelerate the lingering rain.

10.1.3 PSEUDO SCIENCE IN RAIN-MAKING

A step from magic and religion to science was taken when rain-makers observed a natural truth. One of these observations was the occurrence of rainfall after the great battles were over.

The religious explanation of this coincidence, of a battle and the subsequent occurrence of rain was that the gods were offended by the carnage and had sent the rain to purge the land of blood. The materialistic answer for this coincidence was different. Rain was simply the condensation of the blood, sweat and tears of warriors. There were other theories. One was that noise might cause rain. The great noise of firing guns and screams produced rain. All these theories, however, were demolished later. Battles are fought gene-rally in good weather in wet regions and when the battles are over, it was generally the time for rain. People observed that rain might well be inducing lightening and thunder instead of vice versa. An American argument in favour of smoke-noise theory was the 4th of July rainfall and it was argued that fireworks did it. In fact this was, and is, the peak of the rainy season in the USA.

Explosions held sway for a long time. In 1880, a patent was issued in the USA for using balloons loaded with explosive for making rain. Powdered lime was used to stop rain in certain areas and other chemicals were used to induce rain. In 1879, meteorologist Aitken discovered the condensation nuclei particles to explain the phenomena of condensation. So these nuclei were added to induce rain. First it was dust; if this did not work sulphuric acid was used which produced bubbles that flew into air. The explanation given for this experimentation was that chemical action produced hydrogen which being lighter rose high and in doing so created up-currents and carried moisture for condensation. However in later years the actual facts discredited this claim.

10.1.4 SCIENCE IN RAIN-MAKING

In the thirties of the last century it was established that air must rise in the atmosphere so as to reach a saturation point, and then cause precipitation. Since then, the would-be rainmakers have been concentrating in making the air rise. But the puzzling fact was that even when there were clouds, often no precipitation occurred. It was subsequently discovered that the lack of rain from clouds was because sufficient quantities of hygroscopic nuclei were not present for condensation or sublimation to induce the growth of raindrops. In 1930 Bergeron, a Norwegian meteorologist, demonstrated that raindrops start forming in a cloud when ice crystals appear at a temperature below −15°C (Halacy, 1968). These ice crystals grow rapidly at the cost of super-cooled droplets and fall out of the clouds as rain, hail or snow. The ice crystals are in turn formed on aerosol particles in the clouds. Thus, rainfall can be made to occur by introducing suitable hygroscopic nuclei to accelerate the process of formation of ice crystals. After the end of the World War II experiments were conducted and it was demonstrated that ice nuclei in the air could be increased by introducing into the clouds micron-size particles of silver iodide and solid carbon dioxide (Mason, 1975). It was also discovered that comparatively warm clouds could be seeded for rainfall with sodium chloride particles (Anonymous, 1973).

With the discovery of these agents, cloud-seeding experiments were initiated and successfully conducted in the USA, the USSR, Australia and several African and Asian countries.

The seeding of clouds is done either with aircraft, or bombs are shot into clouds from the earth. The time taken from seeding to growth of raindrops is estimated at about 10 minutes.

A much talked about rain-making process devised by Debriddhi Deva Kul in Thailand consists of three basic steps (Warren, 1982). In the first step, necessary weather conditions are created for clouds to form. At altitudes between 1500 and 10,000 feet two giant aircrafts release a fine spray of calcium carbide. These salt nuclei are injected in the windward side. The interaction between these two chemicals bring a sudden drop in temperature and produces clouds.

The aircrafts' repeat the operation several times and alternately spray ammonium nitrate and calcium chloride. Ultimately the clouds change to towering cumuli and rain droplets are formed at their base.

The next operation is done with a smaller aircraft which sprays dry ice (solid CO_2) in the lower reaches of the turbulent cloud. The injection of fine dry ice further results in lowering the temperature which in turn triggers rainfall within minutes.

The Indian Institute of Tropical Meteorology has been using common salt (NaCl) for rain formation in the monsoon clouds. In its cloud-seeding experiments in Maharashtra, the technique involves seeding of clouds with massive doses of common salt. This results in the condensation of water vapour on the salt particles, thus inducing more moisture into the clouds and their explosive growth.

10.2   Modification of Typhoons

Hurricanes, also referred as typhoons, and tropical cyclones, are severe storms ranging in diameter from about 80 to 1600 km and with a wind speed greater than 100 kmph. Both tornados and hurricanes cause human casualties and damage to property worth millions of rupees year after year.

Current approaches to modification of hurricanes involve seeding of outer rain clouds to cause premature precipitation which, in fact, spreads the release of latent heat and hence spreads the storm to minimise its violent force.

The possibility of mitigating the destructive force of a hurricane by seeding with silver iodide was attempted in USA in 1961 (Sumpson, 1963). But strong evidence for the effectiveness of seeding was not obtained until the 1969 experiments on hurricane Debbie.

In the experiment conducted on hurricane Debbie (Gentry, 1970), clouds surrounding the centre of the hurricane were seeded with silver iodide particles five times, at approximately 2 hour intervals, on both 18th and 20th of August. Before the first seeding on 18th August, the maximum speed of wind varied from 360 kmph at the centre to 182 kmph to the outer ring. However five hours later, after the fifth seeding, the winds decreased to 126 kmph. Analysis of data showed that the storm was modified.

The idea of seeding hurricane clouds is to make the hurricane work against itself. Hurricane clouds contain large quantities of water still in the liquid state at a temperature lower than $-4°C$. At these temperatures introduction of silver iodide nuclei should cause water droplets to change into ice crystals, thus releasing latent heat of fusion, providing a possible mechanism for adding heat to the hurricane.

10.3 Tornado Modification

Tornados are atmospheric vortices or rotating funnels of small diameter. These are known to be the most violent type of atmospheric storms. A wind speed exceeding 450 kilometers is often reached in the tornados.

The most distinctive features of tornado are the exceptionally strong winds and low pressure at the centre. These two properties account for the destructiveness of the storm. There are also many references on electrical properties of tornados (Kessler, 1970, 1974). This aspect may prove important in its modification. The lack of sufficient detailed observations, coupled with an insufficient understanding of the nature of the tornado-forming process, prohibits accurate forecasts of specific places and times of funnel occurrence. The modification of a tornado at the present, is a speculative one, with little scientific support. This is because it is a very difficult task to accomplish; only further research can reveal information about what can influence tornados.

The decision to seed a hurricane or modify a tornado imposes a great responsibility on public officials. Either Governments should accept responsibility or leave the public exposed to the danger of these weather hazards, the choices carry equal risks. The assessment of these experiments are also difficult because the decision-maker does not know what amount of property-damage will occur if the hurricane is seeded or left unseeded.

10.4 Hail Suppression

Hailstones are transparent or partially opaque particles of ice that range in size from that of sweet-pea seeds to baseballs; and in shape from spheres to rounded cones.

Hailstones are composed almost exclusively of transparent ice, or of a series of transparent layers of ice, at least 1 mm thick.

Hailfalls are generally observed during heavy thunderstorms.

Haymsfield (1975) explained the formation of hail on the basis of his observations taken in an aircraft; and also from the calculations from the equations he developed. He concluded that nucleation of ice crystals in cirrus unicinus heads, forming at temperatures lower than $-35°C$, generally should occur near the upwind base of the head and in cirrostratus at the top of the cloud.

It has been demonstrated (Chisnell and Latham, 1976) that the multiplication of ice crystal is a consequence of riming and drop splintering processes, or possibly just one of them. In the riming process large ice particles collect water droplets which eject splinters on freezing. In the drop splintering process a super-cooled drop which collides with a splinter is frozen and may eject further splinters.

Hailstones are thought to grow largely between $-20°$ and $-25°C$ levels. This temperature range indicates that they are balanced in the updraft for most of their life history.

Apart from the intelligent guess that introduction of many potential hailstones, all competing for the same finite supply of super-cooled water, inhibit the growth of large hailstones, the precise nature of the process is not understood. Hail-cells may in fact not be a part of cloud systems. Present numerical models are also based on oversimplifying assumptions. Though thousands of experiments over a quarter of century were carried out using silver iodide, important details of how it stimulates freezing are still largely unknown.

Hail suppression projects are being conducted in Canada, the U.S.A., Europe, South America, Africa and the Soviet Union. But in very few of these, efforts were made to monitor and verify the results. Hail suppression experiments in Argentina and Switzerland lead to only negative conclusions. In the U.S.S.R., the scientists are convinced they can suppress hail, and that they do so regularly. But even there, a sound theoretical or physical basis does not appear to have been established.

Statistical randomization was adopted by the National Hail Research Experiment (NHRE, U.S.A.) which focussed on a test area of 1500 sq. km. However, for reliable results, a large number of cases are required. Thus, very long periods of such experiments and in large numbers, will be required, to prove the efficiency of seeding techniques.

Seeding of clouds for hail suppression in the U.S.A. are conducted primarily from aircrafts, using silver iodide in acetone generators, flying below cloud base (Hess, 1974). Silver iodide is normally insoluble in water but is readily soluble in acetone when mixed with another soluble iodide. A three to ten per cent silver iodide mixture in acetone is normally used.

One of the greatest difficulties of hail suppression is the inherent danger to aircraft in potential hail situations. That is why other methods of delivery have been tried. Ground-based generators all have difficulties and uncertainties. They are still being used in certain experiments.

Another method of hail suppression is of dropping of self-consum-ingg enerators from above the target. A third method, mostly tried in U.S.S.R., is the delivery of seeding material to limited regions of clouds with directed projectiles or rockets. This method has some potentiality. Of the various types of projectiles and rockets in use throughout the world only the toysize, vertically firing type, which has been developed in the National Hail Rearch Experiments in U.S.A. appears to be the most effective.

10.5 Dissipation of Fog

The earlier investigations on dissipation of super-cooled fog indicate a high economical gain. Dissipating techniques are slightly different for the two types of fogs, namely cold fog and warm fog.

Cold fog

This occurs during winter in cool, moist temperate latitudes when extremely low temperatures, (up to $-30°C$) occur, resulting in ice fog of small particles.

Seeding with dry ice has proved to be effective in dissipating such fogs (Gaivoronskii et al., 1968). In Paris, ice nuclei seeding is done by means of 60 propane dispensers. Propane can also be effectively used at relatively higher temperatures. Silver iodide has also been used to dissipate cold fogs.

A recent and new vista of fog-dissipation is the development of numerical models of seeded fogs. Theoretical simulations for dispersion techniques by computers might optimize general techniques. Such approaches will be possible when the microstructure of fog, and the physics of artificial disssipation are better understood.

Warm fog

This is the more widely occurring form of fog. Experiments have been conducted to dissipate this fog by helicopters (Plank et al., 1971). The downdraft produced by helicopters can clear the fog, but this proves ineffective for larger areas.

If the mean wind speed on a clear night could be kept artificially above the threshold of 1 m per second, the chances of warm fog are reduced. This can be done by jet engines blowing down a runway. In this way the time of fog formation is delayed but advection of fog formed outside the ventilated area would probably limit the influence of this device. However, the noise level and turbulence caused by the heated air is to be considered before this technique is adopted.

The most encouraging results in warm fog dissipation have been obtained by using giant hygroscopic nuclei. A relatively small number of giant hygroscopic nuclei will grow to a proportionately large size at the expense of the small-droplet population. Common salt has been used in most of the experiments. Although it has been seen that hydroxides and chlorides have greater effectiveness, they are not recommended as these chemicals have more economic value in many other fields of applications.

Some of the salts due to their corrosive and caustic effects limit their usage in this technique.

10.6 Suppressing Lightning

It is believed that most of the cloud to earth lightning strokes originate in that portion of the cloud where temperatures are between —10 and — 15°C. Therefore suppression techniques attempt to introduce silver iodide into those portions. In 1960-61, tests were conducted in Montana (U.S.A.) using ground based generators to seed the clouds with 10 kg of silver iodide per hour. On days when clouds were seeded, cloud to earth lightning discharges were reduced by 38 per cent, as compared to days when clouds were unseeded. Cloud to cloud lightning was also reduced by six per cent, thus indicating that the seeding agents were correctly placed during the experiments.

Scientific experiments in various countries have been conducted to explore possibilities of 'pulling the teeth' out of thunderstorms, by injecting *chaff* into the clouds (Breuer, 1980). *Chaff* are aluminium covered nylon strips one centimeter long. These bits of foil are actually tiny dipoles with opposite electrically charged ends. *Chaff* are used as radar reflector to confuse receivers during war. As used in lightning suppression, the dipoles are intended to act as conductors for the electrical charge in clouds before they reach a high enough potential to cause the giant spark of lightning (Wickmann, 1968). In actual tests *chaff*-seeding produced strong radio noise, which is an indication of coronal activity in the thunderstorm.

10.7 Modification of Field Microclimate

The future trends in agrometeorological research are focussed on efforts to bring about a breakthrough in the field of artificial control of the plant environment, to keep up the optimum conditions for plant growth and crop production. Great efforts are, however, required to achieve this breakthrough. Even if it is anticipated in the very near future, this breakthrough will be on a microlevel and will not cover vast stretches of farmland. Another problem bound to emerge will be from the modified environment itself. A set of conditions artificially created for one type of organism may be detrimental to another, or to neighbouring organisms. Moreover, the optimal conditions are variable with the growth and development of plants. This means that a set of conditions ideally suited for the planting to emergence period, may not be optimal when the plant is in its growth period. Thus, the control of the environment is to be made specific, continuous or intermittent. Further, the interactions within the available energy and physiology of plants are very complex. Therefore all successful practices of environmental control require a complete knowledge of the physiology of plants and the physical environment; a difficult combination indeed.

The control or modifications to the physical environment practised at present can be grouped into three categories (Lowry, 1970). The first is controlling the heat load; the second, controlling the water balance; and the third is the control of atmospheric turbulence or wind velocity.

10.8 Control of Heat Load

The control of heat-balance is achieved in two ways; one through heat-trapping, and the other by heat-evading. Whereas the latter is important in tropical and subtropical arid climates, the former is required in temperate areas with short-growing seasons.

10.8.1 HEAT-EVASION

In many areas in the tropics and subtropics, the heat load on some of the plants is above the tolerance limit. In such cases, it is desirable to evade the thermal energy in order to achieve good results. Shading of plants is a common method of evading solar radiation. A number of shade structures are used and these are opaque. The shade can be from wood or fibre. Its beneficial effects are that it keeps the temperature low and retards evapotranspiration. The material acts as a thermostat and can be applied or removed as required.

10.8.2 HEAT-TRAPPING

The opposite of heat-evasion, heat-trapping is extremely beneficial in temperate climates where the growing period is comparatively short. Heat-trapping can be achieved by taking into account the angle of solar radiation relative to plants. By proper placement of the crop canopy, the flow of solar radiation (or light intensity) and temperature can be increased. Heat-trapping is accomplished by planting the trees on steep and sunny slopes, and erecting alternate rows of low stone walls. These low stone walls reflect the light back towards the lower portions and shaded sides of the trees. Additionally, the thermal capacity of the wall material will increase the local source of heat by night. This type of heat-trapping is practised in cool temperate areas where the summer temperatures are not high.

An alternate method of heat-trapping is the planting of crops on the sunny wall of furrows. The soil itself acts as a reflector during the day. It is also a source of nocturnal heat. This practice is being used in experiments to grow maize in the winter season in Punjab.

Another method of heat-trapping is the adjustment of canopy structures of vegetation, by mere orientation the row direction in such a manner that solar radiation penetrates in the crop canopy rather than reflected away by the upper parts of the canopy. Such trapped solar radiation becomes available to the lower portions of the canopy directly, and also by reflection from the soil.

Experiments have proved that heat can also be trapped by employing an intermittent space covering practice. The soil between plant rows is covered with white plastic sheets. These sheets reflect light to the lower sections of the canopy. An additional benefit of this device is that it directs rainfall towards the plants and reduces evaporative loss from the soil (Anonymous, 1966).

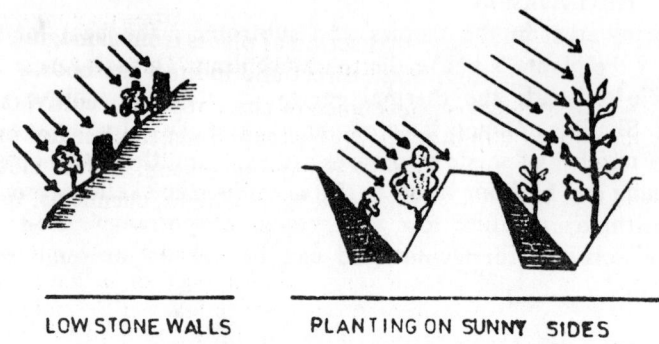

LOW STONE WALLS   PLANTING ON SUNNY SIDES

Fig. 10.1 Heat trapping for climate modification.

10.8.3 RETARDING THE SENSIBLE AND LATENT HEAT FLUX FROM THE SOIL

Heat sensitive crops can be covered with plastic enclosures during the night. These enclosures retard the loss of heat from the surroundings of the crop. This is an effective measure against cold damage. This method, however, cannot be used for larger plants and on a major scale.

Mulching and ploughing are effective methods to retard heat flux from soil and to save crops from excessive cooling. Mulching and ploughing introduce a sort of barrier which reduces the radiation from the soil and tends to decrease transpiration. The mulches used can be of different types. These can be a blanket of particles spread over the soil. For example, sawdust, wood-chips, straw, paper or a shallow ploughing. Plastic sheets, monomolecular films or any impervious fluid can be used as a mulch. Though mulches have many advantages, there are some harmful effects as well. The major limitation is that they are unable to save the aerial sections of plants from heat loss through thermal radiation.

10.8.4 REGULATING THE SOIL HEAT BUDGET

The soil heat budget can be affected by burning crop residues from the previous harvest. The burnt matter decreases the albedo and contributes to soil warming, which in turn increases the growth rate of crops.

10.8.5 PROTECTION AGAINST FROST DAMAGE

At the onset of frost, i.e. when temperatures decrease below freezing, the aqueous solution which fills the intercellular spaces may turn solid.

Prevention of frost and protection of plants from damaging frost can be achieved through both, direct and indirect methods.

Indirect methods include choice of sites, resistant cultivars and the use of crop growth regulators and chemicals, to alter flower and bud formation during the frost occurring season. Direct methods include mulches, screens, heaters, wind machines, chemicals, sprinklers, brushing, sanding and windbreaks.

Indirect Methods

1) *Choice of sites*: Before planning a crop or an orchard, the site should be selected depending on the climatic conditions prevailing in that location, its slope and soil characteristics. If the temperature prevailing in a particular location are not suitable to the crop to be grown, another location should be chosen.

2) *Resistant cultivars*: Depending on the prevailing climatic conditions, cultivars of any appropriate crop should be chosen. For frost-prone climates, cold-resistant varieties are the obvious choice.

3) *Use of crop growth regulators and chemicals*: This is done mainly with the purpose of delaying or advancing the most frost susceptible growth stages of crops to avoid frost damage.

Direct Methods

4) *Mulches*: Mulches are used to protect crops by increasing soil temperatures and reducing the outgoing thermal radiations.

5) *Screens*: Screens made of any material with low transmissivity of long wave radiation can be used to prevent radiation frost. Chemicals have also been used to form smoke cover or fog cover over crop surfaces. Enclosing house orchards in lowcost metal screen and sprinkling water on them was found to increase the temperature by several degrees. Under ideal conditions orchard temperatures may be raised by 1 or 2°C with fog generators. Cetyl alcohol was used to stabilize fog and resulted in an increase of 1 to 1.5°C in air temperatures. Fog cover was found to reduce outgoing radiation by 10 per cent. However fog drift complicated matters by shifting it in the wind direction.

Sodium leuryl sulphate foam has also been used to protect orchards from frost. This foam was found to increase the soil temperatures over a control plot at an ambient temperature of −1°.

The foam froze on the trees forming a desired cover.

6) *Heaters*: Heaters are most effective on nights with a strong temperature inversion. Heaters increase the temperature by radiating energy to plants and soil. They also produce smoke which constitutes a moderate screen against radiation loss from the ground. Heaters fueled with petroleum based products can be used to protect orchards (Geiger, 1965). A heating system must be capable of producing 3.5 to 5.5 million BTUS per acre per hour if the burning is in rows and middles; and from 2 to 3 million BTUS- if the burning is beneath the canopy. This would provide protection by raising temperatures from 3 to 5°C under any condition, and 6 to 10°C under ideal conditions. Under windy conditions less protection will be obtained. This type of heating requires 35–40 heaters per acre, each burning one gallon of fuel per hour. Around the periphery more heaters are required because the ascending plumes of hot air allow an inflow of cold air. The high costs coupled with fuel shortages, air and noise pollution regulations and labour problems, are increasing the interest in other methods of frost protection to substitute for heaters.

7) *Wind machines and helicopters*: The use of wind machines for frost protection is attractive because of the reduction in labour and operating costs. This device is highly advantageous in locations where cold weather is commonly accompanied by rapid warming higher in the atmosphere, an intense inversion of temperature near the earth surface.

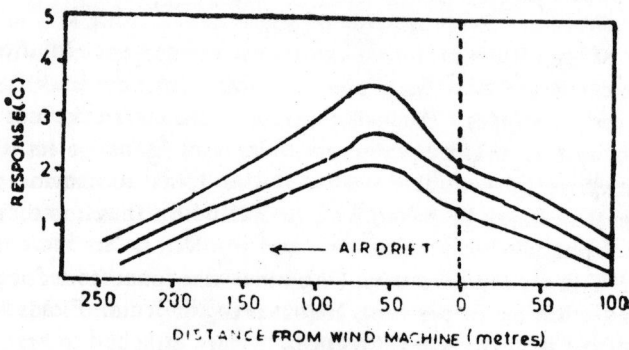

Fig. 10.2 Microclimate modification with wind machine

Wind machines provide protection by utilizing heat stored in the system. Wind machines mix the air and produce turbulence by propeller action. The amount of protection depends on the strength of inversion. Crop protection from frost by a wind machine largely depends on warm air sources, and the ability to create enough turbulence to bring this warmer air to crop level. It has been demonstrated that some protection can be obtained by stirring itself, even with no heat source. This may be due to an increase in turbulent transfer of sensible heat flux toward the plant, which is normally cooled below air temperature by radiation.

Helicopters can also be used as wind machines to provide protection against frost. In one of the experiments, flying over a strawberry crop a helicopter's action raised the temperature by about 2.2°C, to a distance of 30 metres on either side of the flight path (Crawford, 1965).

8) *Overhead sprinkler irrigation*: Sprinkling the canopy with water provides protection from cold by the release of latent heat of fusion, when water turns from liquid to ice. As long as the mixture of ice and water is maintained, the transfer of energy to the plant is efficient.

If too little water is sprinkled, the damage is worse than if no sprinkling was undertaken. When ice forms, energy is released but when evaporation occurs energy is required. In fact as much as seven-and-a-half times more energy is needed to evaporate one gram of water, as is released by freezing. If evaporation occurs at a rate faster than about one-seventh that of freezing, the net result will be a lowering of temperature. The temperature of the wetted plant under these conditions, may reach the wet bulb temperature which is generally lower than air temperature. Thus the leaves must be sprinkled at least once a minute for successful protection. It is necessary to make sure that distribution of water is excellent, the irrigation system is reliable, the sprinklers rotate and eject water each minute, and that enough water can be applied to provide protection. The major disadvantage of this method is that it is difficult to regulate the system.

9) *Brushing*: Brushing is commonly used against frost for protecting tomatoes and other vegetables in California. Fields look brushy, as shields of brown coarse paper are attached to arrowed stems on the north side of the east-west rows of plants. During the day they act as windbreaks against cold wind. At night the shields reduce radiation loss to the sky.

10) *Sanding*: Adding sand in small quantities to the soil every few years reduce frost damage. A sandy surface warms easily and cools slowly, by radiation. Sanding can raise the temperature of clay soil by several degrees.

11) *Windbreaks*: Windbreaks protect crops against advective frost by reducing the intensity of cold winds.

10.9 Improving the Water-balance

Below a certain level of water supply crop production is not possible. Relatively small increases in moisture supply may produce a marked increase in crop yields. Such improved moisture regimes in the soil can be achieved in two ways:

a) by increasing the amounts of water stored in the root zone;

b) by reducing losses due to evapotranspiration.

10.9.1 WATER STORAGE IN THE CROP ROOT ZONE

The amount of precipitation taken in by the soil depends on run-off and infiltration. By reducing run-off and increasing infiltration the amount of water stored in the soil can be increased.

Run-off Control

Most soil conservation methods, such as strip cropping, contour ploughing, terracing, etc. aim at reducing run-off. Various studies on moisture conservation in India, on shallow loam soil receiving 400 mm rainfall annually, showed that bunding increased soil moisture content by 50 to 100 per cent. The protection provided by vegetation is also usually a major factor in run-off control. Plants intercept part of the rainfall and reduce the velocity of raindrops. They also slow down the movement of water on soil surface.

Increasing Infiltration

The rate of infiltration of water into soil depends on the soil structure and texture, soil cover, and on the duration and intensity of rainfall. Mulches of straw or crop residues, by breaking the impact of the raindrops, markedly improve infiltration.

The effect of tillage methods on crop growth and yields are to a large degree attributable to an increased soil moisture reservoir. This is achieved by creating soil conditions that favour root growth and penetration, and improved infiltration and conservation of water (Siddoway *et al.*, 1970).

Tillage can be effective in reducing surface run-off if it is carried out according to soil conservation practices.

By sacrificing a crop, moisture is conserved from one season to the next, so that the combined precipitation of two seasons is sufficient for one crop. This is a common practice in rainfed areas.

Reducing Evaporation from Soil

Evaporation from the soil can be minimised in a number of ways:

1. by decreasing turbulent transfer of water vapour to the atmosphere, by windbreaks, mulches, etc;

2. by decreasing capillary continuity of the surface layer;

3. by decreasing capillary flow and the moisture-holding capacity of the surface soil layers;

4. by chemical treatments to control evaporation. It has been found that hexadecanol, a long chain alcohol, mixed with one-quarter inch of the soil reduced evaporation by 40 per cent. This material which is resistant to microbial activity remains effective for more than a year.

10.9.2 WATER HARVESTING

Several methods are used for water harvesting. Soil surfaces can be treated with chemicals to prevent the water from soaking into the soil. An increased run-off can then be utilized by the crop fields situated at lower levels.

It has been demonstrated that run-off can be increased to a great extent if smooth sandy loam and clay soils are treated with 400 pounds of sodium carbonate per acre. Similar results have been obtained with sodium chloride treatment.

A water repellent catchment involves spraying soil with sodium rosinate. When applied at a rate of 150 pounds per acre, this compound increases the run-off and simultaneously stabilizes the soil. But the limitation of this compound is that it oxidises very rapidly.

Contour ditches constructed downslope of barren lands can be used to collect and convey run-off to adjoining farmlands.

If trees are replaced by short vegetation like grass, run-off is increased, and can be controlled for use in farm areas.

Thin low cost plastic and metallic films can be used as ground cover to collect rainfall Catchments can be installed by spreading plastic films and then covering them with gravel. The gravel protects the plastic against wind and weather damage.

The U.S. Department of Agriculture has developed a unit called raintrap. A rubber sheet spread over the gravel collects rain which is then stored in large rubber bags. The water from these is piped to the desired fields

10.9.3 MODIFICATION OF TRANSPIRATION

Three types of chemicals are being tried to reduce transpiration from plant canopies and evaporation from water bodies (Rosenberg, 1974).

1) The substances which form films on leaves or water bodies include long chain alcohols such as *hexadecanol* which form mono-molecular layers. These are usually used on open water bodies and are unsatisfactory in reducing the transpiration from leaves. Low viscosity silicone was tested and found to reduce the water use by leaves without any detrimental effects on growth.

Thick-film forming materials include latex, waxes and plastics. To be more effective, these materials are made permeable to carbon dioxide diffusion.

2) Stomata closing materials include common herbicides like *Atrazine*. These act like a pump affecting the turgor of the stomata guards.

The anti-transpirant found to be most successful under field conditions is glycoryl half-ester of decenyl succinic acid (Glosa.). A 12 per cent reduction in water loss was reported when this chemical was applied to the under side of leaves of broad-leaf trees.

3) The third type of chemicals used to reduce evapotranspiration are called reflectants. It has been estimated that by doubling the albedo of the plants, transpiration can be reduced by 15 per cent. So far the best reflectant tried is kaolinite, which when applied in a mixture of plant gum and surfactant to a soyabean crop at the rate of 196 kg per hectare produced satisfactory results. The increase in reflection in the visible parts was 20 to 40 per cent. Savings in transpiration, in experiments, was reported to be of the order of 10–15 per cent (Rosenberg, 1974).

10.10 Need for Protection against Wind

Wind is an important weather element and both its direction and velocity are significant. The influence of wind is both local and regional. It influences the configuration and distribution of plants in a region. It influences plant life, both mechanically and physiologically. The influence is more pronounced on plants on flat-lands near the seacoast, and on the higher slopes of mountains. The wind affects plants directly by increasing transpiration and the intake of carbon dioxide, and by causing several types of mechanical damage. Less significant effects are numerous including the generation of cold and heat waves, the movement of clouds and fogs, and the changing of water, light and temperature conditions.

Under normal conditions, wind increases transpiration. However, this increase is only up to a certain point, beyond which either it becomes constant or begins to fall. With increasing wind velocity, there is a greater increase in cuticular transpiration than in stomatal transpiration. Wind increases turbulence in the atmosphere, thus raising the supply of carbon dioxide to the plants and resulting in greater photosynthetic rates. However, the increase in photosynthesis is again up to a certain wind speed, beyond which its rate becomes constant.

When the wind is hot, it accelerates the desiccation of the plants by replacing humid air by dry air in the intercellular spaces. When a hot dry wind blows during the period when cells are expanding and maturing, dwarfing of plants result. This is because the cells cannot attain full turgidity in the absence of optimal hydration, thus remaining at subnormal sizes. When the developing shoots come under the influence of strong wind pressure from a fixed direction, the normal form and position of the shoots are permanently deformed Another severe injury to plants caused by strong winds is lodging. This injury is most common in crop plants such as maize, wheat and sugarcane. Strong winds break the twigs and shed fruit from plants. Further, crops and trees with shallow roots are often uprooted. Trees which bear comparatively large fruits prefer light winds. Crops grown on sandy soils in areas where strong winds prevail are damaged because of abrasion. When the plant cover is not thick, strong winds remove the dry soil, exposing their roots and then killing them. Eroded material from one place becomes a hazard to the existence of small plants in places where it is deposited. This is because the deposited material sharply reduces aeration around the roots of plants. Winds which blow from closed seas and lakes do a lot of salt spraying on the windward coastal areas, making it impossible to grow crops which are sensitive to excessive salts.

10.11 Use of Shelter Belts for Protection against Wind

The use of shelter belts has been one of the oldest methods employed by man for modifying the climate. Properly oriented and designed shelter belts are very effective in stabilizing agriculture in regions where strong winds cause mechanical damage and impose severe moisture stress on growing crops. In cold climates windbreaks save plants from freezing and mechanical damage caused by cold winds. Windbreaks save the loose soil from erosion; aid in the uniform distribution of snow cover; and increase the supply of moisture to the soil in spring.

Various tall crops such as corn, sorghum, sunflower, wheat and oats, are being successfully used as temporary wind barriers to protect crops like sugarbeet, soyabean, groundnut and tomato. Crop yields have been positively affected by these wind barriers in dry continental climates.

10.11.1 WIND SPEED REDUCTION

The reduction in wind speed is the primary objective of a shelter belt. This in turn is responsible for the amelioration of the microclimate of fields, and thus increased production.

The effectiveness of the shelter belt, to reduce wind speed on the leeward side of shelter belts, depends upon the permeability, height, shape and width of the barrier. Wind speed is reduced nearer the shelter belt of low porosity. However, it tends to increase quickly. At higher permeabilities the sheltered area becomes negligible on the leeward side.

What should be the optimum permeability of a shelter belt? The answer to that depends upon the purpose for which the shelter belt is erected. For equal distribution of snow shelter belts should be more porous, than for controlling wind erosion. Numerous research studies can be cited to show that the optimum protection to crop plants is provided by a barrier which has a permeability of 40–50 per cent.

The area protected by a shelter belt increases proportionally with the increase in the height of the barrier. Hence higher trees planted in the belt, result in a greater area protected.

Results of the shelter belt studies have shown that maximum protection was provided by a 10-row plantation. However, narrow width barriers gave nearly as good protection as a 10-row belt. It is of course observed that the shelter belt density improves according to width, but the benefit of the shelter belt decreases. Single row plantations have given quite good results in checking wind velocity.

The area protected by a shelter belt, again, depends upon the angle at which the wind strikes the shelter belt. Maximum protection is provided when wind strikes the belt perpendicularly. With wind blowing at an angle of less than 90°, the area protected is reduced. Results of an experiment (Skidmore and Hagen, 1970), to observe the effect of orientation on the extent of area protected, show that at 25 h (multiples of shelter height) distance on the leeward side of a shelter belt of 47 per cent permeability, the mean wind speed was reduced to 54, 63, 81 and 95 per cent as the wind deviated from the normal by 0°, 25°, 50° and 75° respectively. Even when the wind blow parallel to the shelter belt, the wind velocity was considerably reduced up to a distance of 5 h. In one of the experiments conducted at Ludhiana (Mavi et al, 1983), a medium porosity shelter belt of *guar* resulted in the reduction of wind speed by 68 per cent at a distance of 4 h. From this point, the wind increased up to 8 h and then dropped to 50 per cent of its open speed due to the influence of the next barrier.

10.11.2 MODIFICATION OF OTHER FACTORS OF MICROCLIMATE

Windbreaks have a considerable impact on other factors of the microclimate, of fields they protect. A lot of data from field experiments have proved that the climate that prevails in the leeward side of a shelter belt is more moderate than that in the unsheltered areas.

A shelter belt usually results in the reduction of vertical diffusion and mixing of air. This leads to a higher day and lower night air temperature. If the shelter belt suppresses evaporation as well, additional energy is available during the day to generate sensible heat.

The increase in temperature during the day extends 5 to 10 h leeward. Skidmore and Hagen (1970) observed that over evaporating sudan grass air temperature at 2 h on the leeward, was higher than that at 6 h windward by 0.9°, 1.2° and 1.5°C at 60, 40 and 0 per cent permeability respectively. It has been established that air temperature in the leeward side can be predicted on the basis of the increase or decrease in evapotranspiration. At higher rates of evapotranspiration more of the available energy will be consumed leaving a lesser balance available as sensible component to heat the air resulting in lower air temperatures. The reverse will occur when the rate of evapotranspiration is reduced.

Soil temperature is affected by barriers in two ways. In cold climates in the higher latitudes, increased soil moisture from melting snow on the leeward side of a barrier, lowers soil temperatures due to its greater heat capacity and greater evaporation. Secondly, as the shelter belts alter the air flow and thus, the heat transfer, soil temperatures are modified. A review of the research indicates that soil temperatures in the sheltered areas was higher during the day and lower during the night. The amplitude is maximized when the soil is bare and dry, and lowered when the soil surface is moist.

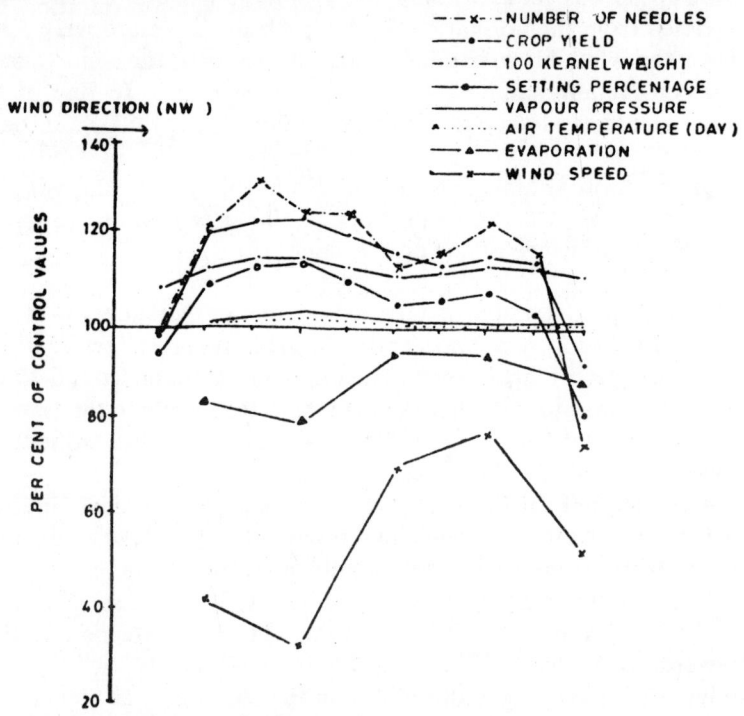

Fig. 10.3 Summary diagram of the effects of a shelter
Shelter belt-guar
Sheltered crop-groundnut

Solar radiation is affected only in the vicinity of the shelter belt and here too depending upon the orientation of the barrier. A shelter belt may reflect, intercept and reradiate the radiation. It may change the albedo and net radiation. The differences caused by the barrier are not of major importance when a shelter belt is oriented in a north-south direction But in an east to west-oriented shelter belt in the northern hemisphere, the area to the north of the shelter belt will be shaded for long periods, while the areas to the south will get more reflected radiation.

The plant canopy acts both, as a sink (assimilation) and source (respiration), of carbon dioxide. In a crop field the processes of respiration, assimilation and turbulence affect carbon dioxide concentration. Respiration in a crop field is a continuous process but assimilation occurs only during the day, consuming carbon dioxide at a much faster rate than that acquired through respiration. Thus at low wind speeds and decreased turbulence during the night, carbon dioxide concentration tends to increase. During the day it decreases.

It has been demonstrated in an unsheltered field that the air one metre above the ground is considerably richer in carbon dioxide between 10 a.m. and 3 p.m. than at other times.

The atmospheric humidity in the leeward side of a barrier is not consistently uniform, and its distribution is complicated by a number of factors like soil moisture, evapotranspiration and diffusion, etc. Results of many of the studies are contrary. Many studies show only slight variations in humidity in a sheltered and an unsheltered crop. On the other hand, some studies indicate that humidity was slightly higher at $2 h$ on the leeward side of the shelter belt.

One of the major objectives of a shelter belt in semi-arid climates is to check the evaporation and evapotranspiration. In order that evaporation should occur, two conditions must exist. A source of energy to provide latent heat of vaporisation, and turbulence for vapour transfer. Energy as latent heat of vaporization is derived from solar radiation. However, reduced wind speed because of a shelter belt tends to reduce turbulence which in turn reduces the rate of transfer of vapour pressure; hence, the rate of evaporation is reduced. Various research studies are available to show that on a relatively calm day the wind component contributes one-third as much as solar radiation towards evaporation. But on a comparatively windy day, the wind component contribution was found to be 56 per cent as against 44 per cent by radiation.

In a sheltered area, the reduction in evaporation is less than a corresponding reduction in wind speed, due to the fact that the contribution of radiation is unaffected. Thus if in an unsheltered area radiation and wind are contributing 50 per cent each in evaporation, then in a sheltered area where wind velocity is reduced by 50 per cent, its contribution towards evaporation will be reduced by 50 per cent; the radiation contribution remaining unaltered.

In a study conducted at Ludhiana (Mavi *et al.*, 1983), the evaporation curve was found to be similar in trend to the wind speed curve in the leeward side of the barrier. A maximum reduction of 20 per cent in evaporation was recorded at 4 *h*. On clear days when the wind was blowing perpendicular to the barrier, evaporation was 4 mm in the open plot and 3.18 mm in the sheltered plot, indicating a 13 per cent reduction in the sheltered plot. For the entire groundnut crop season, the evapotranspiration from the sheltered crop was estimated to be 388 mm as against 422 mm in the unsheltered crop.

10.12 Climate Modification—Inadvertently

Man has been modifying the climate, unconsciously from the day he appeared on the planet. This has been through the tampering of forests, the natural flow of water courses, urbanization, industrialization and the use of chemicals for greater crop production.

The primary concern of each government is to provide the basic necessities of life to its people. To achieve this, a reckless exploitation of natural resources takes place. For example, to increase food production, man has increased the area under cultivation, created irrigation facilities and is using protective chemicals to save his crop from pests and diseases.

Forests and Water Courses

To increase the area under cultivation, man encroached upon forests. An additional and immediate advantage was the cheap availability of fire wood. But steep mountain slopes can seldom sustain the degree of cropping, wood cutting and grazing. The ultimate result is the destruction of forests which in turn adversely affect the intricate link between the land and water interface.

The Himalayas, the Andes and the East African highlands are examples where the degree of cropping to grow more food, woodcutting for firewood, and grazing have caused landslides, erosion of soil and siltation of reservoirs. The lifespan of the Bhakra reservoir was estimated to be eighty eight years when the dam was built. Revised estimates show the reservoir will be filled with sediment in 47 years.

The uncontrolled and reckless destruction of forests is likely to affect food production systems and cause recurring flash floods. At present, diversion of forest land for agriculture, irrigation and power projects, industrial establishments, roads, tribal colonies, settlement of evicted persons, besides indiscriminate private encroachment, account for the depletion of forests.

The effects of forest destruction are formation of gullies and deterioration of water courses. Deposition of silt and sand have raised river-bed levels accentuating the flood problem in some regions. The diversion of flows has accelerated riverbank erosion along the reaches of many water courses.

Man initially irrigated his crops with river water. To achieve this he constructed canals. But the meanderings of rivers is one of the most fundamental of fluvial processes, and is of major importance in maintaining an energy balance within the river system. The elimination of this pattern through channelisation may, therefore, have serious consequences on fluvial morphology and hydrology. Channel enlargement and the construction of uniform trapezoidal cross-sections tend to put rivers in a state of disequilibrium (Nunnally, 1978).

It is revealed that river channel works such as dredging, widening and strengthening used in land drainage improvement, can often severely affect the form of the river environment, and can be seriously detrimental to the wildlife associated with it (Swales, 1982).

Industrial Plumes

Cloud condensation nuclei (CCN) are those aerosols in the air which serve as nuclei upon which cloud and fog droplets form. CCN are important in determining the stability of clouds and the formation of precipitation. Their number is greatly increased by paper mills and oil refineries.

Coal fired power-plants raise serious environmental hazards which are primarily due to the emission of radio nuclei. The air, contaminated in this way, is thus the main source of pollution for the remaining environmental components like water, soil, vegetation and man.

It is now a well known fact that carbon dioxide and other tropospheric gases like methane, nitric oxide and ozone all produce a warming of the earth's atmosphere commonly referred as a "green house" effect.

Auto-exhaust emissions are the major source of a number of deleterious pollutants usually detected in the atmosphere of urban areas. The pollutants are mainly carbon monoxide, lead, nitrogen oxides and reactive hydrocarbons. The carbon dioxide released, mainly by the combustion of chemical fuels has led to the warming of the atmosphere.

Urbanisation

The central segments of cities which are warmer than the surrounding rural areas, particularly at night, are known as urban 'heat islands'. The formation of heat islands is one of the consequences of urbanisation and industrialization. The characteristics of the intensity of heat islands vary from city to city, and from season to season. Urbanisation increases air temperature, dust particles, cloudiness and precipitation; whereas it decreases relative humidity, radiation, albedo and wind speed. These in turn affect the water balance parameters like evapotranspiration, soil moisture storage, run off, etc. (Haske *et al.*, 1981).

Chemicals and Machinery

To protect their crops, farmers began using pesticides and fungicides. These chemicals reduce the environmental quality, and influence essential ecosystem functionings—by reducing species diversity, modifying food chains, changing patterns of energy flow and nutrient cycling (including nitrogen), reducing soil, water and air quality, and changing the stability and resilience of the ecosystem.

The use of heavy equipment, chemical fertilizers, pesticides and high-yielding varieties have helped to increase food production, but at the same time they create imbalance in the microenvironment (Power, 1982).

It has been demonstrated that air pollution turns rain acidic. The effects of this acidic rainfall on plants are: 1) it increases erosion of cuticle on leaves; 2) it increases nutrient leaching from leaves; 3) it induces necrotic lesions on leaves; 4) it inhibits nodulation of legumes leading to decreased nitrogen fixation, and 5) it predisposes plants to increased bacterial and fungal infestation.

To cultivate more land, farmers use hardware equipment. With tractors, farmer can work the soil at above optimum water content, thus causing an aggregate destruction and soil compaction. This leads to decreased infiltration, reduced water holding capacity and restricted root growth.

The use of off-road vehicles on farm-land increases the amount and frequency of water run-off, leading to erosion by decreasing soil porosity and infiltration capacity, effectiveness of surface stabilizers, and hydraulic resistance to over flow (Iverson *et al.*, 1981).

It is now a wellknown fact that the use of combine harvestors for wheat crops in the wheat belts of the USA and Canada, leaves the stalks nearly flat during winter. Consequently, less opportunity exists for catching snow and recharging soil water during the winter months. Larger combines tend to concentrate crop residues behind the machine, with less uniform distribution of crop residues across the field. This can change the energy and water balance of crop fields.

REFERENCES

Anonymous. 1966. Reclaiming sunlight. Agri. Research. 14. U.S. Dept. of Agriculture, Agril. Research Service.

Anonymous. 1973. Weather and Climate Modification. Problems and Progress. National Academy of Sciences. Washington: 47–48.

Anonymous. 1976. Hundred Years of Weather Service, 1875–1975. India Meteorology Department, New Delhi.

Breuer, G. 1980. Weather Modification: Prospects and Problems. Cambridge Univ. Press: 88–89.

Chisnell, R.F. and J. Latham, 1976. Ice Particles multiplication in cumulus clouds. Q.J. Royal Met. Soc.: 133–156

Crawford, V. 1965. Frost protection with wind machines and heaters. Meteorological Monographs, American Meteorological Society: 81–83.

Gaivoronskii, I.I., L.A. Krasnovakaia and A.D. Solovev, 1968. Artificial low cloud and fog dissipation. Proceedings of the International Conference on Cloud Physics. Toronto: 700–706.

Geiger, R. 1965. The Climate near the ground. Harvard Univ. Press: 509.

Gentry, R.C. 1970. Hurricane Debbie modification experiment. Science. 168: 473–475.

Halacy, D.S. Jr. 1968. The Weather Changers. Harper and Row Publishers: 246.

Haske, S., J. Krishnand, P.C. Behere and S.D. Kaehare, 1981. Characteristics of heat-island at Pune. Vayu Mandal: 259.

Hess, W.N. 1974. Cumulus clouds and their modification. J. Atmos. Sci. 32: 229–285.

Hymesfield, A. 1975. Cirrus Uncinus generating cells and the evolution of cirriform clouds. J. Atmos. Sci. 32: 799–803,

Iverson M. Richard, Bern S. Hinckley and Robert M. Webbe, 1981. Physical effects of vehicular disturbances on arid landscape. Science. 212: 915–917.

Kessler, E. 1970. Tornados, Bull. Am. Met. Soc. 51: 926–936.

Kessler, E. 1974. On Tornados and their modification. Technol. Rev. 74: 2–9.

Lowry, W.P. 1970. Weather and Life. An Introduction to Biometeorology. Academic Press: 200–217.

Mason, B.J. 1975. Clouds, Rain and Rainmaking. Cambridge Univ. Press: 124-141.

Mavi, H.S., N.R.K. Rao and S.D. Lall, 1983. Improving field microclimate and crop yield with temporary lowcost shelter belts in Punjab. Proceedings of the International Conference on Biometeorology, New Delhi.

Nunnally, N.R. 1978. Stream renovation: an alternative to channelisation. J. Environ. Mgmt. 2: 403–411.

Plank, V.G., A.A. Spatola and J.R. Micks, 1971. Summary results of Lewisburg fog clearing programme. J. Appl. Meteorology. 10: 763-779.

Power F. James, 1982. Agricultural Ecosystems. A scientist's perspective. J.E. Sciences. Nov-Dec.: 32-33.

Rosenberg, N.J. 1974. Microclimates: The Biological Environment. John Wiley & Sons: 281–293.

Siddoway, F.H., P.W. Unger and A.D. Schneider, 1970. Soil Modification by Improving Plant Water Relations and Effects on E.T. Proceedings of the Seminar on Evapotranspiration in the Great Plains: 181-206.

Skidmore, E.L. and L.J. Hagen, 1970. Evapotranspiration and the Aerial Environment as influenced by Windbreaks. Proceedings of the Seminar on Evapotranspiration in the Great Plains: 339–368.

Sumpson, R.H. and J.S. Malkus, 1963. An experiment in hurricane modification, Preliminary results. Science 142: 498.

Swales, S. 1982. Environmental effects of river channel works used in land drainage improvement. J. Environ. Mgmt. 14: 103–126.

Warren, W. 1982. The remarkable rainmaker of Thailand. Readers Digest. March: 71–74.

Wickmann, H.K. 1968. The programme on Weather modification of the Environmental Sci. Service Admn. Part III. Augmentation of Continuous rain and lightning suppression. 72: 219–232.

CHAPTER 11

WEATHER FORECASTING FOR AGRICULTURE

Weather is the dominant factor determining the success or failure of agricultural enterprises. This is because farmers have no control over this natural force. Weather manifests its influence on agricultural operations and farm production through its effects on soil, plant growth as well as on every phase of animal growth and development. Out of the total annual crop losses, a greater portion is because of aberrant weather. Several years ago, it was estimated in the United States (Noffsinger *et al*, 1964) that annual losses in agriculture are 13 billion dollars; out of this amount about 11 per cent are caused directly by weather hazards like floods, hailstones and storms. At the same time, losses due to conditions affecting harvesting, storage, parasites, crop and animal diseases are highly influenced by weather. In all, directly and indirectly, weather makes a contribution of approximately three fourth of the annual losses in the farm production.

In India, the losses in crop production are even of greater magnitude. Each year, there is an extensive damage due to floods in one part of the country and a severe drought ruining crops in another part. In one season, crops are damaged by a severe attack of pests and diseases, in the other season, the damage can be even more due to some other factor. The total annual pre-harvest losses for the various crops in the country as a whole, are estimated to range between 10 and 100 per cent while the post-harvest losses are estimated to range between 5 and 15 per cent; a 7 per cent average is considered an appropriate figure for all the crops (Atwal, 1983). At these levels, the total loss of food grains and some other important crops for the year 1982–83 have been estimated and are presented in Table 11.1.

No estimates of the losses exclusively due to weather hazards are available for our country. However, it is an established fact that a major part of the crop losses is primarily due to direct and indirect effects of weather. Assuming three fourth of the total losses due to weather, as one study conducted in US has indicated and has been referred earlier, the annual crop losses due to weather in India for the six major crops during the year 1982–83 are estimated at about 26 million tonnes. This loss is worth about Rs. 49570 million.

Table 11.1. Crop Losses in India during 1982–83

| Crop | Total production (m. tonnes) | Per cent losses | | Total losses (m. tonnes) | Value of losses (m. Rs.) |
		Before harvest	After harvest		
Wheat	42.5	10	7	7.22	10974
Rice	46.5	20	7	10.50	20097
Millets	27.8	25	7	8.94	10906
Pulses	11.6	10	7	2.02	8080
Groundnut	5.6	10	7	1.21	4840
Cotton	7.7	50–100	7	4.39	11194
Total	141.7	10–100	7	34.28	66093

For Punjab, accurate figures of crop losses of food grains due to weather phenomena during the year 1981–82 are available and are presented in Table 11.2.

Table 11.2. Crop Losses in Punjab during 1981–82

Cause	Food grain losses (tonnes)	Value of losses (m. Rs.)
1. Floods in monsoon season	11,200	14.5
2. Untimely rains in April-May	8,54,000	1238.3
3. Post harvest transport and storage etc.	6,50,000	942.5
Total	15,15,200	2195.3

Table 11.2 reveals a massive loss of 1.5 million tonnes of food grains worth about Rs. 2200 million. A single rainy weather spell in

April-May of 1982 damaged wheat crop worth Rs. 1238 million. The losses in post-harvest transportation and storage etc. (Gill, 1984) also mainly due to rains and excessive humidity were worth Rs. 942 million.

11.1 Accurate Weather Forecasts can Reduce Crop Losses

There is no doubt that avoidance of all the farm losses due to weather factors is an impractical objective, at the same time it is very much possible to minimise the crop losses to a considerable extent by making adjustments with the coming weather through timely and accurate weather forecasts. When a specifically tailored weather support is available to the needs of agriculture, it can greatly contribute towards making short term adjustments in daily agricultural operations which minimise input losses resulting from adverse weather conditions and can markedly improve the yield and quality of agricultural products. It is estimated that about 8 per cent of the total crop losses can be avoided through improved weather forecasts (Anonymous, 1971). The weather support also provides guidelines for long range or seasonal planning and selection of crops most suited to anticipated climatic conditions.

In Punjab, it is estimated that crops worth Rs. 176 million could be saved through a better weather service. Few examples may suffice to support this projection.

In the month of March, the weather is highly variable and the wheat crop is approaching maturity hence it is at a very critical stage. If, in this month, the farmers of the State are informed two to three days in advance about anticipated heavy rains and strong surface winds and advised to with-hold the irrigation, it can save lakhs of hectares of wheat crop from lodging.

There are 6.23 lakhs tube-wells in the State, of which 3.33 lakhs are operated with electric power and the rest with diesel. The electric power driven tubewells consume about 2115 million KWH of energy which comes to about 41 per cent of the total power consumed in Punjab (Anonymous, 1983). With-holding irrigation and switching off the tubewells in the light of rain forecast, farmers can not only save the crops from lodging but can also save considerable electrical energy for other sectors of the economy. Likewise, farmers can save the wastage of diesel oil.

During April and in early May, there are frequent thunder-storms and squalls which carry away considerable quantities of the harvested crop which is yet to be threshed. If the farmers are informed about the timings of duststorms/thunderstorms which are likely to occur within next several hours or on the next day, they can withhold the harvesting operation of wheat and can collect the harvested crop well in time to save it from being blown away.

The losses in seed, diesel, labour and time can be avoided by not sowing the crops if the anticipated weather is not suitable for the operation.

The consumption of chemical fertilizers (N and P) in the State is about 8.62 lakh tonnes. It is stated that the recovery of applied nutrients is about 40 per cent in case of Nitrogen and about 20 per cent in case of Phosphorus. This shows that about 5.6 lakh tonnes of nutrients, 65 per cent of total, go waste due to various loss mechanisms such as leaching, fixation, gaseous loss, etc. savings worth lakhs of rupees can be achieved if the farmers are informed well in time that the coming weather may not be suitable for fertilizer application. A similar wastage can be minimised in the use of fungicides and insecticides.

There are many more applications of weather forecasts to improve crop yield and to minimise losses of costly inputs in the State (Mavi, 1980).

11.1.1 TIME FACTOR IN WEATHER FORECAST

The weather elements which influence the agricultural operations and crop production can be forecast upto different spans of time; however, with increase in time span, the accuracy of the forecast decreases. With all the forecasting tools at disposal, various weather phenomena can be forecast as below:

i)	Hail	
ii)	Tornados	Less than 12 hours in advance
iii)	Flash floods	
iv)	Heavy rainfall	
v)	Thunderstorms	24 hours in advance
vi)	Wind velocity	
vii)	Rainfall amount	36 hours in advance
viii)	Occurrence of rainfall	
ix)	Temperature intensity	5 days in advance
x)	Temperature departure	
xi)	Precipitation departure	3 months in advance

Based upon the forecasts of these phenomena, decisions can be taken in advance in agricultural operations and planning so as to make the best use of favourable weather conditions and adjustment with the adverse weather (Smith and Strim, 1973).

11.1.2 Types of Weather Forecasts and Their Applications in Agricultural Operations and Planning

Weather forecasts for agriculture can be grouped into *short range forecast* (upto 48 hours) *extended forecast* (upto 5 days) and *long range forecast* (4 weeks to the season). Each has got a role to play in farm operations and planning of agricultural activities (Newman and Stearns, 1957; Noffsinger *et al.*, 1964; Jensen and Davis, 1974; Hudson, 1972).

24–48 Hours Weather Forecast

Forecast emphasis: High and low temperature,
wind velocity and direction,
sunshine duration,
time and amount of precipitation,
relative humidity.

Forecast accuracy: 70-80 per cent

Applications
  i) Irrigation scheduling
 ii) Timing of field operations
iii) Protection of plants from frost
 iv) Efficiency of chemicals
  v) Spray applications
 vi) Labour efficiency—workable hours
vii) Insect-disease effects
viii) Soil workability
 ix) Livestock protection from cold and heat
  x) Animal production rate
 xi) Drying rate of siraw
xii) Drying rate of soil

5 Day Weather Forecast

Forecast emphasis: On change of weather type,
sequence of rainy days,
normal weather hazards in farming such as
strong winds, extended dry or wet spells.

Forecast accuracy: 60-70 per cent

Applications
  i)   To determine the depth at which seed be sown to achieve an optimal rate of seedling emergence
 ii)   To determine whether or not to sow a crop in this period
iii)   To take account of expected rainfall to plan irrigation
 iv)   To decide whether or not to harvest a crop in this period
  v)   To ensure maximum efficiency of spray programme
 vi)   To prepare in time for the protection of crops against frost
vii)   To the management of labour and equipment
viii)   To animal feed requirements

30 *Day Weather Outlook*
Forecast emphasis: Abnormalities in temperature and precipitation.
Forecast accuracy: 60 per cent

Applications
  i)   In soil moisture management
 ii)   In pasture management
iii)   In determining irrigation frequency
 iv)   In harvesting crops for short term storage where adverse conditions are likely to interfere
  v)   To decide whether to put perishable products into short term storage to even out supplies to market
 vi)   In avoiding chemical sprays when diseases or pests are unlikely to be troublesome

Seasonal Outlook
Forecast emphasis: Abnormalities in temperature and precipitation.
Forecast accuracy: 60 per cent

Applications
  i)   To decide whether or not to grow marginal crops
 ii)   To aid in the management of limited water resources
iii)   To plan timely measures against diseases and pests likely to be favoured by the expected weather
 iv)   To choose varieties most likely to thrive in the expected

pattern of the weather
v) To determine the acreage needed to give a required tonnage of a crop
vi) To determine crop yield

11.1.3 PRESENT STATUS OF WEATHER SERVICE FOR AGRICULTURE IN INDIA

In order to harness the weather for more and better farm-produce and to maximise the efficiency of costly inputs, the farmers in our country are to be made weather conscious in their day-to-day farm operations and in planning the entire crop season well in advance.

With this in view, the Punjab Agricultural University started a weather service for the farmers of the State and since 1977, a regular weekly weather bulletin is being issued in which the scientists of various disciplines of the PAU and India Meteorological Department participate. The flow diagram shows the operation of the Weather Service from the PAU. It is now a well known fact that the majority of the educated farmers read the weekly weather bulletins from the PAU in the newspapers and others, uneducated as well as educated listen to the advisory service on radio and television.

11.1.4 SCOPE FOR IMPROVEMENT IN SHORT RANGE AND EXTENDED FORECASTS FOR AGRICULTURE

The accuracy of weather forecasts depends on the availability of detailed weather data for the country and its surroundings. The data needed is on pressure patterns; location and movements of the low pressure and high pressure areas; fronts; upper air troughs; advection of moisture, heat and cold; wind direction and wind speed. Synoptic charts from numerical data are prepared for surface and various heights in the atmosphere to study the phenomena. These charts and other data can be received from far and nearby meteorological stations through radio signals and land lines with the following equipments:
i) Facsimile Weather Chart Recorder
ii) Teleprinter.

The other most important data needed for accurate weather forecasts are on clouds. These data are transmitted by the Meteorological Satellites. The equipment needed to receive these data is a Meteorological Satellite Ground Receiving Station.

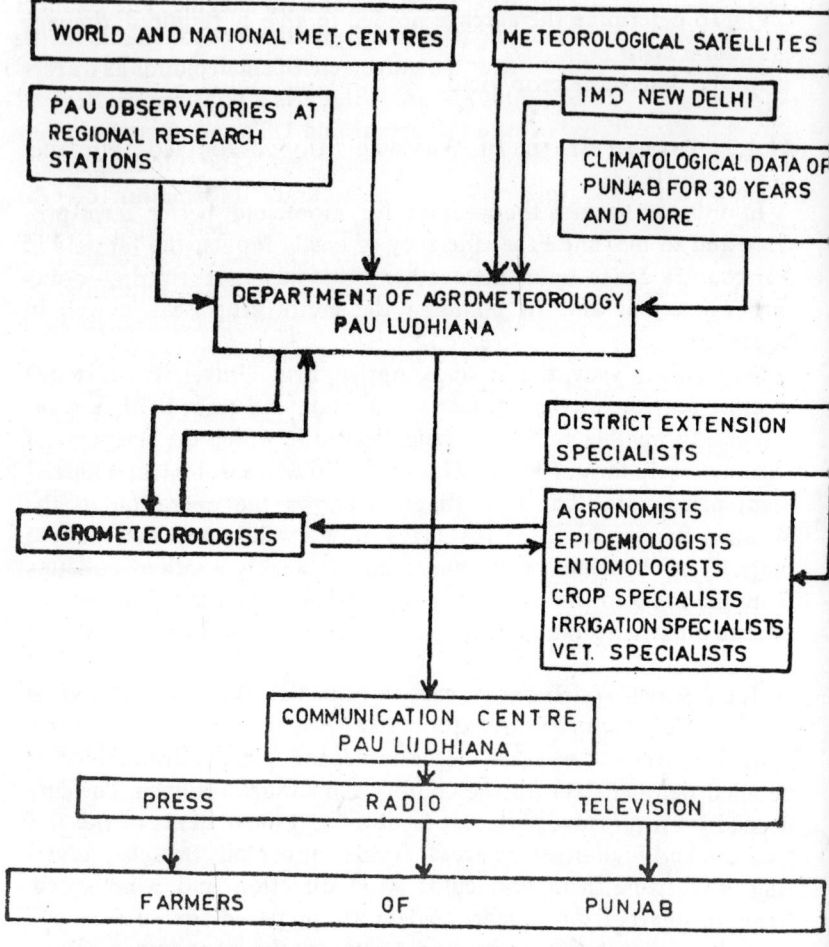

Fig. 11.1. Weather and crop outlook for the Punjab.

11.1.5 METEOROLOGICAL SATELLITE AS A TOOL IN WEATHER FORECASTING

For the meteorological purposes, a satellite takes pictures of the earth and atmosphere in the visible and infra-red spectra and transmits them towards the earth. These pictures can be received at any station by a Meteorological Satelline Ground Receiving Station. Infra-red images make it possible to determine the temperature of earth's surface and cloud temperature and its height. The pictures in the visible spectrum show cloud formations and enable us to calculate wind velocity from the movement of small clouds as tracers. In case of India and adjoining areas there is a continuous flow of cloud pictures from orbiting (Russian and US) and Geostationary (Meteosat Japanese and INSAT–IB) satellites. The cloud pictures received at short intervals provide accurate information on the development and movements of the clouds, their type, height, temperature as well as the wind velocity. The weather forecast with greater accuracy can, therefore, be made by super-imposing the synoptic charts and cloud pictures with respect to the occurrence of the following weather phenomena:

Occurrence of hail storms and squalls,
Flash floods,
Occurrence of rainfall, its amount and time,
Intensity and persistence of cold and heat waves,
Rate of evaporation and evapotranspiration,
Range of wind speed,
Duration of cloudy and sunny hours,
Frost intensity.

The forecast of these weather phenomena will enable agricultural scientists in India to give specific recommendations to farmers for the following operations:

i) To either complete sowing operations or to withhold them.
ii) To irrigate a crop or to withhold the irrigation.
iii) To start and complete the harvesting operation or to withhold it.
iv) To apply fertilizer or not.
v) The appropriate time to spray pesticides and fungicides.
vi) To take measures against frost damage.
vii) Measures to protect young livestock from cold.
viii) Management of farm labour.
ix) Transportation of farm produce to the market.
x) Handling, transportation and storage of foodgrains.

11.2 Preparation of a Weather Outlook for the Farmers

The weather outlook for farmers is an interpretation, of how expected weather in the future and weather conditions accumulated upto the present, will effect crops, livestock and farm operations

(Smith & Walter, 1973). A crop-livestock operations calendar is used to provide the proper weather information at the proper time. This is also done for agronomic operations, diseases and insects. The first part of the farm summary is a synopsis of weather systems expected through the next two to five days' period.

Synopsis

This is a description of locations and movements of low pressure areas, high pressure areas, fronts and upper air troughs, and the associated weather with these systems. This information is derived from guidance charts from National Meteorological Centres. Prognostic charts for surface and upper air conditions are used for preparing this synopsis. The synopsis generally is designed to answer the *why of weather*.

Sunshine

This parameter is provided to give the user an idea of just how much of possible sunshine will be available to dry soil, hay, evaporation of water and to complete farm operations. For minor clouds or mostly sunny conditions, a 90–100 per cent sunshine term is used. Under *partly cloudy* or *scattered cloudiness* usually 50–90 per cent is used; for *considerable cloudiness* 20 to 50 per cent is used and for *mostly cloudy* 20 per cent or less term is used. This is average cloudiness for the entire day-light period; or it can be broken down into morning and afternoon periods. *Forecasting cloud cover* is based on the moisture content of air between 1000–500 mb, stability or lapse rate, vorticity field and the type of average flow (cyclonic, anticyclonic or vertical motion type of advection) at surface and aloft at 500 mb. Generally, positive vertical motion with a mean R.H. of 70 per cent or greater, and conditional instability, with cold air advection at 500 mb and warm surface advection, will produce cloudiness and precipitation. Surface lifting of moist air is necessary, either frontal or convectional. Negative vertical motion, anticyclonic flow, mean RH under 50 per cent, vorticity 10 or less and warm air advection aloft—will produce clear sky conditions. Forecast aids that are helpful in sunshine prediction are satellite charts, weather depiction charts, synoptic cloud observations and radar echos.

Precipitation

A forecast of the precipitation quantity is most important to farmers in planning their operations and estimating its effect on crop health and crop yield. To arrive at such a forecast, precipitable water analysis is necessary for a weather system. This is accomplished using cloud pictures, upper air moisture, dew points, vertical motions, stability and temperature information (Anonymous, 1971). Rainfall is described in the forecast as *isolated* where less than one-third of the rainfall recording stations are expected to receive rains. It is described as *scattered* when one-third to two-third stations are expected to record rains; and it is referred to as *widespread* when more than two-third stations are expected to record rainfall or other forms of precipitation.

Dew

Dew is forecast in six categories, namely: very light, light, moderate, heavy, very heavy and wet. Formation of dew is dependent on cloud cover, wind, surface moisture and temperature-dew point relationships. Clear sky, winds under 8 kmph and moist soil surface will usually permit heavy dew formation, and if surface moisture is surplus, then very heavy dew formation. In any event, for dew formation rapid outgoing radiational cooling, very little surface air mixing and absence of positive vertical motion is necessary. As wind and cloudiness increase dew potential decreases. Usually cloudy skies and winds of 15 km per hour or more permit no dew formation. High pressure areas and associated dense air with drainage is more conducive for dew formation than areas under low pressure systems.

Relative humidity

Relative humidity is forecast by first determining temperature minimums and maximums for high and low R.H. values. A dew-point analysis is made on an observed synoptic charts, then moved with pressure patterns and pressure systems. Air temperature as dry-bulb and dew-point values are then substituted in the R.H. formula to arrive at maximum and minimum relative humidity values. A diurnal curve can be established.

Drying rate

This is forecast by establishing a relationship between wind, temperature, radiation, % sunshine and humidity (or moisture content of air). These can be calculated using an appropriate equation or based on actual observed evaporation and projected conditions to cause changes in intensity.

Thresholds for spraying

The efficiency of spraying insecticides and fertliizer applications, varies according to the weather conditions during which the operations are conducted. It was found that a temperature between 5 and 27°C is ideal for insecticides, fungicides, herbicides, and fertilizer applications. At higher temperatures there was heavy loss by evaporation.

For a six-hour duration subsequent to spraying or application, any rainfall (even of one mm or less) is significant and should be taken into consideration as the chemicals used can get diluted or washed away.

The following wind speed thresholds for spraying have been identified:

Wind speed less than 8 kmph	Ideal
Wind speed 8–15 kmph	Good
Wind speed 16–22 kmph	Fair
Wind speed 23–28 kmph	Marginal

Wind speed exceeding 28 kmph is unfavourable.

Under normal weather conditions, spraying should be undertaken early in the morning or late in the evening, to ensure a minimum three hours of ideal weather.

Interpretation of weather for crops

Interpretation of conditions takes into account the impact of weather on germination, growth rates, freeze protection and irrigation demands. The cumulative effect of weather encountered and that anticipated, is used to determine the necessity of chemical sprays, dates of harvest, duration of harvest, quality and storage capabilities of grains, fruits and vegetables.

Interpretation of weather for farm operations

Interpretation of weather on farm operations takes into account the drying rate of soil; evaporation losses; the effect of heat, cold and wind on appiication of chemicals and fertilizers; the drying rate for curing and wetting and the rewetting of grains and hay.

Interpretation of weather for livestock

Various combinations of heat and moisture in the atmosphere cause comfort and discomfort to humans and livestock. A single index can be used to express this combined temperature-humidity effect on livestock. An index prepared by NOAA (Anonymous, 1971) National Weather Service of USA can be used to give timely warnings of anticipated weather dangerous to the health and safety of livestock. This index provides an indication regarding heat stress, cold stress and shelter requirements; and the effects of weather on the productivity of milk, meat and eggs.

Interpretation of weather for crop diseases

There exists a very close relationship between many plant diseases and the weather. Therefore, the incidence of these diseases can be forecast in the light of accumulated and anticipated weather. Both synoptic and statistical approaches are used for these forecasts, which are concerned with probable development, extent and time-of-spread or suppression of the diseases.

11.3 Operational Forecasts

These are essentially short-range forecasts issued for general farm activities. The forecast period covers two days with an outlook for the third, fourth and fifth (Anonymous, 1971). These forecasts are prepared to guide the farmers for carrying out their farm operations with minimum of risk for their costly inputs and crop losses.

Soil preparation

The important parameters in the forecasts are soil moisture, soil temperature, precipitation and wind.

The required conditions are that: the soil should be in a workable condition with moisture less than 80 per cent of field capacity; soil temperature should be above 0°C; the amount of rainfall less than 1 mm; and the wind speed should be less than 45 kilometres per hour.

Crop planting

a) Seed Crops—The parameters in the forecast are soil moisture, soil and air temperature, precipitation and wind.

The required conditions for the operation are that: soil moisture should be 40 to 80 per cent of field capacity; soil temperatures at depths of 50 to 100 mm should be above 4.5°C, though this varies with the type of crop—for cotton it should be above 15.5°C, and for wheat about 5°C; the rainfall should be less than 1 mm; and the wind speed less than 30 kilometres per hour.

b) Transplants—The parameters are soil moisture, air and soil temperature, precipitation and wind.

The required conditions for operations are: the soil moisture should be 60 to 90 per cent of field capacity up to a depth ranging from 10 to 20 centimetres; the soil temperature should be above 10°C; the air temperature should be above −2°C; and the wind speed below 25 kilometres per hour.

Crop fertilisation

The parameters in the forecast are soil moisture, soil and air temperature, precipitation and wind.

The soil moisture should range from 30 to 80 per cent of the field capacity up to a depth of 15 centimetres. The soil temperature should be below 10°C for higher nitrogen levels. Precipitation should be less than 1 mm and the wind speed below 40 kilometres per hour for granular fertilizers, 30 kilometres per hour for spraying fertilizers and 15 kilometres per hour for dusting fertilizers.

Irrigation

The weather parameters are soil moisture, precipitation, air temperature, wind, evapotranspiration and radiation. The moisture should be less than 50 per cent of field capacity in the root zone. There should be no precipitation, and the wind speed should be less than 25 kilometres per hour.

Spray and dust (aerial application)

The important parameters are cloud ceiling, visibility, low level temperature inversion, air temperature, precipitation, wind and dew.

The cloud ceiling should be greater than 150 metres and visibility greater than 1.5 kilometres; a surface inversion is desirable; air temperature should be below 30°C; and the wind speed should be less than 15 kilometres per hour.

Spray and dust (ground application)

The important parameters are soil moisture, air temperature, precipitation, dew and wind.

The soil moisture should be below 90 per cent of field capacity. No rainfall; and the wind speed should be less than 25 kilometres per hour.

Harvesting

a) Moisture-sensitive crops—The weather parameters are soil moisture, air temperature, precipitation, wind, humidity, sunlight, dew and evapotranspiration.

The soil moisture should be less than 90 per cent of field capacity; no rainfall; and the wind speed 8 to 30 kilometres per hour. The relative humidity should be below 75 per cent.

b) Temperature-sensitive crops—The weather parameters are soil moisture, air temperature, precipitation and wind.

The soil moisture should be below 90 per cent of field capacity up to a depth of 15 centimetres, and the air temperature below 13°C. The rainfall should be less than 1 mm.

c) All hardy crops—The weather parameters in the forecast are soil moisture, air temperature, precipitation and wind.

The soil moisture should be below 90 per cent of field capacity and the rainfall less than 1 mm.

11.4 Fire-Weather Forecasts

The fire-weather forecasts are very necessary in areas where the economy is primarily based on forestry. The main causes of forest fires are lightning, self-combustion and man made. An analysis of forest fires indicates that lightning is the major cause of forest fires. Self-combustion as a source of forest fire is rare. However, there are instances when fires have occurred during dry summers due to self-combustion.

Fire-inducing weather conditions are the lack of rainfall, low humidity and high velocity winds. The types of trees, their moisture content and the stage of foliage also contribute to forest fires. The humidity and wind velocity within the forest, and the air temperature immediately outside the canopy are also contributing factors.

Several methods have been developed for fire-weather forecasts. The most common one is the graphical aid developed by Landberg and Jacob, known as the *Burning Index.*

1) The Burning index is based on relative humidity, precipitation and wind velocity. The warnings against forest fires are grouped into three categories (Anonymous, 1953).

ɔ) *Good fire days*—When the relative humidity is below 40 per cent, precipitation is less than 0.25 mm. and wind speed is greater than 20 kilometres per hour.

b) *Poor fire days*—When the relative humidity is greater than 60 per cent and precipitation is more than 1.0 mm.

c) *Indifferent days*—When the state of weather on a particular day will neither contribute to nor retard fire.

2) Based on relative humidity and the amount of moisture in the litter, measured with a psychrometer and litter hygrometer (Molga, 1962), the fire warning indices are catagorised as given below:

a) *No fire danger*—When relative humidity is above 70 per cent and the content of litter moisture above 26 per cent, most of the causes of fire do not operate.

b) *Possible fire danger*—When relative humidity is below 69 per cent and the content of litter moisture 19 to 25 per cent—lightning can cause fires.

c) *Slight fire hazard*—When relative humidity is 50 to 59 per cent and the content of litter moisture 14 to 18 per cent—campfires and debrisfires can cause a conflagaration.

d) *Moderate fire hazard*—When the relative humidity is 40 to 49 per cent and the content of litter moisture 11 to 13 per cent—fire smoke is sufficient to spread fires.

e) *Fire danger*—When the relative humidity is 30 to 39 per cent and the content of litter moisture 8 to 10 per cent—a railway engine, saw fire and spontaneous combustion can cause fires.

f) *Extreme fire danger*—When the relative humidity is below 29 per cent and the content of litter moisture 2 to 7 per cent—fires can start from a cigarette, or even from railway engine which is passing through the forest.

3) Warnings against fire-weather, or forecasts, are also given with an index of combustibility. The index expression, as proposed by Nestrov (Molga, 1962) is

$$G = \sum_{s=1}^{s=n} T.d$$

where, T is the air temperature in °C, d is the saturation vapour-pressure deficit in mm., and n is the number of days since the last rainfall. This index G is given in the following form:

i) No danger of fire : The index of combustibility is 300.

ii) Slight fire hazard : The index of combustibility is 301 to 500.

iii) Moderate fire hazard : The index of combustibility is 501 to 1,000.

iv) Fire danger : The index of combustibility is 1,001 to 4,000.

v) Extreme fire danger : The index of combustibility is over 4,000.

11.5 Methods of Crop-yield Forecasts

In the following pages some examples of quantitative forecasts, especially crop-yield forecasts based on meteorological parameters, are given. The listed methods are not exhaustive; only the most common, simple ones are included to make the students familiar with the different approaches used in forecasting crop-yields.

Crop-yield and climate change model

A model, to estimate changes in crop-yield with two main climatic variables, was developed for a global study of crop-yield and climatic change (Anonymous, 1978). The climatic variables used in the study are: (1) variance of heading-period temperature (T) from the average; and (2) the variance of crop season rainfall (P) from the average. The model assumes no change in technology.

The yield estimates are expressed as percentages of the yield for years with average weather, i.e. the years for which the variance T and P values are zero. A continuous version of the yield for various combinations of T and P is plotted on a graph as contour lines.

Figs. 11.2 and 11.3 show two such models for India. One for rice crops and the other for wheat crops. The model indicates estimates of crop yield (in %) corresponding to various changes in temperature and rainfall from the average.

The curves in the Figs. 11.2 and 11.3 are the choropleths of the normalized relative yield. In other words, the yields are expressed as percentages of average calculated annual yield for the base period, for which no climatic change is assumed.

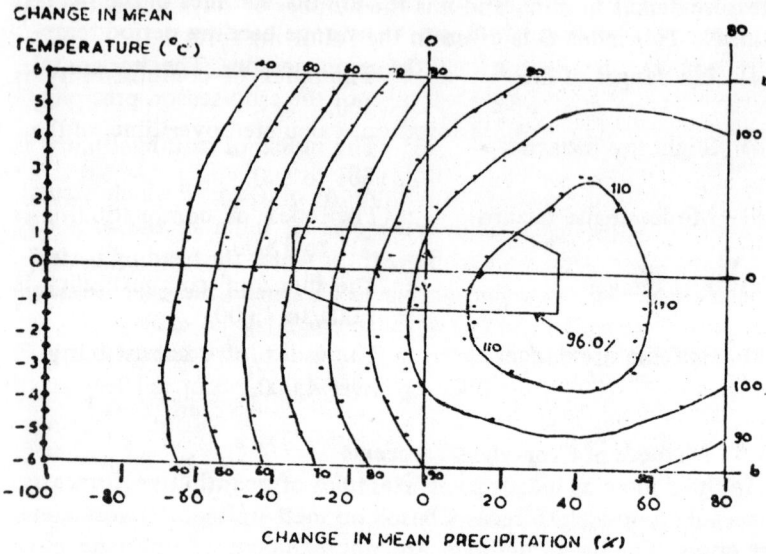

Fig. 11.2   Relative variations of rice-yield in India with variation from mean temperature and rainfall.

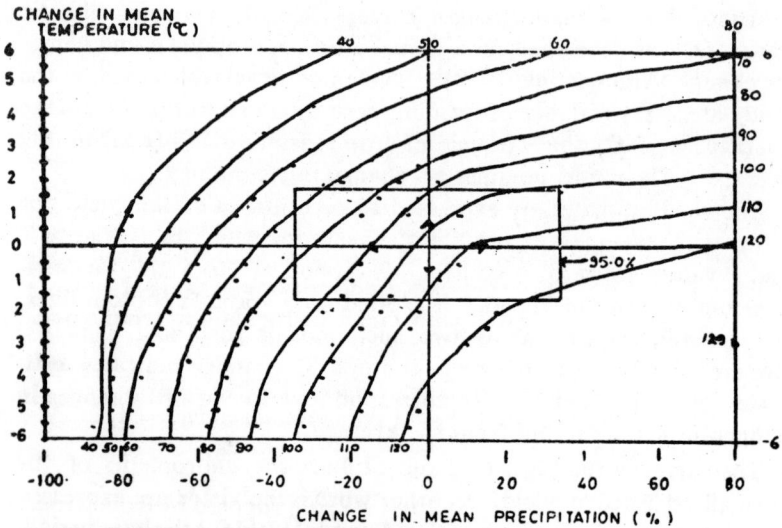

Fig. 11.3 Relative variation of wheat-yield in India with variation from mean temperature and rainfall.

The vertical axis of the graphs measure the variance of the heading period temperature (T) from the average heading period temperature calculated over time, of the crop season. The horizontal axis measure the variance percentage of the crop-season precipitation (P) from the average precipitation, calculated over time, of the crop season.

The curves connect annual combinations of T and P which result in the same relative yield. For example, in India in the case of wheat the relative yield is 80 in an year for which the heading period temperature is 1°C above the average ($T = 1$), and the crop season precipitation is 20 per cent below the average ($P = -20$).

The polygons on the map enclose the limits of the annual combinations of T and P which are most likely to occur in the yearly variation in climate. In other words, there is a probability of 95–96 per cent that a random combination of T and P will fall inside the polygon. The yield contours in polygons thus represent the variations in crop-yield which are most likely to occur from yearly fluctuations in temperature and rainfall.

Statistical climate/Crop-yield models

Linear regression type climate/crop-yield models were developed by Steyaert *et al.* (1981) for selected countries in South and Southeast Asia. Models for rice, maize, wheat and sorghum were developed at the regional and national level depending upon the availability of reliable yield data. These models take the form :

$$Y = a_0 + a_1 (\text{Trend}) + \sum_{i=2}^{N} a_i X_i$$

where Y = the predicted yield (q/ha)

a_0 = the regression constant (intercept)

a_1 = the estimated regression coefficient for the linear time "trend" variable defined, for example, as (1951 = 1..., 1981 = 31) and acting as a surrogata for technology trends in the yield data

a_i = the ith estimated regression coefficient, and

X_i = the ith meteorological predictor variable, $i = 1, 2...N$.

Factorial yieldweather model for wheat

The factorial yieldweather model (FYWM) proposed by Robertson (1974), and as claimed by the author, is readily adaptable for assessing, at any time during the wheat crop development period, the influence of past and current weather on expected yield. The FYWM model is:

$$Y_t = V_1(Y_{t-1}, P_t) \cdot V_2(T_1)_t \cdot V_3(T_2)_t \cdot V_4(Q)_t \tag{1}$$

where V_1, V_2, etc. indicate mathematical functions of the weather elements

Y_t is the yield (or really the condition of the crop in terms of the yield which it will support) as estimated at time t, at the end of a given crop stage

Y_{t-1} is the yield estimated at the end of the previous stage (antecedent crop condition)

P_t is the total precipitation between stages

T_1 is the average of the daily maximum temperature, during the period between stages

T_2 is the average of the daily minimum temperature during the period between stages

Q is the average daily global radiation, during the period between stages,

and where the functions, V_1 etc. are:

$$V_1(Y_{t-1}, P_t) = b_0 + B_1 Y_{t-1} + b_2 P_t \tag{2}$$

$$V_2(T_1) = P_0 + P_1 T_1 + P_2 T_1^2 \tag{3}$$

$$V_3(T_2) = q_0 + q_1 T_2 + q_2 T_2^2 \tag{4}$$

$$V_4(Q) = r_0 + r_1 Q + r_2 Q^2 \tag{5}$$

and where b, p, q and r are regression coefficients to be evaluated for each crop period. The quadratic functions permit an evaluation of the optimum values, as well as values of the lower and upper critical limits for temperatures and global radiation. An equation similar to eq. (1) is required for each significant phenological period of the crop, where $t = 1$, 2. etc., up to as many periods as are desirable.

Maize yield

Huda *et al.* (1976) predicted the maize yield under monsoon conditions with a second degree multiple-regression equation. The equation used is

$$Z = A_0 + a_1 \sum_{i=1}^{n} (t_i^0 y) + a_2 \sum_{i=1}^{n} (t_i^1 y) + a_3 \sum_{i=1}^{n} (t_i^2 y) + DT$$

where Z is the crop yield in quintals/hectare

A_0, a_1, a_2, a_3 and D are constants.

y is any climatic variable for any given 7-day period,

t_1 is the number of each of the 7-day periods
(1 is for the week from June 18–24, and 16 for the week from Oct. 1–7)

n is equal to 16 for a 7-day period in a given season

T is the year number (beginning 1961 = 1 and ending 1972 = 12) which was included to correct for the long term trends in yield.

The equation predicted the maize yield very well and demonstrated that maize yields are closely related to weekly changes in climatic parameters.

Sugar cane yield models

a) A climatological model for sugar cane yield prediction in Andhra Pradesh has been proposed by Subbaramayya and Rupa Kumar (1980). The equation is:

$$Y = 1253.3 + 281.7\,T_{x_3} - 292.5\,T_{n_3} - 4.36\,(T_{x_3})^2$$
$$+ 1.49\,(T_{n_3} \times R_{h_3}) - 1.11\,(T_{x_3} \times R_{h_3}) + 4.84\,(T_{x_3} \times T_{n_3})$$

where Y is the yield in tonnes per hectare

T_{x_3} is mean maxi. temperature (°C) in the 3rd month after sowing.

T_{n_3} is mean mini. temperature (°C) in the 3rd month after sowing.

R_{h_3} is mean morning relative humidity (%) in the 3rd month after sowing.

The equation has been found to predict 62 per cent of variations in the yield. Since the equation involves weather parameters in the third month of the crop-period, a prediction of the yield well in advance can be made with this equation.

b) Thompson (1976) developed a relationship between water use and dry matter production in sugar cane. He obtained a linear equation to forecast the sugar cane yield in Hawaii, South Africa and Australia. The equation takes the form

$$Y = 9.69 \left(\frac{ET}{100} \right) - 2.4$$

where Y is yield of sugar cane in tonnes per hectare

ET is evapotranspiration in mm.

Ulanova's method for wheat yield

Longrange methods of forecasting winter wheat-yields in the Black Sea region of the Soviet Union, have been developed by Ulanova (Munn, 1970). Only two predictors are used:

1) The number of sprouts per m^2.

2) Available soil moisture 'S' in mm in the 0-100 cm layer. Both observations were made in spring.

Y is the yield in 100 kg

a) Equation for 1000 to 2000 sprouts per sq meter is

$$Y = 0.24S - 10.2, r = 0.86$$

b) Equation for 400 to 900 sprouts per sq. meter

$$Y = 0.2S - 11.1, r = 0.89$$

Rice yield

1) The IRRI (Chang, 1981) model on the prediction of maximum rice yield is based on the combined effect of solar radiation and temperature on crop-yields in the tropics. The model is

$$Y = S (278 - 7.07t) \times 0.86 \times 18.1 \times 10^{-5}$$

where $Y = $ Yield in tonnes/hectare

$S = $ Solar radiation in ly/day

$t = $ Temperature in °C during 25 days before flowering

0.86 is the average filled-grain percentage,

18.1 is the average 1000 grain weight and

10^{-5} is a correction factor.

This model can be used to compare different areas for potential yield.

2) A regression model to forecast the rice yield on the basis of nitrogen application and moisture stress has been developed at IRRI (Anonymous, 1972).

The equation for the wet season crop is:

$$Y = 2790 + 41.5N - 0.50N^2 - 50.2S_1 - 20.40S_2 + 0.76NS_1$$

The equation for the dry season crop is:

$$Y = 3600 + 17.9N - 0.14N^2 - 35.2S_1 - 94.4S_2 + 0.54NS_1$$

where Y is yield of paddy in kg per hectare

N is nitrogen applied in kg per hectare

S_1 is the early stress (number of days, in excess of three, that the paddy was subjected to within the period from transplanting to 60 days before harvest).

S_2 is the late stress (number of days in excess of three, that the paddy was subjected to within the period from 60 to 30 days before harvest)

Wang's method for tomato yield

Wang (Mather, 1974) determined that the optimum range of temperature for tomato production lay between 66°F(17°C) and 83°F(28°C). Outside this range the yield declines drastically.

Wang's regression equation to forecast the tomato yield is:

$$Y = -0.29 \, Tf + 13.29 \quad r = -0.9$$

Y = yield of tomato in tons/acre

Tf = Temperature frequency over 83°F in %

11.6 Meteorological Basis of Disease and Insect-Pest Forecasts

There is a close relationship between plant diseases and weather. Therefore, in terms of prevailing weather conditions, the incidence of several diseases can be forecast. The relationship between the weather of an area and the diseases in it, can be visualised as follows (Anonymous, 1970):

Let the range of climatic conditions favourable for the development of the diseases be represented by D, and let C_1, C_2 and C_3 represent the climatic conditions in regions 1, 2 and 3. Three distinct relationships can be established between diseases and weather.

1) In the first case the range of weather conditions favouring a disease (D) or pest is entirely outside the range of weather (C_1) encountered in an area. Therefore the disease or pest cannot flourish in that region.

2) In the second case the weather (C_2) irrespective of the prevailing weather conditions, is always favourable and lies within the limits (D) for the appearance of diseases or insect pests. In such cases, the weather factors are not very important for forecasting disease or pest.

3) In the third case, which is the most frequent and important one, if during the year the weather shifts and is no longer favourable for the disease, then the disease may not occur or spread at all in that year. When weather conditions are close to or favourable for disease, the chances of attack from the disease will be comparatively greater.

Viral and bacterial diseases are more weather-dependent than insects due to the fact that viral and bacterial pathogens remain at fixed locations, consistently exposed to a particular type of weather for a sufficiently long period. Insects however are mobile and move from place to place at different times, and hence are less affected by the uniformity of weather. It is certain that most diseases are more dependent on weather than are insects; however the spread of certain pests is directly weather dependent.

11.6.1 LONG RANGE FORECASTS

The forecasts of crop diseases and pests are based on laboratory research and longterm analysis of diseases and climatological data. These forecasts are concerned with probable development, spread and modification of a disease or pest, over a few months or a year. The purpose of long range forecasts is to give warnings of the probable nature, extent and time of the spread of diseases or pests, and to prepare a control programme for them. A few examples of long-range forecasts of diseases and pests are given as follows.

1) Bacterial wilt and leaf blight

In the United States, this disease is related to the previous winter conditions. When the sum of the average temperatures of December, January and February remains below 38°C, there is no chance of the occurrence of wilt on corn. If the sum of the average temperatures is above 29.5°C, corn blight is likely to occur. This follows that if the winters are mild, the bacterial wilt and leaf blight are likely to spread in an epidemic form in the coming crop: severe winters reduce the chances of blight (Mather, 1974).

2) Corn flea beetle

When the sum of the average temperatures of December, January and February is less than 32°C, the incidence of this pest is very low. If the sum of average temperature is less than 26°C, no incidence of flee beetles is expected. However if the sum of average temperatures is greater than 32°C, then a high incidence of the pest is expected.

3) Blue mold of tobacco

The severity of this disease is directly correlated with climatic conditions, viz. temperature and relative humidity during early spring. The mean temperature for the month of January in all the tobacco-growing areas of the U.S.A. directly affects the time of sowing, and the severity of blue mold. If the mean temperature of January is above normal, blue mold will appear earlier and the disease will be severe. If temperatures are below normal, blue mold will appear later and the disease will be less severe.

11.6.2 MEDIUM RANGE FORECASTS

Both synoptic and statistical approaches are used to make forecasts. These are based on recent climatological data, which give sufficient advance notice on the overall seasonal impact of a particular disease and pest. The purpose of medium range forecasts is to enable the planners to make a complete programme for taking control measures, and for taking such steps which may suppress the spread of the disease.

1) Wheat rust

There are three types of rust for wheat: yellow rust, brown rust and black rust. Each of the three spreads when there exist particular combinations of weather elements.

Yellow rust: In the plains of Northwest India, yellow rust spores come from the Himalayas, and the rust appears by the end of January. The optimum weather conditions for its multiplication are:

 i) Mean temperature 9 — 13°C.
 ii) Relative humidity more than 70%.
 iii) Partly cloudy sky conditions.

If such conditions prevail for a week in mid-January, then yellow rust multiplication is likely to accelerate. Further, if the wind direction is North to Northwest then the attack will be severe.

Brown rust: This appears in Punjab during the month of February. Optimum conditions for its multiplication are:

 i) Mean temperature 15° — 20°C for approximately a week.
 ii) Relative humidity more than 70%.
 iii) Sky conditions: intermittent clouds and sunshine by end-January or first week of February.

Black rust: It appears in Punjab usually from the end of February to middle-March. It comes to Punjab from South. Optimum conditions for its multiplication and spread are:

 i) Mean temperature 16 — 27°C.
 ii) Relative humidity more than 70%.
 iii) Excessive dew.

2) Rice stem borer

A statistical approach was used in Japan for releasing medium range forecasts for the outbreak of rice stem borer. The forecast is prepared on the basis of the following equation:

$$X = 23.3 - 0.537\ Y + 0.456\ Z$$

where X is the date of appearance of stem borer expressed as the number of days after May 31,

Y is mean temperature of the month of March,

Z is date of emergence of the first blossom of cherry in that area.

3) Pecan scab of apple

The following method is commonly used in the U. S. A. for the prediction of pecan scab of apples. Multiply the wetting period (foliage remaining wet) by the mean temperature (°C) during the wetting period. If the result is 140 or more, scab infection is anticipated. This rule works up to a temperature of approximately 27°C. Temperatures above 27°C are quite lethal for the spores of this disease especially when relative humidity is more than 50 per cent.

4) Apple scab

The basic factor which is used to control the apple scab is the wetting period. The forecast is based on the number of hours during which the leaves will remain wet from fog, dew or rain. From Table 11.3 (Valli, 1968), the intensity of the disease can be estimated.

Table 11.3. Length of Wetting Period with Mean Temperatures Necessary to Produce Light, Moderate or Heavy Infection of Scab

Mean temperature during wetting period (°C)	Length of wetting period (hours) necessary to produce		
	Light infection	Moderate infection	Heavy infection
7	20	26	40
13	12	16	24
19	9	12	18
25	12	17	26

5) Downy mildew

The attack of this disease, which affects beans, is forecast in the U. S. A. on the basis of the following meteorological criteria:

a) A five-day moving mean temperature below 27°C but a minimum temperature of 7°C or higher.

b) A ten-day moving rainfall total of 30 mm or more. If these conditions are fulfilled, the downy mildew attack is expected during the following week.

6) Peanut leaf-spot

The forecast of leaf-spot is based on the number of hours during which relative humidity remains 95% or more, and the intensity of the lowest temperature (15–17°C) for more than ten hours. Under these conditions the disease is likely to increase rapidly.

Intensity of the infection rate is expressed in tabular form (Valli, 1968) as in Table 11.4.

Table 11.4. Infection Rate v/s Hours of Relative Humidity (RH) 95% or more and Minimum Temperatures

Hours of more than 95% R.H.	Lowest Temp. (°C) during high R.H. period				
	18	20	22	24	26
20	1	3	3	3	3
16	1	3	3	3	3
12	0	2	3	3	3
8	0	1	2	3	3
4	0	0	0	1	2
0	0	0	0	0	0

0 = No infection 2 = Moderate infection
1 = Light infection 3 = Heavy infection

Maximum attack is in the temperature range of mid-twenties, i.e. 22°–25°C, when R.H. is more than 95% for 12 hours or more. On the basis of this duration the probability of leaf spot infection is forecast.

7) Potato blight

Several rules have been developed to forecast late blight of potatoes for various combinations of meteorological conditions (Bedi *et al.*, 1983).

Dutch rule
1) 4 hours dew in the course of a night.
2) Minimum temperature during the night not below 10°C.
3) Mean cloudiness on the following day not below 8/10,
4) Measurable rainfall in 24 hours not below 0.01 mm following the night of dew.

As a result of this combination of weather conditions, blight will appear within a fortnight.

Cook's rule
1) Weekly mean temperature must be equal or less than 24°C.
2) Weekly cumulative rainfall must equal or surpass a critical rainfall level for two weeks.

Beaumont's rule
1) A period of two days during which the temperature does not fall below 10°C.
2) Relative humidity not below 75% on each of the two days mentioned above.

Blight is expected to appear ten days after a Beaumont period.

Irish rule
1) Twelve hours with temperatures not below 10°C and relative humidity not below 90%.
2) A period of at least four hours during which the foliage is wet either due to rain, drizzle or high humidity.

Under these conditions blight is expected to appear after about a week.

Wallin's rule (I)
1) Concurrent temperature of 24°C or less.
2) Relative humidity 90% or more for at least ten hours or more; subsequent daily maximum temperature remained below 32°C.

Under these conditions blight is expected to appear in a fortnight.

Wallin's rule (II)
Favourable periods for blight development
1) For ten hours temperature between 15.5 − 25°C, relative humidity 90%.
2) For twelve hours temperature between 12 − 15°C, relative humidity 90%.

3) For fourteen hours temperature between 7 — 12°C, relative humidity 90%.

Maximum temperature during the 24-hours should not exceed 35°C.

Smith period

1) A period of two days during which the temperature does not fall below 10°C.

2) Relative humidity of 90% or higher for at least eleven hours on each of the abovementioned two days.

8) Karnal bunt

Multiple regression analysis was used by Srinivasan and Mavi (1983) to develop a model for predicting 'Karnal bunt' disease in Punjab using weather variables. The analysis involves simultaneous regression of a set of independent variables on the dependent variables.

Five meteorological variables—maximum temperature, minimum temperature, relative humidity, cumulative rainfall and number of rainy days—were used as input variables. The data on these variables and the disease incidence in the past fourteen years were used for the analysis. The location was Ludhiana, representing the central plain region of Punjab.

The equation developed based on meteorological conditions during the second week of March predicts the disease fairly accurately. The equation developed was:

$$Y = 18.475 - 0.544 X_1 + 0.108 X_2 - 0.059 X_3$$
$$- 0.118 X_4 + 1.192 X_5$$

where Y = 'Karnal' bunt disease incidence in %.

X_1 = Maximum temperature during 11th week.

X_2 = Minimum temperature during 11th week.

X_3 = Relative humidity during 11th week.

X_4 = Cumulative rainfall during 11th week.

X_5 = No. of rainy days during 11th week.

The equation has a significantly higher R^2 value of 0.9066, significant at $P = 0.005$.

In one test, the predicted incidence of the disease was 5.4 per cent and the actual disease observed in the field was 4.8 per cent. The equation thus demonstrates the relationship of the meteorological factors in outbreaks of *Karnal bunt*, and its subsequent utility in successful forecasting of the disease.

11.7 Minimum Temperature and Frost Forecasts

1) The formula devised by Young (1920) has been widely used in the Orange Belt of California and has been producing fairly good forecasts of minimum temperatures. The formula is:

$$T_m = D - \left(\frac{H - 30}{4}\right) + v + v' \qquad (1)$$

where T_m is the indicated minimum temperature (°F)
  D is the dew point (°F) at 4.45 p.m.
  H is relative humidity (%) at 4.45 p.m.
  v and v' are variable corrections that are functions of D and H respectively. The values of these functions are determined as

$$v = \left(\frac{D - 28}{3}\right) \quad \text{and} \quad v' = \frac{H - 52}{6} \qquad (2)$$

Substituting (2) in (1), the prediction formula takes the form:

$$T_m = \frac{2D}{3} + \frac{98 - H}{12}$$

2) Allen (1957) simplified Young's formula so as to eliminate the use of psychrometric tables. The simplified equation is

$$T_m = T_w - 1/4 \, (T_d + 16)$$

where T_m is the predicted minimum temperature (°F)
  T_w is wet bulb temperature at 4.45 p.m. (°F)
  T_d is dry bulb temperature at 4.45 p.m. (°F)

3) Smith (1973) developed an equation for forecasting the frost occurrence at Christchurch. The formula is:

$$G = \frac{1}{3}\left(T + \frac{E}{2}\right) - c$$

where G is the forecast grass minimum temperature (°C)
  T is the 3 p.m. dry bulb reading (°C)
  E is the 3 p.m. dew point (°C)
  c is a constant with values 8 for May, September and October; 9 for June and August; and 10 for July.

This method gives fairly good predictions when the sky is clear during the night and the wind speed is moderate.

4) Singh and Jaipal's method :

Singh and Jaipal (1983) developed an equation to predict the minimum temperature (°C) at New Delhi. The equation is

$$Tnf = 0.170\ Ta + 0.287\ Tn + 0.319\ Te + 0.081\ Td - 24.87$$

where Tnf is the forecast minimum temperature

Tn is the minimum temperature recorded at New Delhi to be used for the next day's forecast

Ta is the minimum temperature at the place from where the air is likely to come to Delhi

Te is the dry bulb temperature at 12 GMT

Td is the moisture content. It is the mean of the dew-point temperatures for the surface and 900 mb at 12 GMT.

This method gives satisfactory results for the months of December, January and February. The limitation of the method is that it needs data pertaining to other stations which is not usually available.

REFERENCES

Allen, Charles, C. 1957. A simplified equation for minimum temperature prediction, Monthly Weather Review. April 1957 : 119–120.

Anonymous. 1953. Elements of Forest Fire Control. F.A.O. 41–43.

Anonymous. 1970. The forecasting from weather data of potato blight and other plant diseases and pests. WMO. Technical Note No. 10 : 26–28.

Anonymous. 1971. Livestock Hot Weather Stress. National Weather Service, Central region, Kansas City. Missouri, Regional operations manual letter: 71–73.

Anonymous. 1971. Description of the numerical prediction model used at NMC for producing upper air progs. NOAA, WSFH No. I R-19 : 6.1-6.16.

Anonymous. 1971. Federal plan for a national weather service. NOAA. US Department of Commerce, Washington, D.C.

Anonymous, 1972. Annual report —International Rice Research Institute, Los Banos.

Anonymous, 1978. Crop yield and climate change : The year 2000. Progress report. Selected results from a study conducted by Research Directorate of the Defence University. U.S. Dept. of Agri., NOAA and Institute for Future: 3–27.

Anonymous. 1983. Statistical Abstract of Punjab. Economic and Statistical Organisation. Govt. of Punjab. Pub. No. 34.

Atwal, A.S. 1983. The role and use of pesticides in agriculture. Seminar on Pesticides and Human Welfare. New Delhi.

Bedi, P.S., J.S. Dhiman and O.P. Singh. 1983. Basic Epidemiological Techniques in Phytopathology, Pub. Series Epidem/83-2. PAU, Ludhiana.

Chang Jen Hu. 1981. A climatological consideration of the transference of agricultural technology. Agric. Meteorol. 25 : 1–13.

Gill, K.S. 1984. Marketing of wheat. Personal communication. PAU. Ludhiana.

Huda, A.K.S., B.P. Ghildyal and V.S. Tomar. 1976. Contribution of climatic variables in predicting maize yield under monsoon conditions. Agric. Meteorol. 17 : 33–47.

Hudson, J.P. 1972. Agronomic implications of long term weather forecasting. Weather Forecasting for Agriculture and Industry. ed. V.A. Taylor : 44–55.

Jensen, Ray. E. and D.R. Davis. 1974. Expanded Agricultural Weather Service for Alabama, Florida and Georgia. Proc. of Florida State Horticultural Society. 87 : 144–149.

Mather, John. R. 1974. Climatology. Fundamentals and Applications. McGraw-Hill Company : 181–214.

Mavi, H.S. 1980. Weather Forecasting for Agriculture. Proc. First Agrometeorological Conference, Coimbatore: 25–30.

Molga, M. 1962. Agricultural Meteorology. Part II. Outline of Agrometeorological Problems. Warsaw: 293–297.

Munn, R.E. 1970. Biometeorological Methods. Academic Press : 246–254.

Newman, J.E. and F.W. Stearns. 1957. 30 day weather outlook. What's News in Crops and Soil. 9.9.

Noffsinger, T.L., L.L. Means and D.R. Stoffar. 1964. A Weather Service Programme for Agriculture (United States) Agric. Meteorol. 1 : 93–106.

Robertson, G.W. 1974. A factorial yield-weather model for wheat. Agrometeorology of the Wheat Crop. WMO-No. 396 : 242–264.

Singh, Dhanna and Jaipal. 1983. On forecasting night minimum temperatures over New Delhi, Mausam. 34 : 185–188.

Smith, L.H. and Walter L. Strim, 1973. The Agriculture Weather Service in Indiana (Personal Communication).

Smith, R.M. 1973. Frost forecasting for Christchurch. New Zealand. Meteorological Service. Technical Note 217 : 1–5.

Srinivasan, G.S. and H.S. Mavi. 1983. Bioclimatological model to predict Karnal Bunt disease of wheat in Punjab. Proceedings of the International Conference on Biometeorology. New Delhi.

Steyaert, L.T., V. Rao Achutuni and Atanas Todorov. 1981. Agroclimatic Assessment Methods for Drought/food Shortages in South and South East Asia–Proposed Early Warning Programme. Final Report to AID by NOAA, Centre for Environmental Assessment Service. Climate Impact Assessment Division Models Branch and Atmospheric Science Department, University of Missouri, Columbia.

Subbaramayya, I. and K. Rupa Kumar. 1980. Crop Weather Relationships of Sugarcane and Yield Prediction in Northeast Andhra Pradesh, India. Agric. Meteorol. 21: 265–279.

Thompson, G.D. 1976. Water use by sugar cane. Sugar J. 560/593.

Valli, V.J. 1968. Weather and plant disease forecasting. Agroclimatological Methods. Proc. of the Reading Symposium, UNESCO: 341–345.

Young, F.D. 1920. Forecasting minimum temperatures in Oregon and California. Monthly Weather Review Supplement 16: 55–58.

CHAPTER 12

TECHNIQUES AND METHODS OF AGROCLIMATIC REGIONALISATION

Crop production depends on the climate to a much greater extent than any other single factor of the environment. However, a large number of crops are being grown traditionally in areas without any consideration to the fitness of the climate. As a result, on one hand, poor yields of the crops are obtained, and on the other much of the production potentials of the climates go unutilized. With staggering increase in food demands and limits on the availability of land and water, the resource base of agriculture needs careful management to increase farm produce from a unit area. Great advances are being made to properly manage some of the variables involved in crop production, but successes in the management of the climate are still limited. Two different approaches are being tried. One is to control or modify the climate. Here the elements of climate can be controlled with varied degrees of success. This is however, possible at a micro-level, and at a very high cost. The second approach is to make an adjustment with the climate to make the best use of it, without involving any major expenditure. This adjustment is made, first, by determining the agroclimates, and then, delineating these agroclimates into agroclimatic regions. Agroclimates well understood and wisely integrated into agroclimatic regions can become valuable and handy tools for the practical execution of plans for harnessing the potentials of climates, for agricultural production. In fact, many countries have set up agroclimatic regions for the purpose of agricultural landuse planning and management.

12.1 From Climatic Regions to Agroclimatic Regions

The ideas for developing methods of delineating agroclimatic regions originated much after many climatic classifications had been proposed. Thus initially, the purpose was purely academic, and a systematic account of the climates of different areas was sought. Among the pioneer climatic classifications proposed during the nineteenth century were those of Humboldt, Dove, Supan and Voieikov. Coincidently some of the early studies also experimented with developing methods of delineating bioclimatic regions. The early bioclimatic classifications were those of Linsser, de Candolle, Supan, Drude and Schimper (Burgos, 1968).

All these researchers were interested in judging the influence of climate on individual plant species, including agricultural species. Both these classifications, climatic and bioclimatic, were however, arbitrary and lacked precision.

At the beginning of the twentieth century appeared the era of systematic classifications of climates. The most widely quoted, even to this date, is the climatic classification of Koppen (Wilsie, 1962). The criteria used by the author were the annual and monthly means of temperature and rainfall. The second important systematic classification of climates is that of Thornthwaite. Thornthwaite (1948) delineated the climatic regions on the basis of thermal efficiency and moisture index, using temperature, precipitation and potential evapotranspiration as the inputs. In Koppen's classification there is more emphasis on temperature than on precipitation, hence it has little application to agriculture especially in warm climates. In Thornthwaite's classification however, greater emphasis has been placed on effective precipitation, and the climatic regions of the tropics and subtropics bear a somewhat better relationship to plant growth and agriculture.

The third in the series is the climatic classification of Budyko (1956). The author delineated the climatic regions corresponding to the vegetation types, on the basis of the radiational index of dryness.

There are many more though lesser known. Lang, Meyer and Prescott delineated the climatic regions by correlating the natural vegetation with an index expressing a ratio between rainfall and evaporation. Penck, de Martonne, Reichal, Holdrige, Lauer and Walter and Leith suggested climatic regions using some similar index.

No doubt systematic classifications are based on observations of relationships between vegetation and climate. However, on a close examination this relationship is not adequately established. This is because all vegetational and climatic boundaries are transitional in nature. Again, vegetation is doubtless, mainly controlled by the climate; however, boundaries are often redefined by edaphic, biotic and microclimatic factors. Further even within the climate, temperature and rainfall, on which most of these classifications are based, are not the only factors in shaping the vegetation. Other factors like wind and sunshine also have a role to play making the situation more complex. The most important cause of the failure of classifications is that they are based on mean values of climatic elements. Mean values are unreal and extremes are significant in determining the limits of the distribution of vegetation, including crop plants.

Many of these classifications have been applied to measure and compare the agricultural productivity of different areas. When critically examined their application has been found to be most unsatisfactory. All of them fail to establish a relationship between climate and productivity. Climatic regions based on a few climatic elements, synthesised in terms of simplified scales of monthly or yearly averages are utterly inadequate to express the complex bioclimatic relationships. There are numerous examples of regions which, according to even the widely quoted Koppen's and Thornthwaite's classifications, have been defined as having different climates, but are known for the productivity of the same crop. Again, areas in the same group of climate, present marked differences in agricultural production.

It can thus be concluded that while systematic descriptive classifications of climates may have illustrative geographical value, they are of little value in comparing the productivity of different areas, and cannot be put to practical use to solve the problems encountered in agricultural production.

12.2 Agroclimate, Agroclimatic Index and Agroclimatic Region

Agroclimate is defined as the total of 'climatic conditions rendering possible economic cultivation of plant species, expressed either in their values of intensity, duration, frequency and moment of occurrence, or in value of their integral effects upon living organism and soil. The values in the definition refer to the agroclimatic indices which express the relationship between climate and agricultural production in quantitative terms. The indices may be simple values of climatic elements which may be significant from the agricultural point of view or some specially processed climatic values appropriate to crop plants. The data on agroclimates are usually presented through agroclimatic indices, in terms of the agroclimatic regions.

The concept of agroclimates and agroclimatic regions was put forward by the agronomists, crop ecologists and agroclimatologists, who evaluated and then discarded the conventional classifications of climates as being highly deficient for use in the solution of practical problems of agriculture. The agroclimatic indices proposed by these scientists represent some special significance in agriculture because of their nature, intensity or frequency. Based on these indices, agroclimatic regions are delineated which are homogeneous in agricultural fitness. General agroclimatic regions define the degree of favourableness of climates as a whole, and highlight the agroclimatic potentials and problems. Specific or specialized agroclimatic regions define the favourable climate for the growth of specific crops. General agroclimatic regions are useful for planning a uniform agricultural development of the state and for designing the most profitable cropping patterns. Specific agroclimatic regions are useful in specialising farm production, soil management techniques, and in determining agronomic and cultural practices.

12.3   Techniques and Methods of Agroclimatic Regionalisation

The first step towards delineating an agroclimatic region is, to quantify the main climatic characteristics like heat and moisture in the form of agroclimatic indices, which become numerical expressions of crop-climate. The second step is to map the geographical distribution of the indices in the form of an agroclimatic region.

The following weather elements play a role at some stage in the life-cycle of crop plants :

a) *Elements important to vegetative growth of plants*
   i)   Moisture stress.
   ii) Radiation and temperature.
   iii) Duration of the frost-free period.

b) *Elements important to the development of successive phases in plant life*
   i)   Day length.
   ii) Annual variation in radiation and temperature.
   iii) Daily range of temperature.
   iv) Duration of the frost-free period.

v)   Duration of the rainy and dry seasons.

Any attempt to combine all these variables in one or two indices is not likely to succeed. Again, in each territory several of these variables may not play any significant role in agricultural production. Therefore the first task is to identify the principal environmental stresses and to eliminate those which are insignificant. For example, in tropical areas photoperiod and duration of the frost-free period have no bearing on agriculture. On the other hand, the most dominant stress in these areas is the intensity and duration of moisture stress. Once this process of elimination is complete, separate or combined indices are proposed, to build the crop-climate relationship. This objective can be achieved by the evaluation of the agroclimate :

   i)   where the crops have originated ;
   ii)   of other regions where the crops are grown ;
   iii) of regions where experience has shown that the crops cannot be grown.

Based on these lines, scores of methods have been put forward to delineate the agroclimatic regions. Burgos has discussed some of these methods in 'World trends in agroclimatic surveys' (Burgos, 1968). A few of the well known ones, and those proposed recently in India, are discussed here.

Visher's methods of comparing agricultural potentials

On the basis of environmental and crop-yield studies Visher (1955) made a generalized classification of regions of the world, using the parameters of their agricultural potentials. He recognised eighty regions of the world on the following criteria :

Percentage of land under agriculture.

Average rank of crop land.

Average suitability of crops.

Seven criteria were used to determine the suitability for crop raising. These were:

   average topographic suitability
   average soil quality
   average warmth adequacy
   average precipitation adequacy
   suitability of precipitation time distribution
   weather dependability
   accessibility to market

A rating of each of these criteria was given in the following order:

lacking or nearly so	= 0
poor, little or low	= 1
medium, average or fair	= 2
above average or good	= 3
superior, excellent or large	= 4

A summarization of scores for the criteria gives a generalized but comparative evaluation of the regions.

Visher does not claim that this method of evaluation was faultless. The criteria used in rating scores are highly qualitative, and the regions demarcated are generalized and offer no practical utility.

Selianinov's method

Selianinov (1957) demarcated the agroclimatic regions of the USSR. The method is discussed by Burgos (1968). Selianinov first established the broad zones on the following criteria:

sum of active temperature
duration of growth period
photoperiod in summer and winter

Zones demarcated on the above criteria were further divided into agroclimatic regions on the basis of the following criteria:

annual soil moisture regime
spring reserve of moisture
type of rainfall
frequency of dry period
evaporation
drainage

The agroclimatic regions based upon these criteria were further divided into sub-regions. The criteria used were:

degree of frost danger
duration of vegetative period
snow depth and duration
frequency of droughts

The classification of Selianinov is very comprehensive and appears very suitable, especially for areas with vast latitudinal extent. Another merit of this classification is that most of the data used is easily available, while the rest can be interpolated.

Uchijima's method

A heat balance climatological method of agroclimatic classification is proposed by Uchijima (1962). The method is discussed by Yoshino (1974). Uchijima proposed a radiative dry index which is calculated as :

$$\text{Radiative dry index} = \frac{SW}{lr}$$

where SW = Sum of net radiation during cultivation period

l = Latent heat of evaporation

r = Sum of rainfall during cultivation period

The following index of accumulated water temperature is also proposed :

Lable	Summation of water temperature	Thermal condition
A	$3000 > \sum O_w$	— Unfavourable for rice pla··
B	$3000 - 4000$	— Less favourable for rice plant
C	$4000 - 5000$	— Very favourable for rice plant
D	$5000 - < \sum O_w$	— Favourable for double cropping.

O_w = Temperature of Water °C

Using these indices he delineated the regions of Japan showing agroclimatic environment for rice areas.

The radiative dry index used in this method is similar to that of Budyko (1956) except that net radiation values in this case are for the water surface.

Thran and Broakhuizen method

Thran and Broakhuizen (1965) proposed the agroclimatic regions of Europe. They used the following criteria:

annual rainfall

annual temperature

temperature of the warmest month

temperature of the coldest month

specific characters of temperature and rainfall.

The authors demarcrated 76 agroclimatic regions of the continent and described their main agroclimatic characteristics and potential. The classification does not pay any attention to photoperiodism which is an important factor in plant distribution in areas having wide latitudinal extent.

Hargreaves method

Hargreaves (1971) proposed a classification of climates on the basis of the degree of moisture adequacy or deficit for agricultural production. He defined a moisture availability index MAI as a ratio $\frac{PD}{PE}$, where PD is the amount of precipitation at 75% probability level, and PE is the potential evapotranspiration. His classification for agriculture on the basis of monthly values of MAI is as follows:

S.No.	Criteria	Climate	Productivity classification
1.	All monthly values of MAI range between 0.00 to 0.33	Very arid	Not suitable for rainfed agriculture
2.	One or two months with MAI 0.34 or above	Arid	Limited suitability for rainfed agriculture
3.	Three to four months with MAI 0.34 or above	Semi-arid	Production possible for crops requiring 4–8 months
4.	Five or more consecutive months with MAI 0.34 or above.	Wet-dry	Production possible for crops requiring a good level of moisture

The major limitation of the method lies in the difficulty in estimating dependable precipitation. The need for long time-series data further restricts the use of this method in many areas.

OMAI index

Sarker and Biswas (1980) made an agroclimatic classification of India by modifying the Hargreaves MAI as Optimum Moisture Availability Index ($OMAI$). The Index proposed by the authors is :

$$OMAI = \frac{\text{Assumed Rainfall (At 50\% probability level)}}{\text{Potential Evapotranspiration}}$$

They used a scale of increasing $OMAI$ and denoted it in alphabetical order, in this form:

Classification	No. of weeks of OMAI	
	at 0.3	at 0.7
D	10	1
E	10	1
F	11	4
G	14	7

Papadakis method

In defining the agroclimatic regions, more on ecological factors rather than on simple meteorological characteristics, the contribution of J. Papadakis is great. Papadakis (1966) proposed the climatic classification on the basis of winter severity, summer warmth, seasonal distribution and availability of moisture. The scale of winter severity is based on the resistance of crops; and the scale of summer warmth by the series of crops with higher and higher requirements. Moisture classifications are defined on the basis of precipitation/saturation deficit relationships. Later he (Papadakis, 1975) introduced the concept of monthly climate which he claims to be simpler. This classification is based on thermic and hydric indices. In the thermic scale he takes into account

Average daily maximum temperature (T)

Average daily minimum temperature (t)

Average of the lowest temperature (t^1)

Thus T, t and t^1 are the indices of day temperature, night temperature and frost risk respectively.

The hydric scale is based on water balance which is calculated

as

$$\frac{P + W}{E}$$

P = Precipitation

W = Water stored in the soil

E = Monthly potential evapotranspiration

Papadakis has given the details of the definitions of thermic and hydric index classes in meteorological terms (Papadakis, 1975).

The introduction of the concept of monthly climate, permitted the use of graphic representation of the climate. Each monthly climate is shown by a point whose co-ordinates show thermic and hydric type, and by joining the twelve points a climograph can be prepared. The climographs vary in position, length, width and shape and hence show peculiarities of each climate. These can be prepared on transparent paper for comparison, or on computer cards from where climates of common characteristics can be sorted out.

The major limitation of this classification is that it is very complex, and has a very large number of sub-groups.

Williams, Mckenzie and Shepard's Technique of Computer Mapping

Williams, Mckenzie and Shepard (1980) delimited the meso-scale agroclimatic regions of the Peace River Region in Canada, with the help of a computer. Spatial climatic equations were used to estimate the thermal climate of eighty five points which represent the topography of the area. Crop development and freeze data, also determined using equations, were then applied to the point estimates of thermal climate—to assess the suitability for maturing barley and wheat, and were delineated on maps with the SYMAP computer programme. The flow chart of the system used, in analysing and mapping the agroclimatic resources, is given on page 219.

This method appears useful for delimiting the agroclimatic regions of frontier areas, where limited meterological data are available. It however, suffers from a number of flaws and cannot be used in every situation.

12.4 Methods of Agroclimatic Regionalisation for Small Geographical Areas

For small geographical areas in tropical and subtropical countries like India, a uniform diffusion of temperature and photoperiod simplifies to some extent, the problem of delimiting the agroclimatic regions. In these areas it is well recognised that any classification using rainfall and evaporation as the inputs, depicts the ecological characteristics better than other variables. This is due to the fact that moisture adequacy is the major determinant of crop success in these areas, and the moisture availability to the crops is a function of these two elements. However, classifications using precipitation and evaporation inputs define only the humid periods for crop growth. Therefore, the better classifications are those which add soil moisture storage as the other variable in proposing a bioclimatic index, or indices, for delineating the agroclimatic regions. Some of the methods using such indices, for defining the agroclimatic regions in India, are given on next page.

Flow Diagram of Computer Mapping for Agroclimatic Resource
(Williams, Mckenzie, Shepard, 1980)

A	Select study area and topography maps

↓

B	Select points (locations) to represent topography.

↓

C	Use spatial climatic equations based on 1931–60 data, to estimate monthly normals of daily maximum and minimum temperatures for altitude, longitude and latitude.

↓   ↓

D	Use Phenological Dev. equations with temp and photoperiod, reach various stages at each point.	E	Use Freeze data equations to estimate normal, first fall freeze at each point.

↓   ↓

F	For each point, calculate estimated normal number of days from wheat and barley maturity to first fall freeze, if maturity would be reached.

↓

G	Using the information for all the points as to whether the crop would mature, and if so, how long before the first freeze; and using the UTM easting as x and northings as y Co-ordinates, map with SYMAP the climatic resources of the study area for maturing each crop.

↓

H	Reduce the estimated temperature by a given amount, and repeat the calculations and mapping to simulate the possible effect of colder climate.

Krishnan and Mukhtar Singh's method

Krishnan and Mukhtar Singh (1972) divided India into agroclimatic regions on the basis of moisture and thermal indices. The moisture index (MI) is calculated as:

$$MI = \frac{P - PET}{PET} \times 100$$

where MI = Moisture index

P = Precipitation

PET = Potential evapotranspiration

The thermal index (TI) is calculated as:

$$TI = \frac{T \text{ max.} + T \text{ min.}}{2}$$

The moisture index scale recognised eight climates, **and the** thermal index five climates, as given below:

Climates on the basis of moisture index

S.No.	Moisture index value	Climatic group
1.	< -80	Extremely dry
2.	-80 to -60	Semi-dry
3.	-60 to -40	Dry
4.	-40 to -20	Slightly dry
5.	-20 to 0	Slightly moist
6.	0 to 50	Moist
7.	50 to 100	Wet
8.	> 100	Extremely wet

Climates on the basis of thermal index

Zone	Thermal index	Climatic group
A	$> 28°C$	Very hot
B	$25°$ to $28°C$	Hot
C	$20°$ to $25°C$	Mild
D	$10°$ to $20°C$	Cold
E	$< 10°C$	Very cold

The climatic zones based on thermal and moisture indices were super-imposed on a soil map of India to demarcate the agroclimatic. regions of the country.

The authors feel that the major defect of this classification lies in its non-consideration of the soil moisture factor. Further, the thermal scale chosen to define the zones is most elementary, and the limits with mean values have no specific significance in agriculture.

The Method Used by NCA

The National Commission on Agriculture (1976) delineated the agroclimatic regions of each state of India, and evaluated the relationship between the patterns of rainfall, agriculture and live-stock. Because of lower variability, ready availability and greater facility in handling—monthly totals of rainfall formed the criteria of delimiting the regions. The methodology adopted is as follows:

Rainfall pattern and rainfall zone : A distribution of monthly rainfall which is the same over two or more area units, is defined as a rainfall pattern, and the area covered is defined as a rainfall zone.

Cropping pattern: A distribution of crops, the total area of which is not less than 70% of the gross cropped area, and is the same over two or more of the adjoining areas, is defined as the cropping pattern for the area.

Twelve months are arranged in three groups of four months each, and the rainfall intensity is coded as

A = rainfall > 30 mm

B = rainfall   20 to 30 mm

C = rainfall   20 to 10 mm

D = rainfall   10 to 5 mm

E = rainfall < 5 mm

The cropping pattern is coded and the first alphabet of the word stands for the crop. In the cropping pattern, the percentage area occupied by the crop is indicated on the foot of the code word. An example of the agroclimatic regions, delineated on the basis of the above criteria, is given below for Punjab.

Rainfall Zone of Punjab and Associated
Cropping Patterns

Zone	Rainfall pattern	Cropping pattern
I	$E_4 (D_2 E_2) E_4$	$W_{24} F_{18} C_{30} G_{10}$
II	$E_4 (D_3 E_1) E_4$	$W_{27} F_{13} C_{24} G_{17}$
III	$E_4 (C_2 D_1 E_1) E_4$	$W_{43} F_{15} P_7 M_9$
IV	$E_4 (C_3 D_1) E_4$	$W_{45} F_{11} P_7 M_{12}$
V	$E_4 (B_1 C_2 E_1) E_4$	$W_{46} F_{11} P_7 M_{23}$
VI	$E_4 (B_2 C_1 E_1) E_4$	$W_{34} F_{13} P_{14} M_{17}$
VII	$F_4 (A_2 C_1 D_1) E_4$	$W_{26} F_6 P_{18} M_{18}$

This method of classification suffers from a number of serious drawbacks. No consideration has been given to evaporation which is so important in tropical crop production. Soil moisture storage has also not been considered. Further, the monthly total of rainfall carries no significance in an area like Punjab where its variability is extremely high.

Duggal's method:

Duggal and Ram (1978) delineated the agroclimatic regions of the Indus Basin (India) on the basis of the quantity of annual rainfall, the variability of rainfall, and the degree of irrigation needed. He recognised eight regions according to the scales given below:

S. No.	Rainfall (mm)	Variability of rainfall (%)	Degree of irrigation needed
1.	< 500	> 50	Exceptionally high
2.	< 500	30–50	Very high
3.	500–800	30–50	I igh
4.	500–800	20–35	Moderately high
5.	800–1000	20–35	Medium
6.	1000–1250	20–35	Moderately low
7.	1250–2000	15–25	Low
8.	> 2000	< 15	Exceptionally low

This method suffers from two major drawbacks. The annual rainfall and its variability limits chosen, have no ecological significance.

Sharma, Singh and Yadav's method

Sharma, Singh and Yadav (1978) delineated the agroclimatic regions of Haryana (India), with the objective of locating the ecological optimum for important crops of the state; and to indicate the meteorological indices for the crops grown in these environments. The state was divided into seven agroclimatic regions on the basis of the moisture index which is calculated as:

$$\text{Moisture index} = \frac{P + I - PET}{PET} \times 100$$

where $P =$ Precipitation (cm)

  $I =$ Irrigation water (cm per unit area)

  $PET =$ Potential evapotranspiration (cm)

To arrive at homogenous zones, the following moisture index scale was used :

Number	Zone	Moisture Index
I	Extremely dry	< -70
II	Dry	-50 to -70
III	Semidry	-20 to -50
IV	Slightly dry	0 to -20
V	Slightly moist	0 to 20
VI	Moist	20 to 50
VII	Wet	50 to 100
VIII	Extremely wet	> 100

The authors have compared the productivity of these regions and have established their separate identity. The use of seasonal values of precipitation however, is not a very reliable input to establish the real ecological patterns.

Reddy's Method:

Reddy (1983) proposed a method for computation of classificatory variables, for agroclimatic classification of agronomically homogenous zones. This method was based upon rainfall (R) and potential evapotranspiration (PE). A term *available effective rainy period* was introduced for this purpose. He defined it as the number of consecutive weeks in which the fourteen week moving average of R/PE is 0.75, but for the first week the value of R/PE is 0.5. The second week is taken to be the week of commencement of the sowing rains.

It is claimed that the method permits estimation of wet and dry spells during the available effective rainy period; an estimate of the likely percentage of crop failures; and production potentials in different regions.

Mavi and Mahi's method:

Mavi and Mahi (1978) proposed a weekly soil moisture index for the summer season, to delineate the agroclimatic regions of Punjab. The moisture index is calculated as:

$$I = \frac{R + Sm}{PE}$$

where $I =$ Soil moisture index

$R =$ Rainfall at 25% probability level (mm)

$Sm =$ Soil moisture stored in the root zone (mm)

$PE =$ Open-pan evaporation (mm).

Based upon this index, the authors delineated seven agroclimatic regions of Punjab, and assessed the suitability of each of the regions for growing crops with and without irrigation. The authors claim the merits of this index score over the others, as a weekly soil moisture balance is nearer the reality in determining the success or failure of crops, when compared to a monthly or seasonal index.

The method used by Mavi et al.

Mavi *et al.* (1979) delineated the agroclimatic regions of Punjab State. The following criteria were used :

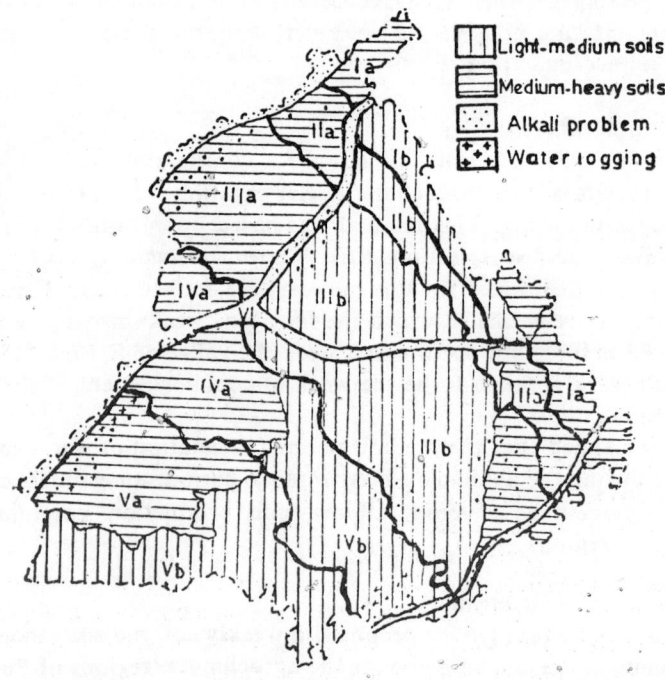

Fig. 12.1   Agroclimatic Regions of Punjab (See Table 12.1)

Main criteria	Sub criteria
1. Physiography	relief
	slope
2. Rainfall	annual
3. Soil moisture	weekly soil moisture index for the kharif season, estimated with the method proposed by Mavi (1978).
4. Soil quality	texture
	alkalinity
	salinity
	water-logging
5. Underground water reservoir	depth of water bearing strata fitness of water for irrigation

Maps of relief, annual rainfall and underground water availability and quality, were superimposed and six main regions were identified. A further study of soil characteristics, and a weekly soil moisture index for the monsoon season of the main regions, resulted in eleven sub-regions. These regions are shown in Fig. 12.1, and their major characteristics are summarised in Table 12.1. These regions reveal their individuality through general environment, ecological characteristics and cropping patterns.

In the author's opinion, an agroclimatic region which represents a uniform resource base for agriculture, should consider all those variables of the physical environment which directly and indirectly have a bearing on crop production. Thus, regions delineated on the basis of homogeneity of physiography, climate, soil, quality and quantity of underground water reservoir and soil moisture storage—identify and present meaningful, significant patterns of environmental conditions, ecological characteristics, and agricultural potentials and problems. Such regions are useful for planners ; for a uniform development of the state; for the management and conservation of natural resources; for reclamation schemes; for bringing adjustments in cropping patterns; for irrigation planning ; and for all the information on crop production which is of agronomic relevance.

REFERENCES

Anonymous. 1976. Report of the National Commission on Agriculture. Part IV. Climatic and Agriculture, Govt. of India, New Delhi: 125-477.

Budyko, M.I. 1956. The Heat Balance of the Earth Surface (English translation from Russian). U.S. Department of Commerce, Washington D.C. 1985.

Burgos, J J. 1968. World trends in agroclimatic surveys. Proceedings of the Reading Symposium on Agro-climatological Methods, UNESCO, Paris: 211-221.

Duggal, S.L. and Daya Ram. 1978. Comparative Production Levels and Potentials in the Agroclimatic Regions of Indus Basin. Proceedings of the Symposium on Land and Water Management in the Indus Basin (India). Vol. II, PAU, Ludhiana: 116-124.

Hargreaves, G.H. 1971. Precipitation dependability and potential for agricultural production in North-East Brazil, EMPRAPA and Utah State University, Publication No. 75-D 158.

Krishnan, A. 1978 A Study of Climatic Delineation and Duration of Crop Growing Season in Indus Basin Proceedings of the Symposium on Land and Water Management in the Indus Basin (India). Vol. II, PAU, Ludhiana: 91-96.

Krishnan, A. and Mukhtar Singh. 1972. Soil Climate Zones in Relation to Cropping Patterns. Proceedings of the Symposium on Cropping Patterns in India, ICAR, New Delhi: 172-185.

Mavi, H.S. and Gian Singh Mahi. 1978. Agroclimatic Regions of Punjab Based on Summer (Kharif) Season Moisture Stress. Proceedings of the Symposium on Land and Water Management in the Indus Basin (India). Vol. II, PAU, Ludhiana: 27-38.

Mavi, H.S., D.S. Tiwana, S.S. Grewal, Raghbir Singh, Bhajan Singh, N.T. Singh, S.D. Khcpar and S.K. Sondhi. 1979. Agroclimatic Regions of the Punjab. Research Bulletin, PAU.

Papadakis, J. 1966. Climates of the World and Their Agricultural Potential. Buenos Aires.

Papadakis, J. 1975. Climates of the World and Their Potentials. Buenos Aires.

Reddy, S. Jeevananda. 1983. Agroclimatic classification of semi-arid tropics. A method for computation of classificatory variables. Agric. Meteorol. 30: 185-200.

Sarker, R.P. and B.C. Biswas. 1980. Climatic Classification. A Consultants Meeting. ICRISAT. 89-107.

Sharma, H.C., Phool Singh and B.S. Yadav. 1978. Principal Climatic Stress and Meteorological Indices for Important Crops in the Semi-arid Region of Indus Basin. Proceedings of the Symposium on Land and Water Management in the Indus Basin (India). Vol. II, 11-20, PAU, Ludhiana : 20-26

Thornthwaite, C.W. 1948. An approach towards a rational classification of climate. Geographical Review, 38: 55-94.

Thran, P. and S. Broekhuizen. S. 1965. Agroecological atlas of cereal growing in Europe. Vol. I. Agroclimatic Atlas of Europe, 36.

Visher, S.S. 1955. Comparative Agricultural Potentials of the World Regions. Econ. Geog. 31: 12–86.

Williams, G.D.V., J.S. Mckenzie and M.I. Shepard. 1980. Mesoscale Agroclimatic Resource Mapping by Computer. An Example for the Peace River Region of Canada. Agric. Meteorol. 21: 93–109.

Wilsie, Carroll P. 1962. Crop Adaptation and Distribution. Freeman and Co. : 313–342.

Yoshino, Masatoshi M. 1974. Agricultural Climatology in Japan. Agricultural Meteorology of Japan, Ed. Yoshiaki Mihara. Univ. of Tokyo Press: 19–21.

CHAPTER 13

MODELLING CROP GROWTH AND PRODUCTION

Traditionally, the scientific methods in biological sciences take a whole mechanism and then divide it into pieces small enough to be preceived. The advent of computer has, however, enabled the scientists to preceive the entire mechanism as a whole rather than as separate parts. This new methodology in biological sciences is referred as dynamic simulation. The dynamic simulation models along with experimental research in agriculture holds a great promise to expand scientific insight, into complex biological systems and will result in huge economic benefits. For thorough understanding of crop-microclimate interactions, and interactions amongst soil, crop insects, weeds and weather, the simulation of these interactions is the best approach. The better understanding of these interactions through simulation modelling will help in controlling the productive ecosystems in an efficient manner. The simulation models will ultimately become the sole tools to be used in policy planning in the field of agriculture.

13.1   What is a Model

A model is a schematic representation of our conception of a system. In a general term, a model brings into mind the thoughts about the form and functional form of a real object, like children's toy, tailor's dummies and mock-ups of building and structure to be later constructed in the real forms. Models also construct the objects or situations not yet in existence in real form. A model can also be referred as a representation of relationship under consideration and may be defined as an act of mimicry.

13.2 Types of Models

Norman (1979) divided the models into three arbitrary categories: simple statistical models, parameterization models and analog-physical models.

Simple Statistical or Empirical Statistical models are those which do not require the detailed information about the plant involved but rely mainly on the statistical techniques such as cor-relation or regression to the appropriate plant and environmental variables. Most statistical models are crop-yield weather models which are applied to estimate yield over large areas with variable success. The regression coefficients themselves are not necessarily related to the important processes and thus are highly variables with crop type, region, etc. Many studies are required to produce the regression equations necessary for the wide spread application of this kind of models. A great advantage of these simple crop-weather models is that they use readily available weather data.

Regression models are attractive because of their simple and straight forward relation between yield and one or more environmental factors, but these are not accurate enough to be used for other areas and other crops. Inspite of this limitation, these are used extensively for the prediction of yield of a single crop over a large region with a variety of soils, agronomic practices and insect-disease problems; a combination of such factors is still beyond the dynamic simulation models.

Parameterization or Crop-Weather analysis models involve the use of differential equations and contain numerous unknown parameters that must be related to properties of the plant and its environment. These models provide information similar to the observed results. The detailed formulation of the models determine whether they are statistical in nature or are closer to the physical models.

Analog-physical models are most detailed plant-environment formulations. This name is used because whenever possible physical models or submodels are used.

The parameterization and analog-physical or complex-physiological models are referred as simulation models.

13.3 Dynamic Simulation Models

Hume and Callander (1990) proposed that a dynamic model is the one whose output varies with time and in which processes are characterised. To characterise processes the state variables must be known. State variables are those necessary to define the state of the system at a point in time. The dynamic simulation crop models predict changes in crop status with time as a function of biogeneous parameters. As example, model which predicts soil water content at a certain depth throughout the season or the one which predicts changing number of bolls on a cotton plant with the march of season are dynamic simulation models.

Simulation means that model acts like a real crop, gradually germinating, growing leaves, stem and roots during the season. In other words, simulation is the process of using a model dynamically by following a system over a time period.

Penning de Vries *et al* (1989) classified the dynamic models as preliminary models, comprehensive models and the summary models. Preliminary models have structure and data that reflect current scientific knowledge. These are simple because insight is at the explanatory level. A comprehensive model is a model of a system of which essential elements are thoroughly understood and in which much of this knowledge is incorporated. Summary models are abstracts of comprehensive models and are found at the levels of production. Models for the lowest production levels are predominantly of the preliminary type. The models of these developmental phases differ considerably in their value for instruction, for prediction, for scientific research, and in simplicity.

Models are also classified on the basis of input output relationships. When the outcome of the model is described in terms of input, the model is named as deterministic. In these models the same input will result in exactly the same output. In cases where some of the processes in the model vary according to some distribution and correspondingly the outcome varies randomly, the model is said to be stochastic. Crop models are mostly deterministic because all plants are of a single genotype and are exposed to a single starting time and a single environment. The deterministic approach provides a prediction of mean behaviour, following the law of large numbers. On a small scale (one cell, one plant), however, there can be large departures from that mean. Methods for introducing probabilistic elements into initial conditions and rate variables are readily available in computer languages for the stochastic models. However, these models are infested with a number of problems. As an example, the "noise" generated by realistic stochastic treatment of 100 variables over 1000 iterations can exceed by many orders of magnitude the variation found in real system.

No doubt, comprehensive dynamic models predict yield much nearer to the reality than the regression models do. However, the more accurate the dynamic model is, the more information is required for initialization and about driving variables. In many of the cases these may not be available, hence the regression models may still be our best option.

Systems analysis is the basis for the development of dynamic simulation models. The word system is commonly used in general sense and usually the meaning inferred is of a complex set of related components within a autonomous frame work. Systems analysis is a procedure for planning, designing, evaluating studying of synthesis and analysis used by various disciplines and incorporates into its procedure, the principles and concepts of science. Computers are used to integrate these elements into a comprehensive process for design, evaluation or study.

A dynamic crop simulation model is most successfully developed by a multi-disciplinary team (Peart and Barrett, 1979). An Agrometeorologist contributes weather data and microclimate fluxes in and around the plant canopies. An Agricultural Engineer, a specialist in system modelling technique, selects the computer language and develops the overall framework of the model. Plant Physiologists, Agronomists and Soil Scientists are needed to help define the overall framework of the problem and define the specificities of the environment and plant growth relationship. Entomologists and Plant Pathologists are required to define the insect and pathogen sub-systems which are the important parts in the crop ecosystems.

13.4 Hierarchy of Models

Peart and Barrett (1979) observed that the concept of the hierarchy of the models is useful to indicate the degree of details and breadth of the scope needed for a particular model. Fig. 13.1 reproduced from his paper represents this hierarchy ranging from world model (used to relate population, food and natural resources) to a micro-component model of processes within a crop.

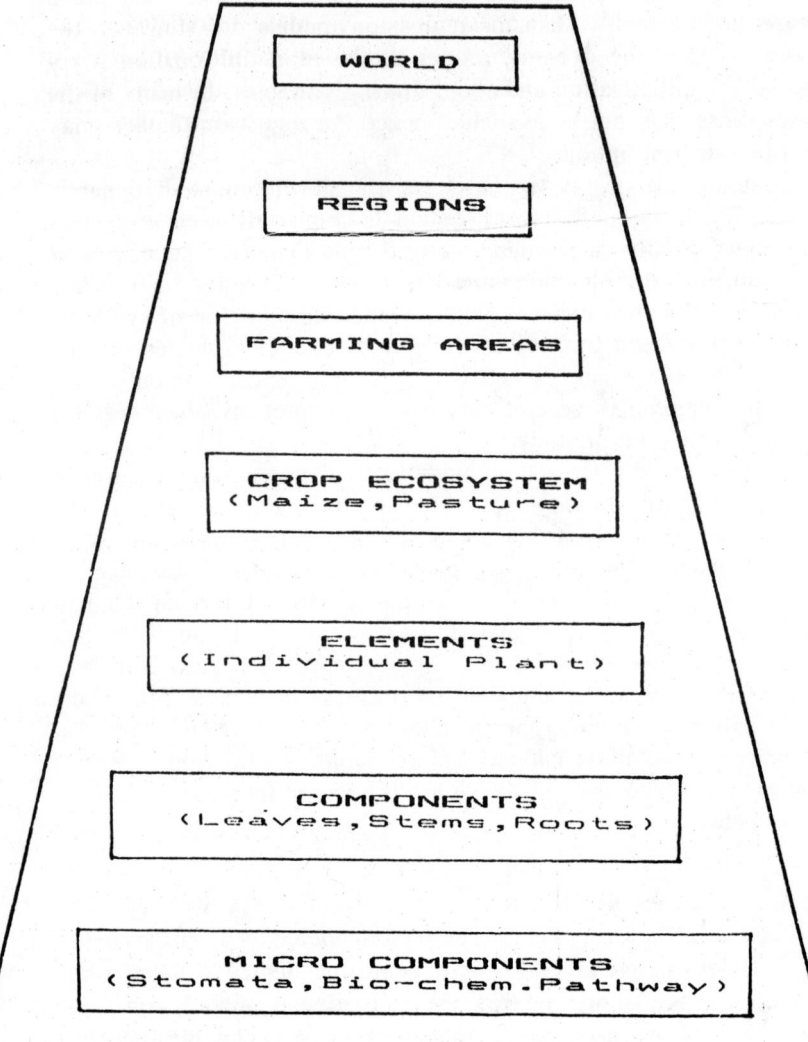

Fig. 13.1 Hierarchy of Models used in Agriculture.

Miles (1974) differentiated the crop ecosystem models from that of element models because of more details involved in those and they also provided output similar to plant physiological research data. The crop ecosystem models, on the other hand, provide output data more nearly like the results of field plot or farm field demonstration results. Models such as those for leaf stomata or plant biochemical reactions are even more detailed and they are closer to the base of modelling hierarchy pyramid. These distinctions do not imply higher importance or complexity for any level of modelling but rather serve to emphasize the appropriate selection of a model based on the desired use.

13.5 Major Characteristics of the Simulation Models

The models are designed to solve specific problems. In order to make their use for diverse purposes and to make them transportable from one region to other, the models should have the following characteristics (Ritchie *et al.*, 1986):

* Use readily available weather, soil and genetic inputs;
* Be written in a familiar and widely used computer language;
* Require minimal computational time;
* Be adoptable for use on both mainframe and micro-computer.

13.6 Steps Involved in Building a Simulation Model

A flow chart of the steps involved in the construction of a simulation model (reproduced from Dent and Balckie, 1979 with some modifications) is presented in Fig. 13.2. These steps are enumerated as follows:

a) Defining the purpose of the model
b) Defining the systems and its boundaries
c) Developing the structure of the model with sufficient accuracy for the unknown parameters
d) Solving the problem of identifying the parameters for the model on the basis of available data
e) Utilizing the results from experiences to determine the range of input and output variables
f) Testing the adequacy of the model i.e. verification of the

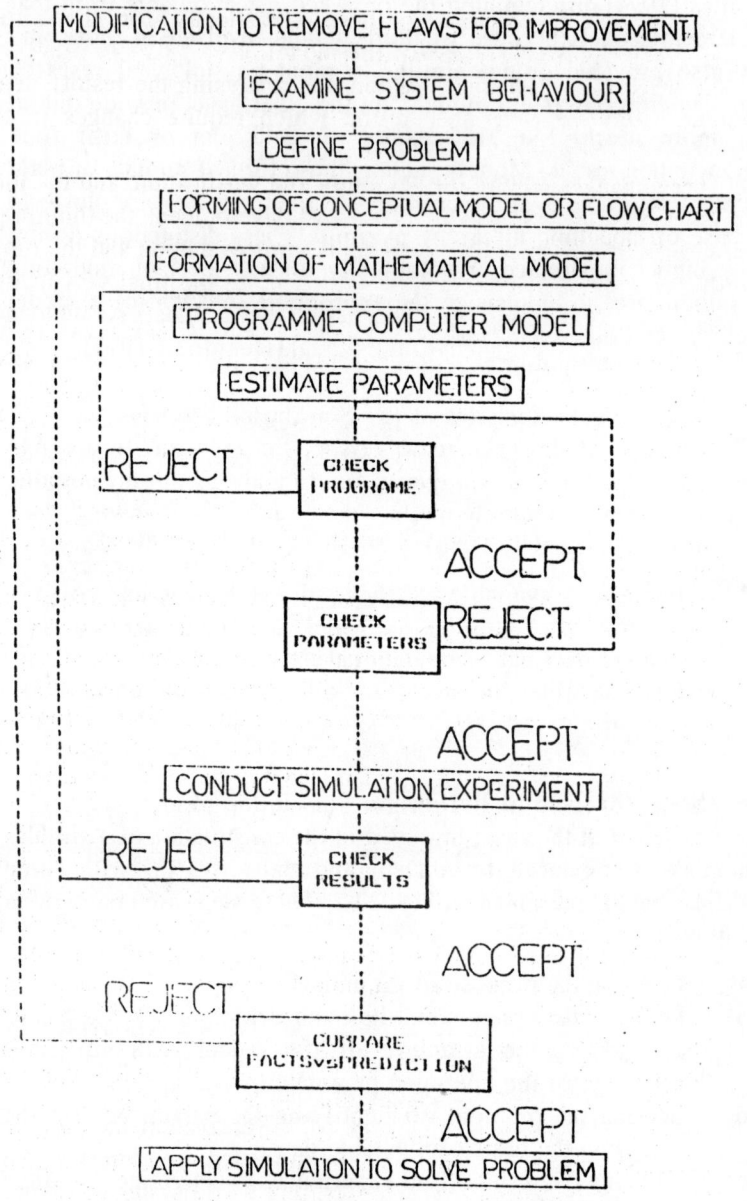

Fig. 13.2 Phases in Construction of a Simulation Model.

results by analysing these statistically for the entire development process of the model.

After designing the first version and analysing the results of its output, faults are invariably found which require changes in the structure of the model.

These changes require further study and verification, and the loop continues. Furthermore, in the process of development, the initial representation of the modelling process is improved upon and the range of the experimental data used is widened. In the final verification process, it is important to consider an independent data set which are not used in the development of the model (Guardrian, 1977).

13.7 Input Data for the Simulation Models

The possibility of using any method of calculation largely depends on the nature and amount of the initial data necessary for the calculations. The data requirement of the dynamic simulation model is divided into following four groups:

a) Constants of time and location-latitude, longitude and altitude.

b) Soil coefficients—soil texture, water holding capacity, chemical properties, etc.

c) Crop coefficients—response to vernalization and photoperiod, tiller formation, leaf appearance rate, grain filling rate and duration etc.

d) Meteorological data—the minimum data required include solar radiation, maximum and minimum temperature and precipitation. In addition, some models use wind speed, relative humidity data also.

13.8 Verification and Validation

Verification and validation are two terms used synonymously in modelling. It is important to describe these words in clear terms wherever these are used. In a literal context "to verify" means "to test the truthfulness or correctness of". Verification therefore certifies that the functional relationships modelled are correct by comparing historical data recorded for the real world systems to what in fact the computer gives as the output of the model used to simulate the real world system. If a model does not behave according to expectations then some correction of the functional relationship may be necessary, or coefficients may need to be adjusted. The latter is called calibrating the model and is an elementary aspect of verification.

Validation, on the other hand, is concerned with the comparison of model predictions with results from independent experiments. Models can be considered valid and useful even though there may be some differences between experimental data and simulation output. If the simulated values lie within the projected confidence band, then the model can be considered valid. The confidence range of the measured experimental data can be fixed by statistical analysis.

In a nutshell, 'Verification' is used for evaluation with emphasis on truthfulness, while 'Validation' is used as evaluation with emphasis on usefulness and relevance of the model.

13.9 Applications of the Models

All models have some value except for those kept in files. Some are scientifically interesting, others are utilised to predict and their results are applied in other fields, and some models are largely used for instructive purposes. But all models have some value in one or the other fields.

A scientifically interesting model contributes to our understanding of the real world because it helps to integrate the relevant processes of the system studied and to bridge areas and levels of knowledge. It helps also to test hypothesis, to generate alternative ones and to suggest experiments to falsify them. Briefly, the scientific value of a model is its contribution to the development of science. A good predictive model simulates accurately the behaviour of a part of the real world in situations where its behaviour has been, or has not yet been, observed. It is therefore a good instrument to apply scientific knowledge in practice. It should predict reasonably well over a range of boundary conditions, to provide its users with alternative solutions of a problem. Good scientific models are often too detailed or too speculative for those who want to apply them, whilst models used for predictive or management purposes are often too trivial or too crude to challenge scientific interest.

Whisler et al. (1986) describe a wide range of major areas in which the application of the models is well established:

Crop Breeding

There are many simulation models which use the genetic characters in the form of rate coefficients or other system constants in crop growth. These coefficients or constants can be evaluated during the validation and sensitivity processes. Duncan *et al.* (1978) have shown with a simulation model of peanut, dramatic yield increases solely from changes in flowering time and some aspect of photosynthates partitioning. The breeding work can thus be undertaken to trade-off these useful characters so as to produce high yielding, insect-disease resistant cultivars capable of competing with weeds.

Physiological Probes

With the traditional scientific techniques, it is almost impossible to obtain data on many physiological processes which are very important from crop physiology point of view. For example, Whisler *et al.* (1986) stated that turgor pressure in the cells is the main driving force for leaf expansion, but unfortunately, it can not be measured directly. These can only be inferred from the measurements made on some other characters using a dynamic simulation model.

If the models are comprehensive in nature, these can then be tested for various growth processes and can help in eliminating the unrealistic hypothesis saving our time and energy. Furthermore, the exercising on a model may give rise to many more experiments to test various hypothesis. This is the way by which the models can be used to probe the physiology of the plants which is not experimentally accessible. Modelling and experimentation can be mutually supportive in developing our understanding of the crop physiology.

Insect and Disease Development

It is an established fact that insect and disease occurrence and development is very closely related to the accumulated and prevailing weather conditions. The models are being used to study the development of the harmful insect-pests and diseases and also being used to apply the chemicals at such a stage so as to reap the maximum economic benefit by involving the minimum chemicals in order to avoid the occurrence of environmental imbalance. According to Loomis *et al.* (1979), most entomological models emphasize the description of insect population, with stochastic submodels to simulate the infection and spread of insects. Combined models have been developed for cotton (Gutierrez *et al.*, 1977, Jones *et al.*, 1975 and Wang *et al.*, 1977), alfalfa (Gutierrez *et al.*, 1976), apple (Rabbinge, 1976), corn (Waggoner *et al.*, 1972) and wheat (Zadoks *et al.*, 1984) to simulate pest or disease development and expected injury to the crops. In some cases these combined models have led to formulation of simplified models for decisions about spraying or not spraying. The combined models also offer a tool for examining biological efficiencies (energy and nutrient transfer) in host-parasite couplings.

Farm Management Decisions

The farmers, in general, have to take farm management decisions on seasonal and on short range basis. On seasonal basis, farmers have to decide about how much area to be planted, when to be planted, which variety to plant, which and how much inputs are needed to be procured. On short range or daily basis, a farmer has to decide when to irrigate, apply fertilizer, spray the crop for control of insect-pests, diseases and weeds, etc.

The packages of management practices are evolved by various agricultural institutions for the respective states. Some farmers follow these practices. i.e. they irrigate according to the schedule given in these practices. Some other follow the established traditions of their area (spraying chemicals when their neighbours are doing so), some other follow their own subjective judgment like replanting the crop if the crop stand looks too thin to produce a reasonable harvest.

These risk management decisions certainly involve the high economic cost. According to Whisler *et al.* (1986), the question being asked by the farmers in general is "Would my profit increase if I act in this way?". The crop simulation models help answer these questions. Observed weather data can be used in the model upto the date of forecast and surrogate data to complete the growing season. The surrogate data may be the daily normals. Historical data can be examined to select the years when the weather data in the area, where the model is to be used resembled the outlook for the region. These data can also be used in the model to arrive at certain management decisions. An almost infinite number of combinations of soil type, weather and agricultural practices exist, however, conducting field experiments on all combinations are impossible. Use of simulation models increase the human efficiency by cutting on time and energy on experimentation. With sequential years of weather data, estimate can be provided for weather related variability in water use and yield. This type of service is in operation in a number of countries. In China and Philippines the models are in use to advise the farmers in rice cultivation (Moris, 1987).

Ng and Loomis (1984) used a simulation model to compare the outputs from different crop husbandry measures such as planting densities. Crop modelling is also used for scheduling irrigation in USA (Anon., 1986) and Canada (Singh, *et al.*, 1991). Simple simulation models which can be used for farm management decisions are now available in almost every country.

Expert System

User friendly models (software) have been developed which are capable of performing at the level of a human expert. The major benefit of such a system is to allow an unavailable human expert to be replaced with a computer. IBSNAT has developed such a system which is capable of providing the answer to the difficult queries of the subscribers because it applies what it does know in a relentlessly thorough manner.

This software system is in form of simulation model and work on mode of hypothesising and testing. It hypothesis a scenario for fertilization and irrigation, and then tests the impact of the scenario on the growth, development and yield with hypothesised values.

Applying models as an expert system lead to more effective use of existing knowledge for extension, agronomic and cropping system research and breeding, to more efficient experimentation and for further integrating the scientific disciplines involved in crop production (Penning de Vries *et al.*, 1989). Using these expert systems, crop performance can be predicted for climates where the crop has not been grown before, or not grown under optimal conditions. This has been used for wheat in Zambia (van Keulen and de Malliano, 1983) and Southeast Asia (Aggarwal and Penning de Vries, 1989). Even though the output may not be accurate, it is probably as good as an expert opinion, and is much easier to get.

Yield Prediction

Crop yields can be predicted sometimes before harvest by using the expected weather data. This is one of the foremost applications of the crop simulation models. Various models (Jones and Kiniry, 1986) have been built to predict the performance of a particular cultivar, sown at any time, on any soil, in any climate. This has been achieved with varying level of success (Hodges *et al.*, 1987, Liu *et al.*, 1989). Long range weather forecasts are not yet possible, however, using a range of expected weather pattern, a fork of yield expectation can be established. As the season progresses, the shorter and narrower the fork becomes and better commercial options are arrived at. The accuracy in the production forecast can help the decision makers in forming the policies for public distribution of such commodities, transportation, storage and price regulations.

The brief review of the available literature outlines the importance of crop modelling in agricultural planning and development. These models are extensively used in the West to assist in crop yield predictions and in policy decision making. In India, the importance of the simulation models is being realised and their use is likely to increase in the years to come. In fact, the simulation models are keys for successful yield prediction, agricultural planning and development in the decades to come.

REFERENCES

Aggarwal, P.K. and F.W.T. Penning de Vries. 1989. Potential production of wheat in Southeast Asia. Agric. Sys., 30: 49-69.

Anon, 1986. Wisconsin Irrigation Scheduling Program. A Computer Tool for Irrigation Management. Developed by the IPM Program University of Wisconsin, WI, USA.

Dent, J.B. and M.J. Blackie. 1979. System Simulation in Agriculture. Applied Science Publishers, London. p. 180.

Duncan, W.G., D.W. McCloud, R.Z. McGraw, and K.J. Boote. 1978. Physiological aspects of peanut yield improvement. Crop Sci., 18: 1015-20.

Guardrian, J. 1977. Crop Micrometeorology: A Simulation Study. PUDDC, Centre for Agric. Publ. and Doc. Wageningen, the Netherlands.

Gutierrez, A.P., T.F. Leigh., Y. Wang, and R.D. Cave. 1977. An analysis of cotton production in California: Lygus hesperus injury-an evaluation. Can. Entomol., 109: 1375-86.

Gutierrez, A.P., J.B. Christensen, C.B. Merritt, W.B. Loew, C.G. Summers, and W.R. Cothran. 1976. Alfalfa and Egyptain alfalfa weevil (Coleoptera, curailionidae). Can. Entomol., 108: 635-48.

Hodges, T., D. Botner., C. Sakamoto, and J.H. Haug. 1987. Using the CERES—Maize model to estimate production for the U.S. Cornbelt. Agric. Meteorol., 40: 293-303.

Hume, C.J. and B.A. Callander. 1990. Agrometeorology and model building. Outlook on Agriculture., 19: 25-30.

Jones, C.A. and J.R. Kiniry. 1986. CERES-Maize. A simulation Model of Maize Grow'ᵗ and Development Texas A&M University Press, Temple, Texas, USA.

Jones, J.W., A.C. Thompson, and J.M. Mckinion. 1975. Developing a computer model with various control methods for eradication of boll weevils. Proc. Beltwide Cotton Prod. Res. Conf. Dallas, USA. p. 118.

Liu, W.T.H., D.M. Botner, and C.M. Sakamoto. 1989. Application of CERES-Maize model to yield predication of a Brazilian Maize hybrid. Agric. Meteorol., 45: 299-312.

Loomis, R.S., R. Rabbinge, and E. Ng. 1979. Explanatory Models in Crop Physiology. Ann. Rev. Plant Physiol., 30: 339-67.

Miles, G.E. 1974. Developing pest management models. Agricultural Experiment Station Research Bulletin No. 50. Purdue Univ., W. Lafayette, IN, USA.

Morris, R.A. 1987. Characterizing rainfall distributions at IRRI cropping systems research sites in Philippines. In: Impact of weather parameters on the growth and yield of rice, International Rice Research Institute, Los Banos. p. 189-214.

Ng, E. and R.S. Loomis. 1984. Simulation of growth and yield of the potato crop. Simulation Monographs, Pudoc. Wageningen, the Netherlands.

Norman, J.M. 1979. Modelling the complete crop canopy. In; Modification of the aerial environment of the crops. ASAE, St. Josephs, Michigan, USA. p. 538.

Peart, R.M. and J.R. Barrett Jr. 1979. The role of simulation. In: Modification of the aerial environment of the crops. ASAE, St. Josephs, Michigan, USA. p. 538.

Penning de Vries, F.W.T., D.M. Jansen, H.F.M. ten Berge, and A. Bakema. 1989. Simulation of ecophysiological processes of growth in several annual crops. Simulation Monograph, Pudoc. Wageningen, the Netherlands.

Rabbinge, R. 1976. Biological control of Fruit-Tree Red Spider mite. Pudoc, Wageningen, the Netherlands.

Ritchie, J.T., J.R. Kiniry, C.A. Jones, and P.T. Dyke. 1986. Model Inputs. In: CERES—Maize. A Simulation Model of Maize Growth and Development. Texas A&M Univ. Press, Temple, TX, USA.

Singh, G., H.S. Mavi, G.S. Mahi, O.S. Singh, O.P. Jhorar and S. Mathauda. 1991. Simulation Models—Tools for Agricultural Planning. Agriculture in Nineties: Challenges and Research Needs. Ed. M.N. Sinha and R.K. Rai. IARI, New Delhi. 22-32.

Van Keulen, H. and W.A.S. de Milliano. 1983. Potential wheat yield in Zambia; a simulation approach. Agric. Sys., 171-192.

Waggoner, P.E., J.G. Horsfall, and R.J. Lukens. 1972. EPIMAY. A simulation of southern corn leaf blight. Conn. Agric. Exp. Sta. Bull, 729. p. 84.

Wang, Y., A.P. Gutierrez. G. Oster, and R. Daxl. 1977. A population model for growth and development: coupling cotton-harbivore interaction. Can Entomol., 109: 1359. 74.

Whisler, F.D., B. Acock, D.N. Baker, R.F. Fye, H.F. Hodges, J.R. Lambert, H.E. Lemmon, J.M. Mckinion, and V.R. Reddy. 1986. Crop simulation models in agronomic systems. Adv. Agron., 40: 141-208.

Zadoks, J.C., F.H. Rijsdijk and R. Rabbinge. 1984. Epipre, a system approach to supervised control of pests and diseases in wheat in the Netherlands. In: G.R. Conway (Ed): Pest and pathogen control: Strategy, tactical and policy models: International series on applied system analysis. Wiley and Sons. 334-351.

Chapter 14

CLIMATE CHANGE AND CROP PRODUCTION

The history of earth's climate for the past 160000 years has been constructed through the analysis of ice and air bubbles that were trapped in the ice when it froze during the course of time. At the time of maximum glaciation, the global mean temperature was supposed to be 5-7°C lower than the present. During the later part of the 13th century AD, temperatures were exceptionally warm over north-western Europe. A pronounced climatic event of the recent past was the little Ice Age between 150 and 450 years back. The decline leading to the Ice Age brought the extinction of Viking Settlement in Greenland. The lowering of the snow line to the extent 200-400 m in Baffin Island during that Age when compared with modern conditions can be accounted for by a summer cooling of about 1.5°C. Following the little Ice Age there was a marked recovery in temperature in the early 20th Century. During the last century earth's climate warmed up by 0.3-0.6°C.

Similar fluctuations are apparent in other parts of the world. Temperature trends in China and Japan compare with those of England. In New Zealand the pattern of fluctuations is the same as that of northern hemisphere. In Chile the information extracted from dendro-climatic reconstruction suggest a long dry period between A.D. 1250 and 1450 and a long wet period from A.D. 1450 to 1600.

During the last 100 to 150 years, for which the records from instruments are available, remarkable climatic fluctuations are identified. During the 20th century abrupt change to warming and then to cooling took place. In Northern-western Europe and North America, records confirm a warming from 1830 to 1930 and then a return to earlier cooling condition.

The Indian subcontinent provides ample evidences to show that the region experienced similar climatic change in the past. Reliable data are available from northwest India suggesting periods with subdued monsoon activity during the recent glacial maxima. The epoch 10,000-4,500 BC experienced warm humid climate with frequent floods. The conditions seem turned more hospitable during the subsequent 1000 year period, when the Harappan civilization flourished in the region. Fluctuations of lake levels and change of salinity of lake sediments also support these century scale changes in the region. The arid conditions with shifting sand dunes are reported to have dominated the region since the last 3000 years or so.

Records of drought occurrence over the Indian subcontinent for the last 200 years are available which indicate that extreme droughts have been occurring due to the high variability of the monsoon rains, Greater frequency of droughts with more number of two consecutive drought years is observed in the 19th century than in the 20th century, which may perhaps suggest an improvement in rainfall amounts with the transition from colder to warmer periods., although the analysis of rainfall series over the past two centuries does not suggest any significant trend (Sikka and Pant, 1991). The mean annual air temperature for the period 1901-88 representing 73 stations of the country shows a significant warming of about 0.4°C/100 years which is comparable to the global mean trend of 0.5°C/100 years.

From the global picture of the recent weather events it looks as if the world climate has gone topsy-turvy. During the last few years, it has rained at wrong times and at wrong places. The weather at many places is amazingly abnormal. Western and Central Europe has experienced the wettest springs. The Alps got a new coat of snow during the month of May which is most unusual. In the eastern Queensland province of Australia floods and subsequently severe droughts have brought havoc to the crops and ranches. In northeast Argentina, heavy rains and consequent floods caused heavy loss to cotton, rice and other crops.

Simultaneously, the reverse of this has been happening in some other areas. When the farmers of North western India were praying for the rains to stop, people as well as the government of Tamil Nadu were asking the scientists to seed the clouds for rain. Southern India was suffering from worst drought and trains were deployed to bring drinking water to Madras city. Drought has also hit Sri Lanka, Bangla Desh, Indonesia and Philippines. Several countries in Africa were in the worst grip of the drought. Ethiopia suffered through a worst drought of this decade with three million people in urgent need of food and water. Republic of South Africa, usually a food surplus country resorted to import, to supplement its drought hit harvest. In Central Mexico, no rainfall has occurred during 2 consecutive years.

What is wrong with the weather? Is it some unique phenomenon or a repetition of the past? Is it going to settle down as a normal weather or will it reverse to the previous weather?

14.1 Probable Causes of Weather and Climate Changes

Natural variability is a characteristic of the global climate and occurs on long and short time scales. Majority of the climatologists believe that both long and short term climatic fluctuations are not a random phenomena, rather these are organised events which are controlled by forces or energy resource either associated with earth itself or with the planetary bodies of our solar system. There is a school of thought which attributes the fluctuations in climate to the periodic tidal pulls exerted by the astronomical bodies on the atmosphere of the earth in a similar fashion as on the oceans (Bryson and Compbell, 1982). Another group of investigators presume that the abnormal patterns in the atmosphere are produced by variations in the amount and quality and solar energy, the solar spectrum, especially the ultra-violet portion which affects the stratospheric ozone concentration (Pittock, 1983). There are others who think that short term fluctuations in the climate are due to El Nino/Southern Oscillation (ENSO). Super imposed on these natural variations are changes induced by human activities. The release of green house gases in the atmosphere in recent years is thought to be the cause of changing climatic patterns. There are few scientists, on the other hand, who question the whole concept of climatic change. According to them, the atmospheric circulation is a stochastic process which allows for the occurrence of irregular fluctuations resulting from the basic sluggish character of the atmosphere or some additional control. The additional control, according to these scientists, could be an extra-terrestrial impulse or an inherent characteristic of the atmosphere which causes the circulation to switch abruptly from one regime to another at irregular intervals (Ross *et al* 1974).

Astronomical Periodicities

There is an evidence of periodicities in the climatic records in different areas of the world. A scientific analysis of the past climate data may provide explanation to the past fluctuations and give some clues to forecast the future fluctuations. However, till this date, the investigations have been quite confusing because every conceivable period of 1 to 36 years has been suggested by the various investigators. Further many of the claimed periodicities in climate may not be existing in reality (Pittock, 1983). For some, of course, sound physical reasonings have been put forward.

Periodicities of about 23, 45, 60, 100 and 170 years in winter severity and summer wetness have been recorded in Europe since A.D. 1100. A peak of mean sea level pressure at a twenty one year period has been noticed over the desert and semi-desert areas of the Northern Hemisphere. A twenty two to twenty three years periodicity is apparent in the frequency of blocking highs over Europe. A quasi-biennial (26 to 28 month) oscillation is well represented in winter over north western India (Chowdhry and Rao, 1978). A 770 years record of the 180 variations in ice core from northern Greenland revealed poriodicities of 78 and 181 years.

Many investigators of the climatic changes come to the conclusion that astronomical periodicities influence the atmosphere directly or indirectly and bring periodic variations in climate.

The time scale of many of the astronomical periodicities influencing the atmosphere cannot be demonstrated with certainty. It is, however, widely accepted that they have a relationship with the sequence of ice ages and the intervening warmers and colder periods. There is also some evidence of temperature fluctuations in Europe and rainfall fluctuations in central Asia at almost similar long cycles.

Lunar Cycles

Apart from the well known 18 year lunar cycle, there are three more lunar cycles of the frequency of 13.6, 27.2 and 44 year periods (Lamb, 1972). After 13.6 years comes the first approach to simultaneous completion of whole number of 29.53 day lunar synodic months and 27.55 day lunar anomalistic months. A period of 27.2

years beings the corresponding first near repetition of the phase of lunar month with the earth in its original position in its orbit. A period of 44 years brings the first near coincidence between the completion of whole numbers.

These period lengths could account for some analog sequence of weather patterns at odd times of the year apparently unrelated to the natural season.

Per incidence or as a cause of lunar tides, the 25+2 year abnormal rainfall cycle in April and May over north western India coincides with a 27 year lunar cycle. It, however, needs investigation and confirmation.

Sun-Spot Cycle

The most important periodicity is associated with the tidal forces of the sun, planets and the moon. The varying tidal pull exerted by the planets on the sun is thought to be controlling the amount of disturbance on the sun's face and these disturbances are referred as sun spots.

The tidal pull seems to attain maximum force when two or more of the planets of our solar system are in line. Jupitar, Venus and Earth at their mean distances, collectively account for 83 per cent of the total tidal pull on sun. Conjunctions of the Earth, Jupiter and Venus occur at interval of 24 years; and alignments, with either Venus or Jupiter in opposition, occur every 12 years (Lamb, 1972). This period length almost coincides with the most prominent and best known solar disturbance of 11.08 years known as sun spot cycle. Some scientists think that there is a strong case for accepting the existance of some long cycles in weather phenomena which may be of the same length as the planet induced sun-tide sun spot cycle (Barry and Perry, 1972). The rainfall data for north-western India, however, did not show any apparent periodicity coinciding with the 11 year sun spot cycles or even double the sun spot cycle.

Soli-Lunar Tides

The gravitational tides associated with the earth-sun-moon interaction are referred as soli-lunar tides. Campbell et al. (1983) studied the soli-lunar tides and their effects on the monthly characteristics of the June rainfall at the interannual scale over north western India. Periodiograms of the mean tidal potential time series had their two largest peaks at 0.054 and at 0.262 per year. The precipitation data also yield similar spatial and spectral characteristics which indicate that in June the atmosphere in northern India responds strongly at the two frequencies of 0.05 and 0.26 per year.

This analysis lead the authors to develop a hypothesis based on soli-lunar tidal force. In simple terms, the hypothesis is, that mechanical soli-lunar tidal effect on the atmosphere modulate the monsoon frontal position, resulting in an element of the inter-annual variability of June rainfall observed over northern India. In this region small anomalies in the monsoon frontal position can have a significant effect on the amount of rainfall received in June.

The two peaks observed in the soli-lunar tidal potential periodiograms seems to result from characteristics of the moon's orbit. One characteristic which contributes to the peak around 0.26 per year is the lunar synodic period of 29.5306 days. This frequency is also found in meteorological data. The other lunar spectral peak at 0.054 per year is associated with the nodal period, which is the time it takes the pole of the moon's orbit to revolve once about the pole of the ecliptic.

The authors (Campbell et al. 1983) advocate that the year to year fluctuations in the precipitations of northern India might result from this tidal forcing. The soli-lunar force shifts the position of the south Indian Ocean high in a periodic fashion as Bryson showed for the eastern south Pacific high. This periodic movement may effect the delicate momentum balance which determines how the monsoon front advances and subsequently produces a response in the June rainfall with a similar periodicity.

The second explanation could be through the soli-lunar force effect on sea surface temperature. The authors observed periodicities around the lunar fortnightly and half-synodical period in travelling waves along the northern coast of the Guinea Gulf. These waves effect the thermal structure of the ocean with the associated sea surface temperature oscillation possibly reaching 2.5°C in the up-welling season. It may be that the 0.25 per year frequency observed in Indian June precipitation is indirectly related to tidal forcing via the ocean-atmosphere feedback characteristic of the Southern Oscillation.

The third and more appealing alternative is that the soli-lunar force responsible for the periodicities observed in the precipitation amount results from an amplitude modulation of the lunar fortnightly tide at the semi-nodal period. So they conclude that rainfall spectral peaks observed in June rainfall of India could be the result of soli-lunar tides.

A critical examination of rainfall data of north-western India for April and May plotted on the graphs, however, did not show any noticeable peaks at these frequencies.

Chandler Compensation

Although the total angular momentum of the earth-ocean-atmosphere system as a result of soli-lunar tides, is constant, however, there is some redistribution of angular momentum and inertia between the solid earth, ocean and the atmosphere. Such transfers of momentum and inertia have been assumed to cause changes in the rotation rate of the earth. Further, the spin axis of the earth undergoes a complex periodic wobble of small magnitude. The polar oscillation taking place at several frequencies is called Chandler motion. Chandler motion is centered one cycle per 437 days or so. It has been observed that hydrosphere and atmosphere both respond to Chandler motion and the atmospheric effects are referred as Chandler compensation.

Bryson and Starr (1978) observed the indication of Chandler tide in climatic data of India. They advanced the hypothesis that there is a transpolar displacement of mass from one hemisphere to the other along some meridian with a fixed phase relationship to the polar position. However, the pattern produced is complex bécause of the distribution of land, sea and mountains and also by the baroclinic effects. Bryson calculated the amplitude of the wave number one of the anomly field for each phase of Chandler tide at a frequency of 60 cycles per 70 years. The authors observed that Chandler tide significantly modulates the rainfall in India. If it is accepted then the interférence at a 14 month period in the atmospheric pressure should produce a seven year periodicity in the behaviour of various climatic parameters. According to Bryson the 14th month pressure wave travelling west to east attains its maximum amplitude of 2.7 mb near 70° latitude. This seems to be a significant pressure rise and may result in blocking anticyclones.

Blocking Highs

If the hypothesis of shifting poles of the earth is accepted then over the 7 year cycle the amplitude of atmospheric pressure at about 70° N may reach 2.7 mb level. This is thought to be a significant amplitude and may be instrumental in the formation of blocking anticyclones also referred as blocking highs.

The pre-requisite for the formation of blocking highs seem to be a meandering sub-tropical westerly jet stream which gives rise to ridges and troughs of increasing amplitude in upper troposphere.

Blocking anticyclones are produced due to the shifts in the mean position of the long waves in the upper tropospheric westerlies. Over Asia, the waves are believed to be forced partly by the Himalayas and partly by the adiabatic heating of the cold Asiatic air coming off the land (Lamb, 1972). Similar factors operate to generate these waves in America and Europe. Once a wave is generated in any area, it will tend to force in other areas. As the westerlies flow strikes the mountains, it produces a ridge or a northward bulge in the contours over the mountains and a southward bulge towards farther east.

With increased amplitude of the waves, the warm air moves northwards and the cold air moves southwards. As soon as this process is set in motion, it brings cold Siberian air far to the south, and on the east side it deploys the tropical air ahead of it forming a surface of discontinuity alongwhich the storms occur. Although there is a mean latitudinal position of the long waves, but it shows marked north south variations. This may be explained by the shifts in the mean positions of the polar ice and snow margins (Barry and Perry, 1973).

A well developed blocking situation result in the splitting of the upper westerlies into two branches, one taking its course to north and the other to the south of the block. In this way the normal track of the western disturbance over extreme north India is shifted to the south. Under such situations, the frequency of western disturbance in the north western parts of the country increases and an abnormal weather situation is created.

Ocean Surface Temperature

The atmosphere has very little memory, so after every short period everything that happened to it is forgotten by its internal mechanisms. Some investigators think that it is the ocean which brings the atmosphere to come back on the previous track. Ocean is sluggish and its time constant is entirely different from that of the atmosphere. So, once it adopts an abnormal thermal property it transports the same from the surface to as deep as three or four hundred meters. There is, thus, a tremendous heat storage over vast area of ocean. Perhaps the long lasting heat storage could in some complex way force the atmosphere to come back, from time to time, to a certain pattern. According to this hypothesis, during the turbulent seasons when the wind is strong the sea is stirred up and the anomalies of temperature work their way downward to deeper layers. With the onset of the season when the winds die down, the water generated in turbulent season, whether cool or warm, stays at depths and remains hidden until the next start of stormy season when it is resurrected and brought upto the surface. Frequently there is a correlation between the sea-surface-temperature pattern of one winter with that of the next. From this, it could be concluded if the sea-temperature really affects the atmosphere, it might be one of the reasons why on occasions there are two years in a row with the same weather pattern. This is one of the hypothesis for short term climatic fluctuations advocated by Namais (Namais, 1976). By making a forecast of the sea surface temperature and then translating it into the atmospheric phenomena, Namais (Namias, 1980) made a successful forecast about the termination of the drought in California in 1977. Pisharoty has also demonstrated above normal rainfall over north western India with positive anomalies in sea surface temperature over north eastern Arabian Sea (Pisharoty, 1981).

Snow Cover

Another important variable that may cause fluctuations in weather is the coverage of snow. If there is snow on the ground where it is uncommon phenomena, it begins to affect the environment. It increases the reflection of solar radiation which is absorbed by the atmosphere. It may accentuate the gradient of temperature between two areas in the track of cyclones. This contrast in temperature, then feeds the storms. When this occurs, the storms develop rapidly and they travel too far in the east. In the process, the cold air is brought down which helps the storms to replenish the snow in a self-generating, self-aggravating process. There is a relationship between December snow cover and the snow cover for the rest of the winter in Eurasia. Namais (1980) considers this fact to be important because when the snow falls in an area where it is not common, it not only influences the overlying air masses but also the storm tracks. The storms develop and move along the boundary of the snow where the gradient of temperature is large and the storms replenish the snow. If this hypothesis is accepted then there should be a strong case for a positive relationship between excessive snowfall over Western Himalayas in winter and abnormal frequency of western disturbances in April-May over plain areas of north western India lying south of the snow clad western Himalayas.

Concentration of Green House Gases

World wide monitoring of the composition of the atmosphere has provided enough evidence that human activities like fossil fuel combustion, production of synthetic chemicals, biomass burning and deforestation are significantly changing the chemical composition of the atmosphere thereby enhancing the green house effect. The green houses gases (GHGs) are the major agents of climate change and the present growth rate is 1 per cent for CH_4 0.4-0.5 per cent for CO_2 and 0.2-0.3 per cent for N_2O (Baker, 1989). The combined effect of other GHGs; CFC 11, CFC 12 and O_3 etc. (30 identified so far) are contributing significantly to the green house effect. Further most of the GHGs have greater growth rates, longer resistance time and greater green house effect.

Pre-industrial revolution atmospheric CO_2 is estimated within the range of 250 to 290 ppm. Precise measurements made at Manua Loa showed a concentration of 354 ppm in 1984 as against 315 ppm in 1958 indicating a growth rate of 1.6 ppm per year. Future CO_2 level scenarios have been made on the basis of the rates of emission and transfer processes between major carbon reservoirs like oceans and terrestrial ecosystems. There appears to be a general agreement that CO_2 concentration will continue to increase. The concentration by the year 2030 will cross 370 ppm but its doubling (550 ppm) since the pre-industrial period may not occur till the second half of the 21st century (Bach, 1989, Keeling et al, 1976).

The projected concentration of other GHGs have also been radiatively similar to CO_2, therefore their approximate effects are measured in terms of equivalent amounts of CO_2. At present their combined effect is equivalent to an additional 40-50 ppm increase of CO_2. During the next 50 years their concentration will reach a level which will result in green house situation equivalent to a CO_2 doubling in the first half of the 21st century.

The climatic response to the increasing CO_2 and other GHGs has been assessed through mathematical models. The surface air temperature due to CO_2 doubling as simulated by a variety of general atmospheric circulation models yields warming of the order of 4.2°C. The GHGs induced warming for the period 1950 to 2030 will be 1.5 to 6.1°C. More realistic models of climate which combine atmospheric and oceanic models yield warming to the order of 0.5 to 0.7°C from the years 1850 to 1980. This figure agrees well with the observed Northern Hemisphere warming of 0.6°C in this period. Thus taking into consideration the thermal inertia of oceans, the warming process will be slowed down and the assessment suggests that in comparison to 1850, the earth will be warmer by 1 to 3°C by the year 2030. As mentioned earlier, the earth surface air temperature is already higher by 0.6°C as compared to the year 1850. An average rate of increase of global temperature during the next century is projected as 0.3°C per decade with an uncertainity range of 0.2-0.5°C (Kellogg, 1983, WMO, 1986). Simple calculations show that other things being equal, it will result in an increase in surface temperature and a decrease in temperature in the upper atmosphere. More elaborate two and three-dimensional calculations, performed with computer models of climate, indicate that this effect is reinforced by two positive feed back effects (Pittock, 1983). One is that higher surface temperature causes more evaporation and thus higher water vapour concentrations, and water vapour is itself an important infra-red absorber. Another is that higher surface temperatures will lead to more melting of snow and ice cover on land and sea which will lead to greater absorption of incoming solar radiation instead of its reflection back into space.

On the other hand, negative feedback effects include the possibility that higher surface temperatures might lead to increased cloudiness and thus reduced incoming solar radiation. The cloudiness effect could, however, lead to further warming in some circumstances as the clouds will also decrease infra-red heat loss from the surface.

Fairly simple physical arguments can be used to anticipiate the nature of likely regional changes in climate due to increased carbon dioxide. For example, it is well known that the land heats up more rapidly than the oceans, so a little more warming of the Indian subcontinent may lead to increase in monsoon activity. It can also be expected that in general a warmer earth will lead to longer summer rainy season in low latitudes, and a shorter winter rainy season in middle latitudes. If high latitudes indeed heat up more rapidly than low latitudes the equator to pole temperature gradient will be reduced which will lead to weaker westerly winds in mid-latitudes and a polewards migration of the climate zones. This may adversely affect the frequency of western disturbances over north-western India (Pittock, 1983).

14.2 Climate Changes and Ecosystems

Ecosystem Structure

Species respond differently to climatic change, hence some will increase in abundance while other will decrease. Ecosystems will therefore change in structure. Over time some species may be displaced to higher latitudes or altitudes. Rare species with small ranges may be prone to local or even global extinction. Ecosystems, of large stature such as forests may not migrate fast enough to keep pace with climate change because of the barriers to migration such as human settlements and highways (Melillo et al., 1990).

Ozone Layer Depletion and Consequences

So far important sinks for CFCs in the lower layer of the atmosphere are not known. The CFCs are ultimately broken down in the atmosphere above 25 Kms by photolysis which frees the highly reflective chlorine. The chlorine competes with nitrogen oxides for odd oxygen species including O_3, and the result is an efficient catalytic destruction of O_3 by chlorine until it is removed from the system as HCL. At the present rates of emission of CFCs, severe O_3 reduction ranging from 15 % near 30 km to about 40% near 45 km will result. Since the thermal balance of the atmosphere is maintained by O_3 which absorbs solar radiation, therefore, the destruction of O_3 would cool the stratosphere. For example, a 50% reduction in O_3 would cool the upper stratosphere by as much as 20°C. Furthermore, O_3 modulates the solar and IR flux incident on the troposphere. A reduction in stratospheric O_3 would allow more sunlight to reach the surface and tend to warm it. This warming will be offset by reduced IR fluxes emitted by the cooler atmosphere and also by a reduced O_3 green house effect.

The ozone depletion will show its impact on the atmospheric dynamics. Reduced ozone has already started reducing stratospheric heating rates. There is evidence, that, in mid-October, the lower stratospher over Antarctica is now 5 degree Celcius cooler than it was 15 years ago.

The greatest changes between 1979-1980 and 1986-1987 reduced ozone amounts, by 10 per cent or more over the Antarctica from September to November. Ozone reduction of 5 per cent over 8 years have occurred at 50 degree latitude south during most months of the year. This is uncomfortably 'close to home' for people living in Tasmania, New Zealand and southern South America.

If the observed yearly average Antarctica ozone reduction over 8 years (which is about 10 per cent) spread over the globe, the depletion would effectively be diluted to about half a per cent in the 8 years. But the global mean indicates a global depletion of about 2 per cent in the 8 years. So some other—as yet unknown—processes of ozone depletion are working world wise.

If the ozone layer continues to be depleted in the atmosphere then more UV radiation will reach ground level. For a 10 per cent ozone reduction, the flux of the biologically damaging UV radiation at the Earth's surface increases by 20 per cent. Such a change will have far reaching consequences. The incidence of cataracts and skin cancer, particularly in the fair—skinned population will increase alarmingly. Non-melanomic cancers are expected to increase by 40 per cent, for a 10 per cent ozone depletion.

Increased UV radiation could damage the eyes of seals basking on the ice and of penguins and their chicks—who stand for many weeks under the depleted ozone region. The increased intensity of UV radiation under the ozone hole could reduce the rate at which phytoplankton are produced. Diatom are produced at and near the surface of the southern ocean. Phytoplankton, by photosynthesis, use chlorophyll to convert visible sunlight into carbohydrates. Since the organisms form the basis of the southern ocean food web, on which the krill feed, which in this situation would be under-nourished. In turn, this would reduce the food source for fish, birds, seals and whales, all of which feed on krill. The entire southern ocean ecosystems could be harmed.

Snow Cover Reduction and Sea Level Rise

The global warming will reduce the size of snow cover over the earth surface. The reduction of snow surface will enhance the absorption of more solar radiation which is turn will further warm the atmosphere. The melting snow will add more water to the oceans. As a result, the sea level could rise any where between 4 and 40 cm by the year 2030.

The best estimate is between 14-24 cm higher than today. The implied rate of rise is about 4-6 cm per annum, which is 2-6 times faster than that over the last one hundred years. Regional changes in sea level may differ from the global average. Even if changes in green house forcing stopped abruptly in the year 2030, global sea level would continue to rise for many decades, and possibly for hundreds of years due to increase of the long response time of the polar ice sheets and the slow processes of heat transfer from the atmosphere to the ocean.

The Ganges-Brahmaputra delta, much of which is less than one meter above sea level may be submerged in Bay of Bengal. Encrochment of the sea in the Nile delta also threatens to rob Egypt of a substantial portion of agricultural land apart from making thousands of people homeless. Other deltas at risk include the Huang-Ho, Indus, Amazon, Mississipi and Po.

Most of the land area of small islands constituting the Republic of Maldives is less than two meters above mean sea level. Two important resources of the Republic, coral and mangrove forests face imminent threat if the sea level rises beyond the existing level. Many Pacific islands are dependent on root crops for a principal part of their diet. These are grown in shallow pits which risk salt contamination with invasion of ocean water. Sea level is a problem of coastal region of Holland which is already below sea level. Any further rise of sea level will robe the country much of its beautiful land. The impending problems of global warming and its consequences through rise in sea level is causing alarm in almost all the Island Nations of the Indian and Pacific Oceans.

14.3 Climate Changes and Agroecosystems

By now it is very clear that the atmosphere is being constantly enriched with CO_2 and is warmed up. However, what else less clear is how the expected rise in CO_2 level and air temperature will interact to affect plant processes. If LAI increases with elevated CO_2 concentrations, the ET is expected to rise further with increase in temperture because increased temperature is associated with greater vapour pressure deficits, hence greater moisture stress (Allen, 1990). The occurrence of moisture stress during critical stages of crop like flowering and grain filling may result in steep reduction in post anthesis photosynthesis and grain yield. Higher temperatures also accelerate plant development and shorten the growth period.

Carbon Dioxide increase can effect the crop productivity directly and indirectly (through climate change). Further the effects are both positive and negative.

Direct Positive Effects

It has been proved experimentally that for a single leaf photosynthesis rate increases with the increased CO_2 level especially in C_3 plants. When these experiments were extended to crop levels, it was found that increased CO_2 to 600 ppm increased the number of tillers and branches and hence higher leaf area resulting in higher solar radiation interception and resulting about 25 per cent increase in photosynthesis rate. At leaf level, it was also found that increased CO_2 reduced transpiration due to decreased stomatal aperture and may result in higher water use efficiency. Since these results were obtained from studies conducted in leaf chambers, green houses and growth chambers (phytotrons) where the other environmental factors were controlled at desired level, these may not be applicable under realistic situations.

Direct Negative Effects

The increased LAI may result in self shading and thus reduces the net assimilation rate. It has been found that in Northern India, the incident PAR always remain below 1600 $\mu E\ m^{-2}\ s^{-1}$ in winter and it was found that this PAR is not adequate to saturate the present day available canopy of the most of the winter season crops at 330 ppmv CO_2 conc. It has been reported that under low light intensity, the net photosynthesis do not differ in water-lily between 340 and 640 ppmv CO_2 concentration. Photosynthetic acclimation is quite common and can result from imbalance in source/sink ratio which slow down the photosynthesis rate at source. Increased CO_2 results in higher LAI, thus more transpiring surface is available which might compensate the increased water use efficiency on per plant basis.

14.4 Indirect Negative Effects through Climate Change (Higher Temperature)

Crop Phenology

There may be about 6-8% reduction in maturity duration for each 1°C rise in temperature. In wheat for each °C rise in temperature, the reduction of about 5 days in flowering date and 4 days from flowering to maturity have been recorded in North India.

Increased temperature during critical periods of crop development (grain filling in wheat) result in accelerated leaf senescence, decline in canopy photosynthesis and forced maturity in winter cereal crops.

Yield

Increased temperature by 1 to 2°C above mean temperature of 17°C during grain filling period reduces yield due to increased rate of senescence of flag leaf and reduction in grain filling duration.

Evapotranspiration

Vapour pressure deficit, one of the governing factors for ET will increase by 7 per cent for each 1°C rise in temperature, provided RH remains unchanged. Increased temperature from 28 to 35°C caused 30 per cent increase in transpiration in soybean at both 330 and 800 ppm CO_2 concentration. A linear increase in chickpea transpiration was also observed with increase in temperature from 10 to 42°C at 330 ppm CO_2 concentration. Under field conditions, a sudden rise in ET with increased temperature above 20°C in barley, chickpea, mustard and wheat is recorded (Singh *et. al.* 1991, Yadav *et al.* 1987).

Evidence suggests that rising emission of carbon dioxide, methane, nitrous oxide and other radiatively active gases will lead to an increase in the average surface temperature of the Earth. In addition to changes in global temperature there will be changes in precipitation. The rate and magnitude of these climatic changes is such that they could have a significant impact on agricultural potential in many parts of the world. The nature and extent of such changes will vary regionally and are dependent upon the level of climatic change in each region, the agricultural and management practices| used at present and the ability of agricultural systems to adapt to changes (Singh 1991).

In cool temperate regions beyond 45° N, the rainfall may increase by 5% in summer and possibly upto 15% in winter. In Warm Temperates (30°–45°N and S), summer rainfall is likely to become very limited and winter rainfall may decrease by 5-10%. Global warming may shift Prairie grass's southern border to north, decrease crop yield by 3-17 per cent and shift the geographical locations of potential crop regions. Warming in high latitudes will reduce temperature constraints on agriculture, increase the competition for land use and result in the northward retreat of the southern margin of boreal forest. In Tropical areas (0–10°N and S) rainfall is expected to be enhanced by about 5–10%. Increases in potential evaporation can be expected to accompany the increase in temperature. Marked water stress may occur in areas where there is no accompanying increase in precipitation. In a warmer world Intertropical Convergence Zone would advance further northward into Africa and Asia. If this were to occur then the total rainfall in the Sahel and India could increase. Rainfall could also be more intense in its occurrence which may propagate flooding and erosion.

Important consequences for agriculture would arise from a reduction in soil moisture due to high rate of transpiration from plants and of evaporation from soil surfaces exposed to higher temperatures. There are several regions where decreases in soil water are predicted. Areas which may suffer decreases of soil water between December and February include the Horn of Africa, Southern Africa, and Western West Africa, parts of southern Asia, Arabian Peninsula, eastern Australia, and the southern half of North America. Decreases in soil water between June and August may occur in West Africa, the Maghreb and Horn of Africa, Western Europe, China, Central Asia, S.W. United States, Mexico and Central America, Eastern Brazil and North eastern and western Australia (Singh, 1991).

Experimental results suggest that a doubling of CO_2 will lead to a 10 to 15% increase in dry matter production of many species provided all other factors remain constant. For wheat and barley, yield increases of as much as 40% have been predicted. The typical aerial crops of central and Northern Europe and similar latitudes should benefit from water stress when evaporative demands are greater than water supply.

The agricultural potential in Cool Temperates decrease towards the poles due to smaller thermal inputs, so the global warming will have greater relative effects on crop potential in higher latitudes than in lower latitudes. In addition the CO_2 induced temperature increase is likely to be greater at higher latitudes, substantial effects on crop potential can be anticipated in the northern regions. In Northern Europe there would be an increase in the potential growing periods, whereas around the Mediterranean the growing season could shorten significantly due to warming and drier conditions in spring and autumn.

Scientific examination of the changes in the climatic limits for a range of crops in Northern Hemisphere countries under a variety of climatic scenarios have been suggested. A 1°C increase in mean annual temperature would advance the thermal limit of cereal cropping in mid-latitude Northern Hemisphere regions by about 150-200 km or an altitudinal limit by about 150–200 m. A 4°C warming would probably raise climatic zones in the European Alps by 450–650 m. making them similar to the levels of those today in the Pyrennes which lie 300 km south of the Alps. It follows that in cold regions yields of most crops will increase with increasing temperature, except where moisture is a limiting factor. Under a doubling of CO_2 climate, yield of barley and oat in Finland would be raised by 9–18%. In Iceland the carrying capacity of improved grassland for sheep is estimated to increase by about two and a half times, and on unimproved range land by more than a half. This increase of biomass potential in northern Europe is in contrast in the decreases in southern Europe. Thus, it could be a significant northward shift of the balance of agricultural resources in the Europe.

Global warming could lead to a decrease in cereal production in North America mainly due to the accompanying reduction in soil moisture. Under a double of CO_2 climate the yield of maize is likely to fall by 16–25%, even assuming the crop is irrigated. In other areas, such as Mexico the combination of decreases in soil moisture and increases in thermal stress are likely to result in a lowering of wheat yields.

In north western parts of Russia, anticipated warmer and moist climate could initially raise the yields of rye. However, the higher rainfall is likely to cause more leaching and erosion, eventually decreasing soil fertility and therefore, rye yields. In China there are indications that global warming could lead to increased rainfall during the summer monsoon. Under a 1°C warming with precipitation increases of 100 mm, national yield of rice, maize and wheat are expected to increase by 10%. Rice yields are also expected to increase in Japan, but decrease in other regions of Southern Asia due to more rapid crop growth. In North and East Africa any change in rainfall could significantly affect maize yield and grass growth and thus the carrying capacity of range lands. Any change in the frequency of dry years would adversely influence the average output of agriculture in these areas. In U.K. the northern temperature limit for the successful ripening of maize, which at present lies in the extreme south of England, would gradually shift northwards as temperatures begin to rise.

In mid-continental Temperate areas, the reduced amounts of rainfall and snowfall could significantly reduce the rates of ground water re-charge and accelerate the rates of gound-water depletion. In areas where increases in the intensity of rainfall occur, there may be more surface runoff, less percolation of water through the soil and less available soil moisture. Such effects could occur in tropical regions, particularly with monsoon rainfall, and in some maritime mid-latitude regions where it has been suggested that more rain may fall as convective thunder-storms. In these areas any decrease in water availability will place an additional strain on crops already stressed by higher temperature. It has been estimated that the yield of quick maturing rice varieties currently grown in northern Japan would probably increase by about 4% with the temperature increase estimated for a doubled CO_2 in atmosphere. In mid-continental parts of Canada and Russia, winter wheat would give higher yields than spring cereals in a high CO_2 environments. The potential for the production of sunflower in the UK could shift northwards by about 300 km for each 1°C rise in mean annual temperature. Similarly, northward shifts of citrus, olives and vines have been projected for southern Europe. Southward shifts of land use have also been suggested in the Southern Hemisphere.

In areas of reduced rainfall, substantial increases in the need for irrigation are likely to occur which will probably lead to significantly higher costs of production. On the other hand, increases in the amount of intensity of rainfall particularly in regions characterized by monsoon rainfall, will require changes in management to prevent soil erosion.

14.5 Impact of Climate Changes on Crop Production in India

In an agrarian country like India with staggering increase in population and food demands, even a slight decline in annual food production is a matter of great concern. Therefore attention has been focussed to visualise the food scenario in the light of climate change. Rice and wheat are the most dominant cereal crops of India, a picture of the likely performance of these two crops is emerging from results of studies which have been conducted during the recent years.

Rice

Murty (1991) studied the impact of likely global weather and associated changes in carbondioxide, temperature, UV radiation, drought spells, flooding and salinity on tropical rice. His analysis showed that favourable influence on photosynthesis by 1.5 to 2.0 fold increase in CO_2 and other gases may not out weigh the unfavourable affects of rising temperature. The increase in temperature by 2 to 4°C in tropical rice areas may reduce net photosynthesis due to high photorespiration and dark respiration. The average temperature during the wet season may exceed the optimum of 30°C for various growth processes. Increase in temperature especially night temperature during reproductive and ripening stages of rice is detrimental for spikelet production and sink potential. The dry season temperature may exceed the threshold value of 35°C during anthesis of rice resulting in acute spikelet sterlity. These affects are further aggravated by low solar radiation during wet season.

Mathauda and Mavi (1994) simulated the variabilities in the rice yield in the Indian Punjab under different climate scenarios (Table 14.1). The simulated rice yields are in close agreement with the findings of the above said study. The rice yield simulated in this study therefore seems to be a good pointer towards the rice production trends in Punjab during the 21st century considering not any major change in land use and assuming that the technology will remain constant. Under the warm climate scenarios (where temperature was +0.5,+1.0,+1.5 and +2.0°C above normal climate scenario) the decline in the grain yield over the normal was to the tune of

Table 14.1 Rice Crop Response to Variations in Temperature

Temperature Change		Crop Duration (Days)	Grain Yield Kg/h	Grains per sq meter	Grains Per Ear	Maxi-mum LAI	Bio-mass Kg/h	Straw Kg/h
				Yield and Yield Attributes				
+2.0°C	P E R C E N T	−3.3	−8.4	−8.4	−12.4	−3.9	−7.4	−6.4
+1.5°C		−2.6	−8.2	−8.2	−8.3	−3.9	−6.5	−4.7
+1.0°C		−2.0	−4.9	−4.9	−6.1	−2.4	−3.6	−2.2
+0.5°C		−1.3	−3.2	−3.2	−2.4	−1.1	−1.3	−0.7
Normal	D E V I A T I O N	153	6136	18846	494	6.2	10220	49.43
−0.5°C		0	+0.3	−0.3	+1.4	+0.2	+1.9	+4.2
−1.0°C		+1.3	+2.7	+2.7	+3.4	+0.5	+2.4	+2.0
−1.5°C		+2.0	+4.6	+4.6	+3.9	+1.1	+4.0	+3.5
−2.0°C		+13.1	+21.7	+21.7	+12.6	+13.6	+18.5	+15.1

-3.18, -4.94, -8.23 and -8.41 per cent respectively. Under the cool climate scenarios (where temperature was -0.5, -1.0, -1.5 and -2.0°C below the normal climate scenario) the increase in the grain yield was to the tune of +0.28, +2.71, +4.60 and +21.69 per cent respectively. The decline in grain yield under the warm climate scenarios indicated the dire need for selecting/evolving suitable genotypes which will have the potentials to produce as good as under present climate conditions.

14.6 Wheat

Abrol *et. al.* (1991) analysed the role of expected increase in CO_2 levels concurrent with the increase in mean annual temperature above the existing normal seasonal fluctuations on the wheat crop in India. Increase in CO_2 concentration will enhance the photosynthetic rates and productivity. They reviewed a number of reports which suggest that wheat yields may increase by about 35–40 per cent by doubling of CO_2. It is likely that the temperature may rise to as much as 4°C at this level of CO_2. Thus the situation will not be grim since such an increase in CO_2 concentration would counterbalance the deleterious effect of temperature on grain yield. However, the country may have to confront with the problem of shifting of wheat area more towards north as a result of global warming. This will not, however, acquire the dimensions which we perceive now as our conventional breeding methods have been able to isolate promising varieties tolerant to high temperatures existing in Central and Southern part of India.

Mavi *et. al.* (1993) conducted a study to assess the impact of climate changes on the performance of wheat crop in Punjab through the simulation technique. Historical daily weather data from November to April (normal wheat crop season in the state) were collected for the 30 years period (1960-61 to 1989-90) on solar radiation, maximum and minimum temperatures and rainfall. The data were averaged out in order to smoothen it and to obtain the normals. Since no Global Circulation Model (GCM) was applied to generate climate scenarios, it was assumed that solar radiation will remain normal and it will be the temperature which will increase. It was also assumed that the crop will be grown under non-limiting (optimum) water and nutrient supply, since the wheat is grown mainly (97.55%) under assured irrigation conditions in the state. The yields thus obtained will be the potential yields.

Both the maximum and minimum temperatures were increased and decreased by 0.5, 1.0, 1.5 and 2.0°C over normal. It is not definitely known that the temperature increase trend will continue. There are, on the other hand, reports in the literature (WMO, 1986) that temperature may decrease in eventuality of a nuclear war. Thus in all 9 climatic scenarios were generated for evaluating their impact on the wheat crop growth and yields.

A number of models have been suggested for assessing the impact of climate change on crop yield (Rosenberg, 1989). The CERES Wheat model has been successfully validated for different environmental conditions (created by planting the crop on different dates). This model was therefore the natural choice for evaluating the climate change impact assessment on wheat crop development and yields under non-limiting (adequate) water and nutrient supply in the Punjab state.

The CERES Wheat model uses the weather, soil and crop data and simulate the crop phenology, leaf area development, dry matter accumulation and partitioning, yield and yield characteristics. The simulation of crop phenology, yield and yield characteristics are generated from the nine climatic scenarios. The same are presented in Fig. 14.1 and Table 14.2.

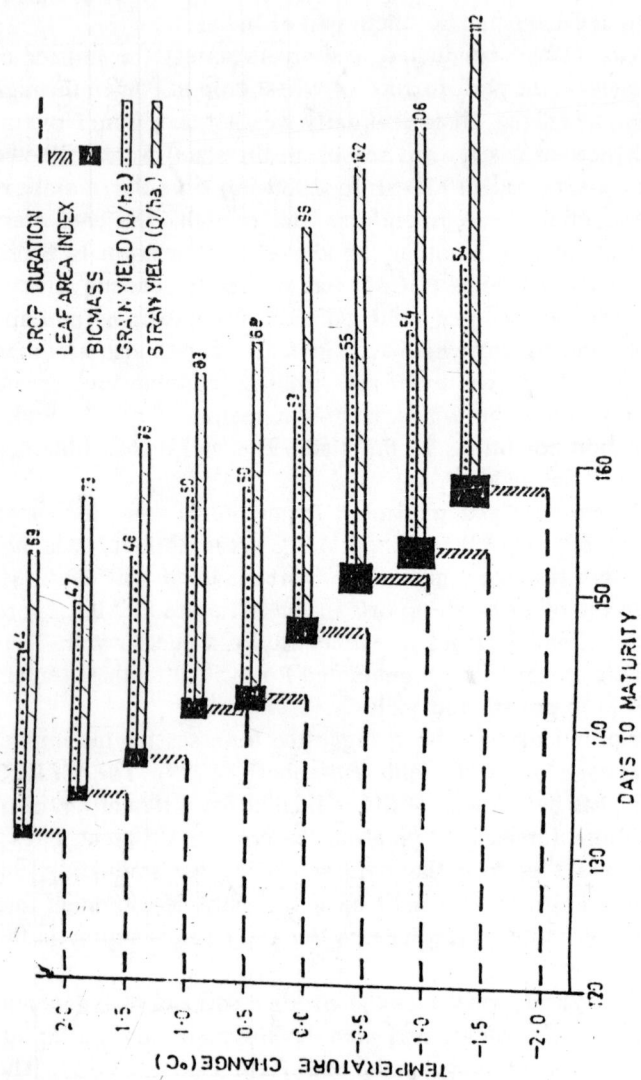

Fig. 14.1. Wheat Crop Performance in Various Temperature Scenarios in Punjab.

Table 14.2 : Wheat Crop Response to Variations in Temperature

Temperature Change		Crop Duration (Days)	Grain Yield (kg/ha)	Kernel Weight (mg)	Grains m^{-2}	Grains per ear	Maximum LAI	Biomass (kg/ha)	Straw (kg/ha)	Harvest Index
						Yield and Yield Attributes				
+2.0°C	% DEVIATION	-7.7	-12.2	1.2	-13.2	+4.1	-23.9	-18.1	-21.6	+2.6
+1.5°C		-5.6	-7.2	+3.8	-10.6	+3.0	-17.6	-13.9	-17.7	+2.8
+1.0°C		-3.5	-4.9	+3.6	-8.1	-0.3	-12.1	-9.0	-11.5	+1.6
+0.5°C		-0.7	-0.2	+3.6	-3.4	+0.2	-6.8	-3.9	-6.0	+1.4
Normal	Absolute Values	143	5043	42.1	11968	24.12	3.8	13871	8829	36.4
-0.5°C	% DEVIATION	+3.5	+5.9	0	+6.0	-1.0	+16.6	+9.0	+10.9	-1.1
-1.0°C		+6.3	+9.4	+0.2	+9.2	-1.7	+23.4	+13.0	+15.2	-1.2
-1.5°C		+7.7	+7.0	-6.4	+14.3	-0.4	+26.3	+15.6	+20.5	-2.8
-2.0°C		+11.2	+7.7	-6.4	+15.2	-1.7	+37.8	+20.0	+27.1	-3.8

Normal Weather Scenario

Under the normal weather conditions, the crop completes its life cycle by the last week of March particularly on March 23, when the crop is planted on November 1. The crop attains a maximum LAI of 3.8 under this scenario.

The total biomass yield is 13.9 t ha^{-1} and the potential grain yield simulated by the CERES Wheat model under normal weather situations is a little over 5.0 t ha^{-1}. Thus the harvest index will be 0.364.

Slightly Warming Scenario

The rise in average temperature by 0.5°C over the normal is expected to occur towards the end of the first decade of the next century. The adverse impact of the rise in temperature of this magnitude during grain filling is neutralized by its positive role during the early stages. This type of climatic change has only a little effect on the total crop duration.

The maximum LAI during the vegetative phase decreases by almost 7 per cent (3.54 from 3.8) under the slightly warm climatic conditions. However, the total biomass production is reduced by 4 per cent. The reduction in grain yield under such climate is a fraction of one per cent as compared to the normal weather. The partitioning to the grains however improves by 1.4% under this scenario.

Moderate Warming Scenario

The moderate warming climatic scenario occurs when the average temperature rises by 1°C. This type of warming is reached by the year 2020. The performance of the crop is adversely affected in all respects. The crop duration under this scenario is reduced by 3.5 per cent. The maximum LAI reduction is by a little over 12 per cent under moderate warming of climate.

The total biomass of the wheat crop reduces by about 9 per cent. There is comparatively large reduction in the grain yield when compared to the slightly warming scenario. The yield is reduced by almost 5 per cent i.e. by 0.25 t ha^{-1} as compared to normal weather, although the moderate warming slightly improves the harvest index (0.2%) over the slightly warming climatic conditions.

High/Greater Warming Scenario

This type of situation is expected to occur by the year 2035. The expected rise in the average temperature is to the tune of 1.5°C. The total crop duration under the high warm climatic scenario shortens by 5.6 per cent i.e. the crop matures 8 days in advance as compared to the crop maturity under normal weather conditions. The maximum LAI of the crop decreases by 17.6 per cent.

The total biomass yield obtained under high warming scenario is 11.94 t ha^{-1} which is almost 14 per cent lower than the biomass obtained under normal weather. The grain yield will decrease by 7.2 per cent over normal although the harvest index will improve by 2.8 per cent.

Severe/Extreme Warming Scenario

When the average temperature rises by 2°C over the normal weather, severe warming climatic conditions occur. This situation is expected to occur by the middle of next century with almost doubling of the CO_2 in comparison to 1990 level. Under such climatic situation, the maturity of the crop is advanced by 11 days. The maximum LAI decreases by almost 25 per cent under the severe warming climatic scenario over the normal weather conditions because of the accelerated leaf senescence.

Increased temperature by 2°C reduces the biomass production by more than 18 per cent. The reduction in grain yield is more severe, it reduces by 12.2 per cent over the normal yield of 5.0 t ha^{-1}. This might have occurred due to increased respiration from the grains of the wheat crop.

Slightly Cool Scenario

In the eventuality of a nuclear war, the average temperature is likely to decrease. This climatic scenario was generated by reducing the crop season daily average temperature by 0.5°C.

This scenario has a pronounced effect on the crop duration which enhances by 5 days over the normal weather conditions (registering 3.5 per cent increased duration) and increases the maximum LAI by over 16 per cent. The total biomass under the scenario increased by 9 per cent over the normal weather conditions, whereas the grain yield increases by almost 6 per cent although the harvest index decreased by 1.1 per cent.

Moderate Cool Scenario

This scenario was generated by reducing the daily mean temperature of the crop season by 1°C. Under moderate cool climatic conditions, the crop growth duration increases by a little over 6 per cent whereas the maximum LAI increases by a little lesser than 25 per cent over the normal weather conditions. The total biomass increased by 13 per cent whereas the grain yield increases by almost 9 per cent over the normal weather even though the harvest index further reduces by 0.1 per cent over the slightly cool weather conditions.

High/Greater Cool Scenario

This scenario occurred where the average normal temperature declines by 1.5°C. Under this scenario, the wheat crop duration increases by 7.7 per cent and the maximum LAI increases by 26.3 per cent over the normal weather conditions. The total biomass increases by 15.6 per cent whereas the grain yield increases by 7 per cent over the normal weather yield. This yield is, however, 2.5 per cent lower than the yield under moderate cool climatic scenario. The harvest index decreases by 2.8 per cent under this scenario when compared to normal weather.

Severe/Extreme Cool Scenario

This scenario was generated by reducing the crop season daily normal mean temperature by 2°C. The crop duration under this scenario increases by a little over 11 per cent and LAI by 37.8 per cent over the normal weather conditions. The increase in the attributes is by 3.5 and 11.5 per cent, a comparatively sharp increase over the greater cool scenario. The total biomass registers 20 per cent increase and the grain yield increase is also slightly higher than the greater cool scenario. The harvest index under this scenario declines by 3.8 per cent over the normal weather.

As can be observed from the simulated results, the total crop duration, maximum LAI, total biomass and grain yield decreases with each 0.5°C rise in temperature above the normal during the crop season. On the other hand, all these attributes increase with decline in temperature. The harvest index, however, increases with increase in temperature and decreases with decrease in temperature as compared to that under normal weather conditions.

Under the warm climate scenarios, the reduced source size (leaf area) coupled with the decreased life span of the crop and reduced tiller number, as depicted by the number of grains m^{-2}, resulted in considerable decline in biomass and grain yield of the wheat crop. Although, increased kernel weight, grains ear^{-1} and harvest index indicate the increased sink strength and rapid rate of translocation of photosynthates towards the grains (sink). Since wheat is a C_3 plant and has higher CO_2 compensation point, increased CO_2 concentration could have increased activity of CO_2 reduction enzyme (Ribose i.e. Diphosphatase). In addition, the higher temperature might be within the thermal kinetic window resulting in increased CO_2 reduction and the translocation of photosynthates to the sink. However, the decreased crop duration and leaf area reduced the total solar radiation harvesting resulting in considerable reduction in grain yield.

The cooler climate, on the other hand resulted in longer crop duration and higher biomass, grain yield, tiller number (as depicted by grains m^{-2} and maximum LAI but decreased kernel weight, grains ear^{-1} and harvest index. This indicates that under cool climates, the sink strength will decline in addition to the poor translocation of photosynthates. However, the increased duration and size of the source (leaf area) will be highly beneficial resulting in considerably higher yields. Under the greater and extreme cool climates, the yields are poorer than the moderate cool climatic conditions. This might have happened due to the fact that temperature might have fallen outside the thermal kinetic window range, the indication of this type is available from the reduction in kernel weight. The slight increase in the grain yield in severe cool conditions as compared to high cool conditions can be attributed to the higher LAI and longer crop duration.

In the field studies conducted by Dhiman *et. al.* (1985) and Saini and Nanda (1987) it was found that increased temperature hasten the rate of leaf senescence resulting in lower leaf area and total biomass. The decreased crop duration with increased temperature is in confirmation with the studies conducted by Mavi and Chaurasia (1974), Bagga and Rowson (1977), Singh *et. al.* (1987, 1988, 1990, 1991). Similarly the decline in grain yield with the increased temperature climate scenario is in agreement with the results of Wardlaw (1970), Wardlaw *et. al.* (1989) and Dawson and Wardlaw (1990). The decline is of the order of 5 per cent with 1°C increase in temperature over the normal weather and 12.2 per cent with increase in temperature by 2°C. The simulated results conform to the observations of Mahi *et. al.* (1991). They revealed that an increase of 1°C temperature decreased the wheat yield in the Punjab by about 5 per cent. An earlier model used in the study of Crop Yield and Climate Change (Natl, Def. Univ., 1978) predicted a 4 per cent decrease in wheat yield in Punjab with 1°C rise in temperature while 15 per cent reduction with 2°C increase in temperature.

The decrease is in the potential yield and yield attributes, when the crop is free from stresses of water, nutrients, insects, diseases and weeds. It has been reported that competition from weeds and incidences of insects and diseases are expected to increase with rise in temperature (Singh *et. al.*, 1991). Incident PAR is expected to decline slightly (Hume and Cattle, 1990) negating any beneficial effects of increased CO_2 concentration. Onset of summer is likely to advance in north-west India by a couple of weeks resulting in the forced maturity and therefore decreased grain filling duration and increased respiration from the grains resulting in shrivelled grains.

The above said studies have been referred here to show that CERES model simulated wheat yield in Punjab under different warming scenarios as a result of increasing green house gases is in close agreement with the findings of the earlier studies. The wheat yield simulated in this study therefore, seems to be a good pointer towards the wheat production trends in Punjab during the 21st Century considering not any major shift in land use and assuming that the technology will remain constant.

REFERENCES

Abrol, Y.P., A.K. Bagga, N.V.K. Chakravarty and P.N. Wattal. 1991. Impact of Rise in Temperature on the Productivity of Wheat in India. Proce. Symp. on Impact of Global Climatic Changes on Photosynthesis and Plant Productivity. Oxford & IBH. 551-552.

Allen, L.H. Jr. 1990. Plant Response to Rising Carbon Dioxide and Potential interaction with Air Pollutants. J. Environ. Qual. 19: 15-34.

Bach, W. 1989. Growing Consensus and Challenges Regarding a Greenhouse Climate. Climate and food Security. IRRI, P.O. Box 933, Manilla, Philipines. pp. 289-304.

Bagga, A.K. and H.M. Rawson. 1977. Contrasting Response of Morphologically Similar Wheat Cultivars to Temperature appropriate to Warm Temperature Climates with Hot Summers. A Study in Controlled Environments. Aust. J. Plant Physiol. 4: 877-887.

Baker, F.W.G. 1989. The International Geosphere-Biosphere Programme: A study of Global Change. WMO Bulletin. 31: 197-214.

Barry, R.G. and A.H. Perry 1973. Synoptic Climatology–Methods and Applications. Methuen. pp. 555.

Bryson, R.A. and T.B. Starr 1978. Indication of Chandler Compensation in the Atmosphere. Climate Change and Food Production. Tokyo Edn. Koichiro Taka Hashi and Masatoshi M. Yoshino. pp. 257-278.

Campbell, W.H., J.B. Blechman and Reid A Bryson. 1983. Long Period Tidal Forcing in Indian Monsoon Rainfall. An Hypothesis. Jour. of Climate and Applied Meteorology. Vol. 22, No. 2. pp. 287-296.

Chowdhary, A. and G.A. Rao. 1978. Climatic change and the Wheat yield in North Western Parts of India. Climate Change and Food Production. International Symp. on Recent Climatic Change and Food Production. Tokyo Ed. Koichiro Taka Hashi and Masatoshi. M. Yoshino. pp. 125-135.

Dawson, I.A. and I.F. Wardlaw. 1989. The Tolerance of Wheat to High Temperature during Reproductive Growth. III. Booting to Anthesis. Aust. J. Agric. Res. 40: 965-980.

Dhiman, S.D., D.P. Singh and H.C. Sharma. 1985. Grain Growth of Wheat as influenced by time of sowing and Nitrogen Fertilization. Haryana Agric. Univ. J. Res. 15: 158-163.

Hume, C.J. and H. Cattle. 1990. The Greenhouse effect-Meteorological Mechanisms and Models. Outlook Agric. 19: 17-23.

Keeling, C.D., R.B. Bacestow, A.E. Bainbridge, C.A. Eddahll Jr. P.R. Guenther, T.S. Waterman and J.F.S. Chin. 1976. Atmospheric carbon dioxide variations in Mauna Loa Observatory, Hawaii. Tellus 28, 538-551.

Kellogg, W.W. 1983. Identification of the Climatic Change Induced by Increasing Carbon Dioxide and other Trace Gases in the Atmosphere. WMO Bulletin. 32: 23-32.

Lamb, H.H. 1966. The Changing Climate. Selected papers by H.H. Lamb. Methuen. pp. 235.

Lamb, H.H. 1972. Climate: Present, Past and Future. Methuen. pp. 613.

Mahi, G.S., H.S. Mavi, R. Chaurasia, G. Singh and O.P. Jhorar. 1991. Climate Based Wheat Yield Model. Proc. Natl. Symp. on Statistical Methodology for Dryland Agri. CRIDA. Hyderabad. 28-30 Jan., 1991. pp. 187-195.

Mathauda, S.S. and H.S. Mavi. 1994. Impact of Climate Change in Rice Production in Punjab (India). Climate Change and Rice Symp. International Rice Research Institute, Manila, Philippines. (submitted).

Mavi, H.S., G. Singh, S.S. Mathauda, R. Singh, G.S. Mahi and O.P. Jhorar. 1993. Climate Change and Wheat Yield in the Punjab. (India). Proc. Symp. on Climate Change, Natural Disasters and Agricultural Strategies. BAU, Beijing: 58-65.

Melillo, J.M., T.V. Callaghan, F.I. Woodword, E. Salt and S.K. Sinha. 1990. Effect on Ecosystem. Climate Change. The IPCC Scientific Assessment WMO/UNEP, 283-310.

Murty, K.S. 1991. Impact of Global climatic changes on photosynthates and Productivity of Rice. Proce Symp. on Impact of Global climatic changes on photosynthates and plant productivity. Oxford & IBH. 673-683.

Namias Jeroma. 1976. Seasonal Forecasting Experiments using North Pacific air/sea Interactions. Proc. of Sixth Conference on Weather Forecasting and Analysis. American Meteorological Society. pp. 13-16.

Namias Jeroma. 1980. Recent Climate Trends. Prospects for Man. Climate Change. Centre for Research on Environmental Quality. York University, Toronto. pp. 17-18.

Namias Jeroma. 1980. The Art and Science of Long Range Forecasting. E.O.S. Vol. 61 pp. 449-450.

National Defence University, Directorate of Research. 1980. Crop Yield and Climate Change in the Year 2000. Vol. 1. Report on the Second Phase of a Climate Impact Assessment. Washington., D.C.

National Defense University. 1978. Crop Yield and Climate Change to the Year 2000

Volume 1. Washington, D.C. p. 128.

Pisharoty, P.R. 1981. Sea Surface Temperature and the Monsoon. Monsoon Dynamics. Eds. J. Light Hill and R.P. Pearce. Cambridge University Press. 237-252.

Pittock, A. Barrie. 1983. Solar Variability, Weather and Climate: an update. Chart. J.R. Met. Soc., 109. pp. 23-35.

Pittock, A. Barrie. 1983. Carbon-Dioxide Problem and its Impact. Meteorology Australia. Feb. pp. 7-10.

Rao, Y.P. and V. Srinivasan. 1969. Winter–Western Disturbances and Their Associated Features. Forecasting Manual Part II. Indian Meteorological Department.

Ross, John E. and Raid. A. Bryson. 1974. The Technical Front. Food, Man and Weather. War on Hunger. A Report for the Agency for International Development. pp. 13-19.

Rosenberg, N.J. 1989. Potential effects on Crop Production of Carbon Dioxide Enrichment in the Atmosphere and Greenhouse—Induced Climate Change. Climate and Food Security. IRRI, P.O. Box 933, Manilla, Philipines. pp. 359-373.

Saini, A.D. and R. Nanda. 1987. Analysis of Temperature and Photoperiodic Response to Flowering in Wheat. Indian J. Agric. Sci. 57: 351-359.

Singh, D.P., B.D. Chaudhry, P. Singh, H.C. Sharma and S.P.S. Karwasra. 1990. Drought Tolerance in Oilseed Brassica and Chickpea. Directorate of Research, Haryana Agric. Univ., Hissar. 60 p.

Singh, D.P., D.B. Peters. P. Singh and M. Singh. 1987. Diurnal Pattern of Canopy Photosynthesis, Evapotranspiration and Water Use Efficiency in Chickpea (Cicer arietinum L.) under field conditions. Photosynthesis Research. 11: 61-69.

Singh, D.P., P. Singh, R.K. Pannu and H.C. Sharma. 1991. Carbon Dioxide Enrichment, Climate Change and Indian Agriculture: A Preliminary Analysis. Proc. Symp. on Impact of Global Climatic Changes on Photosynthesis and Plant Productivity. Oxford and IBH, p. 279-296.

Singh, D.P., R.K. Behl, B.D. Chaudhry and P. Singh. 1988. Rainfed Wheats in Indian subcontinent: An Overview. Paper Presented at Intern. Symp. Drought Resistance in Cereals. ICSU (Paris), Cairo, Egypt.

Singh Phool. 1991. What Drives Global Climate and Ecosystems?: An Over View. Proc. of Symp. on Impact of Climatic Changes on Photosynthesis and Plant Productivity Oxford & IBH. 685-710.

Sikka, D.R. and G.B. Pant 1991. Global Climatic Change: Regional Scenario over India. Proce. of the Symp. on Impact of Climatic Changes on the Photosynthesis and Plant Productivity. Oxford & IBH. 551-572.

Wardlaw, I.F. 1970. The Early Stages of Grain Development in Wheat: Response to Light and Temperature in a Single Variety. Aust. J. Biol. Sci. 23: 765-774.

Wardlaw, I.F., I.A. Dawson and P. Munibi. 1989. The Tolerance of Wheat to High Temperatures during Reproductive Growth. II. Grain Development. Aust. J. Agric. Res. 40: 15-24.

WMO. 1986. Possible Climatic Consequences of a Large-scale Nuclear War. 35: 134-138.

Yadav, S.K., D.P. Singh, P. Singh and A. Kumar. 1987. Diurnal Pattern of Photosynthesis, Evapotranspiration and Water Use Efficiency in Barley under Field conditions. Indian J. Plant Physiol. 30: 233-238.

AUTHOR INDEX

SUBJECT INDEX

277